CANADIAN ISSUES / THÈMES CANADIENS

Volume XVIII, 1996

Immigration and Ethnicity in Canada

Immigration et ethnicité au Canada

Edited by / Sous la direction de

Anne Laperrière, Varpu Lindström, Tamara Palmer Seiler

Selected proceedings of the 22nd Annual Conference
of the Association for Canadian Studies held at the
Université du Québec à Montréal, 7-9 June 1995.

Choix de communications présentées lors du 22ᵉ congrès annuel
de l'Association d'études canadiennes qui se tenait à
l'Université du Québec à Montréal, du 7 au 9 juin 1995.

Association for Canadian Studies
Association d'études canadiennes
Montréal
1996

Canadian Cataloguing in Publication Data

Association for Canadian Studies. Conference (22nd : 1995 : Université du Québec à Montréal)
   Immigration and Ethnicity in Canada = Immigration et ethnicité au Canada

(Canadian issues = Thèmes canadiens, ISSN 0318-8442 ; v. XVIII)
Text in English and French.
Includes bibliographical references.
ISBN 0-919363-33-4

   1. Ethnic Groups—Canada—Congresses. 2. Immigrants—Canada—Congresses. 3. Canada—Emigration and immigration—Congresses. 4. Minorities—Canada—Economic conditions—Congresses. I. Laperrière, Anne, 1947- II. Lindström, Varpu, 1948- III. Seiler, Tamara Palmer IV. Title. V. Title: Immigration et ethnicité au Canada. VI. Series: Canadian issues (Association for Canadian Studies) ; v. XVIII.

FC104.A87 1995   305.8'00971   C96-900411-7E
F1035.A1A87 1995

Données de catalogage avant publication (Canada)

Association d'études canadiennes. Congrès (22ᵉ : 1995 : Université du Québec à Montréal)
   Immigration and Ethnicity in Canada = Immigration et ethnicité au Canada

(Canadian issues = Thèmes canadiens, ISSN 0318-8442 ; v. XVIII)
Texte en anglais et en français.
Comprend des références bibliographiques.
ISBN 0-919363-33-4

   1. Groupes ethniques—Canada—Congrès. 2. Immigrants—Canada—Congrès. 3. Canada—Émigration et immigration—Congrès. 4. Minorités—Canada—Conditions économiques—Congrès. I. Laperrière, Anne, 1947- II. Lindström, Varpu, 1948- III. Seiler, Tamara Palmer IV. Titre. V. Titre: Immigration et ethnicité au Canada. VI. Collection: Canadian Issues (Association d'études canadiennes) ; v. XVIII.

FC104.A87 1995   305.8'00971   C96-900411-7F
F1035.A1A87 1995

Managing Editor / Gérante de la rédaction : Danielle Comeau
Copy editing and proofreading/Révision des textes et des épreuves : Vincent Masciotra, Keith Lowther, Claire Martin, Aurora Wallace
Translation/Traduction : Élise de Bellefeuille (français)
Typesetting/Photocomposition : Danielle Comeau
Cover design/Conception de la couverture : Communication Synergik MPC Inc.

Legal Deposit, National Library of Canada, Second trimester, 1996
Dépôt légal, Bibliothèque nationale du Canada, Bibliothèque nationale du Québec, 2ᵉ trimestre, 1996

Acknowledgments/Remerciements

This publication was made possible thanks to a grant from the
Social Science and Humanities Research Council of Canada

Cette publication a été rendue possible grâce à une subvention
du Conseil de recherches en sciences humaines du Canada

This publication was made possible thanks to a grant from
' the Multiculturalism Secretariat,
Department of Canadian Heritage

Cette publication a été rendue possible grâce à une subvention
fournie par le Secrétariat au multiculturalisme,
ministère du Patrimoine canadien

• • •

The conference was made possible thanks to the financial support of:
Le congrès a été rendu possible grâce au soutien financier de :

International Council for Canadian Studies/
Conseil international d'études canadiennes

Multiculturalism Secretariat, Department of Canadian Heritage/
Le Secrétariat au multiculturalisme, ministère du Patrimoine canadien

Social Sciences and Humanities Research Council of Canada/
Le Conseil de recherches en sciences humaines du Canada

Social Science Federation of Canada/
Fédération canadienne des sciences sociales

Canadian Issues / Thèmes canadiens (ISSN 0318-8442) is an annual publication of the Association for Canadian Studies (ACS). It features papers presented at the annual conference of the ACS. Copies of this volume may be purchased for CAN$15 (plus 7% GST in Canada, CAN$20 abroad) from:

Association for Canadian Studies
c/o UQAM V-5130
P.O. Box 8888, Station Centre-Ville
Montréal, Québec
Canada H3C 3P8
Tel.: (514) 987-7784. Fax: (514) 987-8210.
Email: acs-aec@uqam.ca.
Web site: http://www.er.uqam.ca/nobel/c1015/

ACS Members receive a copy free of charge as part of their membership.

Canadian Issues / Thèmes canadiens (ISSN 0318-8442) est publié par l'Association d'études canadiennes (AEC). Y sont rassemblées des communications présentées dans le cadre du congrès annuel de l'AEC. On peut se procurer ce volume au coût de 15 $CAN l'unité (au Canada 7 % TPS en sus, 20 $CAN à l'étranger) en s'adressant à :

Association d'études canadiennes
a/s UQAM V-5130
C.P. 8888, succ. Centre-Ville
Montréal (Québec)
Canada H3C 3P8
Tél. : (514) 987-7784. Télécopieur : (514) 987-8210.
Courrier électronique : acs-aec@uqam.ca.
Site Web : http://www.er.uqam.ca/nobel/c1015/

Les membres de l'AEC reçoivent gratuitement un exemplaire de *Thèmes canadiens*.

Conference Organizing Committee/Comité d'organisation du congrès
Roberto Perin, Département d'histoire, Université York (Président du comité/ Committee Chair)
Anne Laperrière, Département de sociologie, Université du Québec à Montréal
Varpu Lindström, Department of History, York University
Tamara Palmer Seiler, Canadian Studies Program, University of Calgary
Jean-Guy Bigeau, Directeur général de l'AEC/Executive Director, ACS

Conference Coordination/Coordination du congrès
José Cadorette, Agent de programme de l'AEC/Programme Officer, ACS

Table of Contents / Table des matières

The articles contained in Volume 18 of *Canadian Issues/Thèmes canadiens* are culled from the papers presented at the 1995 Annual Conference of the Association for Canadian Studies, held at the Université du Québec à Montréal from June 7 to 9. The conference theme of "Immigration and Ethnicity in a Comparative Context" attracted a wide range of responses from a diversity of disciplines and perspectives, both from within and outside of Canada. Although only ten of these papers are reprinted here, they are representative of the breadth and quality of all the presentations. A complete list of all the papers presented at the conference can be found at the end of this volume (on page 211).

The purpose of the conference was to challenge scholars of immigration to explore the potential benefits of a comparative analysis of Canada's ethnic communities. Several scholars met the challenge with innovative articles questioning aspects of immigrant/minority experience. Alexander Freund and Laura Quilici used oral interviews to find out whether and how Vancouver's German domestic servants and Italian housewives with boarders, respectively, altered their feminine identity models in the new social and economic conditions of Canada. By studying these women's "construction of identity" within their historical context, the authors discovered that while women of each of the two cultures partially accepted the new power relations in Canada, they were also clearly capable of selective dissent.

Similarly, the comparative approach encouraged Robin Ostow and Maryka Omatsu to explore the disenfranchisement and rehabilitation of Japanese Canadians and East German Jews. The authors also compare the restitution and rebuilding of these ethnic communities in the late twentieth century. In their study, Ostow and Omatsu demonstrate the growing strength of minorities and the success of recent ethnic/national restitution appeals. Their comparative analysis provides interesting insights into how different states have learned to use minorities to advance and legitimate their own domestic and international objectives.

Angelika E. Sauer argues that Canadian and Australian immigration policy towards the Germans (1947-1952) was motivated by self-interest and economic opportunism. She finds a parallel opportunism on the local level by comparing the motives of the Lutheran church and its "Christian charity" work among the German refugees in postwar Canada and Australia. Sauer concludes that in both countries, assistance was well-calculated and came "with strings attached."

Serge Jaumain and Matteo Sanfilippo examine a different wave of immigration to the U.S. and Canada, that of the Belgians. They argue that although North America was not a significant destination for Belgian immigrants prior to World War I, it is nonetheless possible to distinguish three distinct waves of immigration between 1840 and 1914. Drawing upon a wealth of information from the Vatican archives, Jaumain and Sanfilippo provide a topography of Wallon and Flemish communities in Canada and the U.S., and trace out their social and economic integration into North American society.

Marilyn J. Rose questions "the idea of pure or unfettered translation" in her essay in which she considers the translations of *Songs of Ukraina* and *Stone Voices*. Rose argues that, far from being seamless and transparent, the translation of minority or ethnic writing is subject to the cultural and ideological contexts of its production. In her close analysis of the two works, she demonstrates that they are not only "translated" but "transliterated," or moved from one value-laden context to another.

Comparative statistical analyses allow Jiajian Chen, Russell Wilkins and Edward Ng to distinguish between the life and health expectancy of recent Canadian immigrants and Canadian-born populations. Their study concludes that immigrants are in better health, have fewer disabilities, and a longer life-expectancy than the Canadian-born population. This difference, they argue, is caused by Canada's restrictive immigration policy, as well as by the fact that only healthy persons are likely to emigrate. In addition, Chen, Wilkins and Ng question why non-European immigrants have the longest life-expectancy in Canada, and offer some preliminary structural and cultural explanations for this phenomenon.

Similarly, Oscar E. Firbank uses Statistics Canada data in his comparative analysis of retirement patterns among immigrants, as compared to those of the Canadian-born population. Firbank's study is especially interesting because he also looks at the differences *between* immigrant groups. His research shows that immigrant populations in Canada have found a number of distinctive ways to exit the workforce for retirement. He ends his study with a series of recommendations for policy changes regarding retirement security for immigrant workers.

Fernando Mata uses statistical analysis of Canadian census data to assess the relationship between birthplace and economic status in Toronto. He compares male and female immigrants from twelve different places of origin, ranging from the U.K. and Europe, to Africa and Asia, with the Canadian-born population, and demonstrates that "Toronto's labour force continues to be stratified along ethnic and nationality lines."

In a broader study, Eran Razin and André Langlois present a comparative analysis of immigrant and ethnic entrepreneurs in both Canadian and American metropolitan areas. Their analysis clearly demonstrates that immigrants and ethnic minorities which stand out from the mainstream population have a tendency to seek out self-employment in peripheral metropolitan areas, rather than in larger metropolitan areas. Razin and Langlois also show that some differences can be found between Canada and the U.S., mainly because entrepreneurial non-mainstream minority communities in the U.S. tend to be much larger than in Canada.

Carlos Teixeira uses the Portuguese communities in Toronto and Montréal as a case study of the movement of immigrant populations from traditional urban communities to new suburban enclaves. Teixeira looks at the settlement patterns, geographical distribution, residential mobility, and housing choices of Portuguese households who move from the city to new residences in the suburbs of Mississauga and Laval. Among the many interesting findings is that, despite the move to the suburbs, most Portuguese still maintain regular contact with social and religious institutions in the "core" urban neighourhoods.

We would like to thank all those who participated in the Montréal conference and helped make it a great success. This success is due in large part to the hard work of the conference organizing committee (Roberto Perin, Anne Laperrière, Varpu Lindström, and Tamara Palmer Seiler) and the staff at the ACS Secretariat (Jean-Guy Bigeau and, most notably, José Cadorette, the former Programme and Liaison Officer). As well, we wish to thank all the authors for their diligent work in preparing their texts for publication, and Danielle Comeau for managing the production of this volume in a timely fashion.

Finally, we would like to thank the institutions whose generous financial assistance have made both the conference and this volume of *Canadian Issues/Thèmes canadiens* possible. We thank the Multiculturalism Secretariat of the Department of Canadian Heritage, the International Council for Canadian Studies, the Social Sciences and Humanities Research Council of Canada, and the Social Science Federation of Canada for their financial support of the conference. This publication was made possible thanks to generous grants from the Multiculturalism Secretariat of the Department

of Canadian Heritage and the Social Sciences and Humanities Research Council of Canada.

The editors

Les articles qui composent ce volume de *Canadian Issues/Thèmes canadiens* sont tirés des communications présentées lors du Congrès annuel de l'Association d'études canadiennes, qui s'est tenu à l'Université du Québec à Montréal du 7 au 9 juin 1995. Le thème du congrès, « Approche comparative de l'immigration et de l'ethnicité », a suscité de nombreuses contributions, s'inscrivant dans diverses disciplines et perspectives, de chercheurs du Canada et de l'étranger. Bien que seulement dix de ces articles soient repris ici, ils sont représentatifs de la richesse et de la qualité de toutes les communications présentées lors du congrès, dont la liste complète est fournie à la fin de ce volume (page 211).

Le thème du congrès de l'AEC visait à inciter les spécialistes de l'immigration à explorer les avantages potentiels d'une analyse comparative des différentes communautés ethniques du Canada. Plusieurs chercheurs ont relevé ce défi de façon innovatrice en s'interrogeant sur certains aspects de l'expérience des immigrants et des minorités. Alexander Freund et Laura Quilici se sont basés sur des entrevues orales pour examiner de quelle façon, à Vancouver, les immigrantes allemandes travaillant comme domestiques et les ménagères italiennes hébergeant des pensionnaires avaient respectivement modifié leurs modèles d'identité féminine dans leur nouvel environnement socio-économique. En étudiant la « construction d'identité » de ces femmes dans son contexte historique, les auteurs ont découvert que même si les femmes de chacune de ces deux cultures avaient accepté, en partie, les nouvelles relations de pouvoir prévalant au Canada, elles étaient aussi nettement capables de dissidence sélective.

De même, l'approche comparative a amené Robin Ostow et Maryka Omatsu à explorer l'exclusion et la réhabilitation des Canadiens japonais et des juifs d'Allemagne de l'Est. Les auteurs comparent également l'indemnisation et la reconstruction de ces communautés ethniques à la fin du vingtième siècle. Dans leur étude, Ostow et Omatsu décrivent la force croissante des minorités et le succès des récentes campagnes de réparation

ethniques/nationales. Leur analyse illustre comment différents États ont appris à utiliser leurs minorités pour promouvoir et légitimer leurs propres objectifs nationaux et internationaux.

Angelika E. Sauer soutient, pour sa part, que les politiques d'immigration du Canada et de l'Australie à l'égard des Allemands (1947-1952) étaient motivées par l'intérêt et l'opportunisme économique. Elle décrit un opportunisme parallèle au niveau local en comparant les motivations soustendant les « bonnes oeuvres » de l'Église luthérienne à l'égard des réfugiés allemands dans la période d'après-guerre au Canada et en Australie. Elle conclut que, dans les deux pays, l'aide apportée aux réfugiés était calculée et loin d'être gratuite et désintéressée.

Serge Jaumain et Matteo Sanfilippo examinent une autre vague d'immigration aux États-Unis et au Canada, soit celle des Belges. Ils avancent que bien que l'Amérique du Nord n'ait pas été une destination importante pour les immigrants belges avant la Première Guerre mondiale, il est néanmoins possible de distinguer trois différentes vagues d'immigration belge entre 1840 et 1914. Se fondant sur une mine de renseignements provenant des archives du Vatican, Jaumain et Sanfilippo tracent la topographie des communautés wallonnes et flamandes au Canada et aux États-Unis et décrivent leur intégration sociale et économique à la société nord-américaine.

Marilyn J. Rose remet en question la notion de «traduction pure ou objective» dans son essai sur les traductions de *Songs of Ukraina* et de *Stone Voices*. Elle soutient que, loin d'être transparentes, les traductions de textes littéraires émanant de groupes minoritaires ou ethniques sont assujetties aux contextes culturel et idéologique dans lesquels elles sont produites. Son analyse détaillée des deux textes démontre qu'ils sont non seulement « traduits », mais aussi « translittérés » d'un système de valeurs à un autre.

Jiajian Chen, Russell Wilkins et Edward Ng utilisent l'analyse statistique comparative pour établir des distinctions entre l'espérance de vie et l'espérance de vie sans incapacité des immigrants récents et de la population née au Canada. Ils concluent que les immigrants sont en meilleure santé, ont moins d'invalidités et jouissent d'une espérance de vie supérieure à celle des Canadiens de naissance. Cette différence, soutiennent-ils, est attribuable à la politique d'immigration restrictive du Canada, ainsi qu'au fait que seules des personnes en bonne santé sont susceptibles d'émigrer. Les auteurs examinent également pourquoi les immigrants non européens ont la plus longue espérance de vie au Canada et proposent quelques explications structurelles et culturelles préliminaires de ce phénomène.

De même, Oscar E. Firbank utilise les données de Statistique Canada pour analyser les schémas de retraite des immigrants et les comparer à ceux de la population née au Canada. Son étude est particulièrement intéressante

en ce qu'elle examine également les différences *entre* divers groupes d'immigrants. Sa recherche revèle que les populations qui ont immigré au Canada ont trouvé plusieurs façons particulières de quitter la vie active pour entrer dans la retraite. Firbank propose une série de recommandations pour améliorer la sécurité de la retraite des travailleurs immigrants.

Fernando Mata utilise l'analyse statistique des données de recensements canadiens pour évaluer les relations entre le lieu de naissance, le sexe et le statut économique à Toronto. Il compare les immigrants et les immigrantes de douze lieux d'origine différents, y compris le Royaume-Uni, l'Europe, l'Afrique et l'Asie, avec la population née au Canada, et démontre que la main-d'oeuvre torontoise continue à être stratifiée en fonction de l'origine ethnique et de la nationalité.

Dans une étude plus étendue, Eran Razin et André Langlois présentent une analyse comparative des entrepreneurs immigrants et appartenant à des minorités ethniques dans les régions métropolitaines du Canada et des États-Unis. Leur analyse démontre clairement que les immigrants et les minorités ethniques qui se distinguent nettement de la population majoritaire tendent davantage à s'orienter vers le travail autonome dans les régions métropolitaines périphériques que dans les grands centres urbains. Razin et Langlois décrivent également certaines différences entre le Canada et les États-Unis, surtout attribuables au fait que les communautés minoritaires entreprenariales tendent à être beaucoup plus nombreuses aux États-Unis qu'au Canada.

Carlos Teixeira utilise le cas des communautés portugaises de Toronto et de Montréal pour étudier le phénomène des immigrants qui quittent les communautés urbaines traditionnelles pour créer de nouvelles enclaves dans les banlieues. Il examine les schémas d'implantation, la distribution géographique, la mobilité résidentielle et les choix d'habitations des ménages portugais qui se sont installés dans les banlieues de Mississauga et de Laval. Parmi les nombreuses constatations intéressantes de son étude, Teixeira indique que, malgré leur déménagement en banlieue, beaucoup de Portugais restent en contact avec les institutions sociales et religieuses établies dans les quartiers urbains « centraux ».

Nous aimerions remercier toutes les personnes qui ont participé au congrès de Montréal et contribué à son grand succès. Ce succès repose en grande partie sur les efforts du comité d'organisation (Roberto Perin, Anne Laperrière, Varpu Lindström et Tamara Palmer Seiler) et du personnel du Secrétariat de l'AEC (Jean-Guy Bigeau et, en particulier, José Cadorette, ex-agent de programme et de liaison). Nous tenons également à remercier tous les auteurs qui ont préparé leur manuscrit pour la publication, ainsi que Danielle Comeau qui a géré de main de maître la publication de ce volume.

Nous tenons enfin à remercier toutes les institutions qui ont généreusement contribué à la tenue du congrès et à la publication de ce volume de *Canadian Issues/Thèmes canadiens*. Nous remercions le Secrétariat au multiculturalisme du ministère du Patrimoine canadien, le Conseil international d'études canadiennes, le Conseil de recherches en sciences humaines du Canada et la Fédération canadienne des sciences sociales qui ont fourni une aide financière au congrès. Cette publication a été rendue possible grâce à des subventions du Secrétariat au multiculturalisme du ministère du Patrimoine canadien et du Conseil de recherches en sciences humaines du Canada.

Le comité de rédaction

Jiajian Chen, Russell Wilkins and Edward Ng

Life Expectancy and Health Expectancy of Canadian Immigrants from 1986 to 1991

Abstract

This paper presents the life and health expectancies of Canadian immigrants in 1986 and 1991. The calculations are based on data from the censuses of 1986 and 1991, vital statistics for 1985-1987 and 1990-1992, and the Health and Activity Limitation Surveys (HALS) of 1986-1987 and 1991. For both periods, our results show that immigrants, especially non-European immigrants, had longer life expectancies and more years of life free of disability and dependency than did the Canadian-born population. While immigrants were much less likely than the Canadian-born population to be disabled, they were only slightly less likely to be dependent on others for help with their activities.

Résumé

Cet article présente l'espérance de vie et l'espérance de vie sans incapacité des immigrants au Canada en 1986 et 1991. Les calculs sont basés sur des données des recensements de 1986 et 1991, les statistiques démographiques de 1985-1987 et de 1990-1992, ainsi que sur les Enquêtes sur la santé et les limitations d'activités (ESLA) de 1986-1987 et 1991. Pour ces deux périodes, nos résultats indiquent que les immigrants, en particulier les immigrants non européens, ont une espérance de vie et une espérance de vie sans incapacité supérieures à celles des personnes nées au Canada. Les immigrants sont beaucoup moins susceptibles d'être frappés d'incapacité que la population originaire du Canada, mais ils ne sont que légèrement moins susceptibles d'être dépendants des autres pour leurs activités quotidiennes.

Introduction

Canada's health care system and immigration policies are currently under review, and there is growing concern over the health status of Canadian immigrants. Since the 1950s, immigrants to Canada have consistently rep-

resented about 16 per cent of the total population and accounted for about 26 per cent of Canada's population growth.[1] While the socio-economic and demographic characteristics of immigrants have been well documented, studies on the health of immigrants have been scant. As immigrants come to Canada from countries with diverse socio-economic and cultural backgrounds and environments, their health status and health care needs could be quite different from those of the Canadian-born population.

Conventionally, death rates and life expectancy have provided the most important indicators for assessing the health consequences of illness. Most studies of the health of immigrants in Canada have also focused on mortality,[2] while few have examined other dimensions of health.[3] Recently, it has been increasingly recognized that the consequences of disease affect not only longevity but also health-related quality of life, which is mainly measured by another important indicator: disablement.[4]

According to the World Health Organization (WHO),[5] disablement includes impairment, disability, and handicap. Impairment refers to a loss of normal performance of an organ or organs. Disability refers to limitations in functional abilities such as speaking, listening, seeing, dressing, walking, and so forth. Physical independence handicap refers to the social disadvantage that results from a disabled person's loss of independence in a given physical and social environment. Thus, disability is related to a person's ability to perform specific functions or activities, and handicap is related to a person's autonomy within a particular social context.

Health expectancy, which integrates both mortality and disability or dependence into a simple and understandable indicator, is widely regarded as the most comprehensive indicator for measuring health status.[6] In this study, our objective is to assess the life expectancy and health expectancy of Canadian immigrants compared to those of the Canadian-born population.

Data and Methods

In this study, immigration status was defined by place of birth into three large groups: Canadian, European, and non-European. The Canadian group included all persons born in Canada. The European group included persons born in the United States, Australia, New Zealand, and Europe. The non-European group included persons born in all other countries.

We distinguished European from other immigrants for two reasons. First, there has been a major shift in the source of immigrants since the 1960s, with increasing numbers coming from non-European countries.[7] Second, European immigrants were expected to have cultural backgrounds and life-styles more like that of the Canadian-born population than were

non-European immigrants. Thus it is important to distinguish health differentials between these two broad categories of immigrants.

Mortality

The mortality data used for this study were taken from vital statistics for 1985-1987 and 1990-1992. The population data needed for calculating mortality rates were taken from the 1986 and 1991 census total populations, including both household and institutional residents. However, the censuses only collected information on place of birth for the non-institutional population. We estimated the institutional population (and health-related institutional population) by place of birth using mother tongue information. For purposes of comparison, we excluded non-permanent residents from the estimation of the total population in 1991 because the 1986 census did not collect information on this population.

The populations used in this study were census population estimates not adjusted for net undercount, since adjustments were not available by place of birth or immigration status. As a result, the estimated mortality rates for the total population would be slightly higher than shown in the standard tabulations by Statistics Canada.

Disability and Dependency

The data on disability and dependency were taken from the HALS of 1986-1987 and 1991. For the total population of all ages, disability was classified by severity into four levels: severe disability, moderate disability, slight disability, and no disability.[8] For persons aged 15 and over residing in private households, dependency was defined by degree into four levels:

> *Heavily dependent*: dependent on others for personal care (such as washing, grooming, dressing, or eating), or for moving about within the residence.

> *Moderately dependent*: dependent on others for going out, or normal everyday housework (such as dusting, tidying up), or meal preparation.

> *Somewhat dependent*: dependent or partially dependent on others for heavy housework (such as washing walls, yard work or snow removal), or groceries, or partially dependent on others for normal everyday housework or meal preparation.

> *Not dependent*: neither dependent nor partially dependent.

For persons aged 15 and over residing in health-related institutions, depend-

ency was subdivided into three states only (the category "Not dependent" was not applicable since all persons living in health-related institutions were presumed to be at least somewhat dependent):

> *Heavily dependent*: dependent on others for personal care (such as washing, grooming, dressing, or eating), or for moving about within the residence (i.e., same as defined for the household population).

> *Moderately dependent*: dependent on others for going out, or for shopping for clothing or other necessities. (Questions about dependency for housework and meal preparation were not asked of the institutional population.)

> *Somewhat dependent*: all other persons residing in health-related institutions.

For children under age 15, direct information on degree of dependence was not available. However, based on their severity of disability by place of birth, we estimated their prevalence of dependency using the distribution of persons aged 15-24 by disability and dependency.

For the HALS data, information on place of birth was also limited to the household population only, as these data were derived from the censuses. Therefore, we used a special procedure to estimate the HALS institutional population by place of birth and various states of disability and dependence using the aforementioned distribution of the health-related institutional population by place of birth as determined by the censuses.

Because of sample size considerations, further breakdown of the immigrant population by place of birth was limited. For the same reason, persons aged 65 and over were grouped together. Although the data are not shown here, the estimated median ages of the household population aged 65 and over by place of birth were quite similar for both males and females. This indicates that the estimated prevalence of disability and dependency of seniors by place of birth should not be affected by differences in the age structures of the senior populations.

Calculation of Life Expectancy and Health Expectancy

Life expectancy by place of birth was derived from abridged life tables using Chiang's method.[9] The life table values were from cross-sectional age-specific mortality schedules of the Canadian population by place of birth in 1986 and 1991. As such, the current life table reflects the combined mortality experience of age groups representing different birth cohorts, rather than mortality experienced by the same cohort over time.

For each age group, sex, and place of birth, the estimated number of

person-years of life in each health state was calculated by applying the prevalence of disability and dependency in that population subgroup to the expected total person years of life lived by that subgroup. By accumulating from highest to lowest ages the expected persons-years lived in a given state of health, and subsequently dividing those cumulative sums by the number of persons who survived to a specific age, we obtained the expected years of life in that state of health for the people surviving to that age.

We also calculated disability-adjusted and dependency-adjusted health expectancies.[10] Health-adjusted life expectancy is a summary indicator based on a weighted average of all health states. While health-adjusted life expectancies were calculated for convenience in making comparisons, health expectancy for each discrete state is more easily interpretable. In this study, the expected years of life spent in each of the discrete health states were given an arbitrary set of weights. For disability-adjusted life expectancy, the weights ranged from 1.0 for no disability to 0.3 for the most severe disability (severe level 3). For dependency-adjusted life expectancy, the weights ranged from 1.0 for independent, to 0.4 for heavily dependent.

Results

Life Expectancy

Figure 1 shows the survival curves by place of birth for males and females in 1991. The topmost curve is for non-European immigrants, the middle curve is for European immigrants, and the lowest curve is for the Canadian-born population. The area under each curve represents the expected years of life for each group. The survival curves indicate that immigrants, especially non-European immigrants, had longer life expectancy and older median ages at death than did the Canadian-born population. As well, compared to the Canadian-born population, immigrants, especially non-European immigrants, were more likely to survive to age 85.

Table 1 shows the life expectancy by place of birth in 1986 and 1991. In 1991, the differences in life expectancy at birth between the Canadian-born population and European immigrants were 2.7 years for males (73.6 vs. 76.3 years), and 1.4 years for females (80.4 vs. 81.8 years). Between the Canadian-born population and non-European immigrants, the differences in life expectancy were more pronounced: 6.7 years for males (73.6 vs. 80.3 years), and 5.3 years for females (80.4 vs. 85.7 years).

Disability and Dependency

Table 2 shows the age-adjusted prevalence of disability by severity and place of birth in 1986 and 1991, for males and females respectively. Immigrants,

especially non-European immigrants, were less likely than the Canadian-born population to have any disability, or severe and/or moderate disability. The differences in the severe and/or moderate disability rates between immigrants and their Canadian-born counterparts were more pronounced among males than among females. Between 1986 and 1991, the trends in the prevalence of disability by place of birth were quite stable, especially for severe or moderate disability.

While differentials in *disability* by place of birth were *more* pronounced (see Table 2), the differentials in *dependency* by place of birth were *less* pronounced (see Table 3). In general, the prevalence rates for any dependency were relatively low (about half the level of any disability) regardless of place of birth. While immigrants, especially those non-European immigrants, were also less likely than the Canadian-born to have any dependency, their levels of heavy or moderate dependency were quite similar to those of the Canadian-born population.

Health Expectancy

Table 4 shows health expectancy at birth and at age 65 by level of disability and place of birth in 1991. For disability-adjusted life expectancy at birth, the highest values were for non-European immigrants (77 years for males and 81 years for females), followed by European immigrants (72 years for males and 76 years for females), and then by the Canadian-born population (68 years for males and 74 years for females). The same rank order by place of birth also held for all other disability-based health expectancies, both at birth and at age 65.

Table 4 also shows the changes in health expectancy by place of birth between 1986 and 1991. In general, the expected years of life free of severe or moderate disability increased for each of the three groups from 1986 to 1991, both at birth and at age 65. The highest increase in life expectancy free of severe or moderate disability at birth was for non-European immigrants (3.5 years for males and females), followed by European immigrants (0.9 year for males and 1.6 years for females), and then by the Canadian-born (0.8 year for males and 0.3 year for females).

Table 5 shows health expectancy by degree of dependency at birth and at age 65 by place of birth in 1991. The values in each column show a rank order consistently the same as those of health expectancy by level of disability: the highest health expectancy was for non-European immigrants, followed by European immigrants, and then the Canadian-born population. As shown in Table 5, between 1986 and 1991, generally there were increases in life expectancies free of dependence by various degrees at birth and at

age 65. For almost all of the health expectancies free of heavy and/or moderate dependence, the largest increases were for non-European immigrants.

Discussion

Immigrants, especially non-European immigrants, had longer life expectancy and more years of life free of disability and dependency than did the Canadian-born population. Immigrants were more likely to survive to a given age, and to experience lower rates of disability and dependency. As the consequences of illness include death and disablement, the present findings clearly suggest that the immigrants, especially non-European immigrants, were healthier than the Canadian-born population. In fact, without immigrants as part of the population, life expectancy at birth in Canada in 1991 would have been about 6 months less.

The reasons why immigrants are healthier is likely related to the well known "healthy migrant effect." That is, immigrants are healthier because persons in ill health are less likely to try to migrate to a new country;[11] and because, except for refugees and family class applicants, immigrants are selected by the host country based in part on employability (which implies reasonably sound health), and because before admission to Canada, all immigrants must undergo medical screening.[12]

Other factors may also play important roles in determining health differentials by immigration status. These include: length of residence in Canada, lifestyle, culture, and socio-economic characteristics. As we observed, the differences in life expectancy and health expectancy between non-European immigrants and the Canadian-born were sharper than those between European immigrants and the Canadian-born. This can be explained partly by a duration of residency effect,[13] since recent immigrants were more likely to be non-European.[14] The healthier status of non-European immigrants could also be partially attributable to the effect of other socio-economic characteristics, cultural and lifestyle differences. As a recent finding from the National Population Survey (NPHS) of 1994 shows, immigrants, especially non-European immigrants, were less likely than the Canadian-born to have ever smoked.[15]

While immigrants were less likely than the Canadian-born population to have any disability or any dependency, their levels of heavy and/or moderate dependency were quite similar to the Canadian-born. Is that because disabled immigrants were more likely to be handicapped in the new environments or simply because the observed levels of heavy and/or moderate dependency (about 4 per cent) were so low for each group that there was not much room left for differentials? Could it also be due to the fact that dependency in this study was defined based on receipt of help as opposed

to need for help? As female immigrants (especially non-European immigrants) were reportedly more likely to live with family and/or relatives,[16] could it be possible that immigrants compared to the Canadian-born would be more likely to receive help from family members even though they were less likely to have severe disability?

The findings of the present study raise many questions which will require further investigation into the health of immigrants. We should also bear in mind that since immigrants are very heterogeneous in terms of their socio-economic characteristics and countries of birth, studying the health of immigrants by a simple breakdown into European and non-European groups is only a beginning. Further investigation based on a finer breakdown by place of birth or ethnicity may shed more light on understanding the health status and health care needs of Canada's diverse population.

Notes

1. K.G. Basavarajappa, R.P. Beaujot, and T.J. Samuel, "Canada," in L.A. Kosinski (ed.), *The Impact of Migration in the Receiving Countries* (Geneva: International Organization on Migration, 1993).

2. F. Travato, "Mortality differences among Canada's indigenous and foreign-born population, 1951-1971," *Canadian Studies in Population*, 12:1 (1985), 49-80; R.C. Sharma, M. Michalowski, and R. Verma, "Mortality Differentials Among Immigrant Populations in Canada," paper presented at the 21st IUSSP meetings in New Delhi, India, September 1989; C. Nair, M. Nargundkar, H. Johansen, and J. Strachan, "Canadian Cardiovascular Disease Mortality: First Generation Immigrants versus Canadian Born," *Health Reports*, 2:3 (1990), 203-228; M. Michalowski, "Mortality Patterns of Immigrants: Can They Measure the Adaptation?" Paper presented at the XIIth World Congress of Sociology, Spain: July 9-13, 1990; F. Travato and C. Clogg, "General and Cause-specific Adult Mortality Among Immigrants in Canada, 1971 and 1981," *Canadian Studies in Population*, 19:1 (1992), 47-80.

3. R. Wilkins and O. Adams, "Health Expectancy of Canada's Seniors in 1986." Report to Health and Welfare Canada, 1989 (unpublished).

4. R. Wilkins and O. Adams, *Healthfulness of Life* (Montreal: Institute for Research on Public Policy, 1983); J.-M. Robine, C.D. Mathers, M.R. Bone, and I. Romieu (eds), *Calculation of Health Expectancies: Harmonization, Consensus Achieved and Future Perspectives: 6th REVES International Workshop*, Colloques INSERM, vol. 226. (London: John Libbey Eurotext, 1993); C. Mathers, J. McCallum, and J. Robine (eds), *Advances in Health Expectancies: Proceedings of the 7th Meeting of the International Network on Health Expectancy (REVES)* (Canberra: Australian Institute of Health

and Welfare, December, 1994); World Bank, *World Development Report 1993: Investing in Health* (New York: Oxford University Press, 1993.)

5. World Health Organization, *International Classification of Impairments, Disabilities and Handicaps (ICIDH): A Manual of Classification Relating to the Consequences of Disease* (Geneva: World Health Organization, 1980.)

6. D.F. Sullivan, "A single index of mortality and morbidity," *HSMHA Health Reports*, 86:4 (1971), 347-354; R. Wilkins and O. Adams, "Health Expectancy in Canada, Late 1970s: Demographic, Regional, and Social Dimensions," *American Journal of Public Health*, 73:9 (1983), 1073-1080; R. Wilkins and O. Adams, *Healthfulness of Life*; J.-M. Robine, *et al.* (eds), *Calculation of Health Expectancies*; C. Mathers, *et al.* (eds), *Advances in Health Expectancies*; World Bank, *World Development Report 1993.*

7. J. Badets, "Canada's Immigrants: Recent Trends," *Canadian Social Trends*, (Summer 1993), 8-11; J. Badets and T. Chui, *Canada's Changing Immigrant Population* (Ottawa: Minister of Supply and Service Canada, 1994).

8. I. McDowell, *A Disability Score for the Health and Activity Limitation Survey (For Adults in the Household Population).* Disability Database Program, Statistics Canada (Ottawa: 8 July 1988); M. Brodeur, *Severity Score for Adult Residents of Institutions.* Health and Activity Limitation Survey, Disability Database Program, Statistics Canada (Ottawa: 28 October 1988); M. Brodeur, *Severity Score for Children.* Health and Activity Limitation Survey, Disability Database Program, Statistics Canada (Ottawa: 1988)

9. C.L. Chiang, *The Life Table and Its Applications* (Malabar, Florida: Krieger Publishing, 1984.)

10. R. Wilkins, J. Chen, E. Ng, "Changes in Health Expectancy in Canada from 1986 to 1991," in C. Mathers, J. McCallum and J.-M. Robine (eds), *Advances in Health Expectancies: Proceedings of the 7th Meeting of the International Network on Health Expectancy (REVES)* (Canberra: Australian Institute of Health and Welfare, 1994) 115-132; R. Wilkins and O. Adams, *Healthfulness of Life.*

11. M.G. Marmot, A.M. Adekstein and L. Bulusu, "Lessons From the Study of Immigrant Mortality," *Lancet*, (June 30, 1984), 1455-1457; C.M. Young, "Changes in the Demographic Behaviour of Migrants in Australia and the Transition Between Generations," *Population Studies*, 4 (1990), 68-89; E. Kliewer, "Epidemiology of Disease Among Migrants," *International Migration*, XXX (1992), 141-165.

12. F.N. Marrocco and H.M. Goslett (eds), *The Annotated Immigration Act of Canada* (Toronto: Thomson Professional Publishing, 1993), Sections 11 (1), 19 (1) (a).

13. M.G. Marmot, *et al.*, "Lessons From the Study of Immigrant Mortality"; E. Kliewer, "Epidemiology of Disease Among Migrants."

14. J. Badets, "Canada's Immigrants: Recent Trends"; J. Badets and T. Chui, *Canada's Changing Immigrant Population.*

15. J. Chen, E. Ng, and R. Wilkins, "Health Profile of Canadian Immigrants," *Health Reports,* forthcoming, 1996.
16. M. Boyd, "Immigration and Living Arrangements: Elderly Women in Canada," *International Migration Review,* XXV (1991), 4-27.

Acknowledgements

We thank Peggy Cyr and Pierre Lalonde (Health Statistics Division) for their help in preparing the mortality data files by place of birth, and Danielle Bélisle for her help in preparing the figures. Thanks also to Jean-Pierre Morin, Jenny Lynch and Diane Stukel (Social Survey Methods Division) for their help in reweighting the HALS household sample data for the oldest age groups. We are grateful for the support of Health Canada and of Statistics Canada (Post Censal Survey Program and Health Statistics Division). The views expressed in this study are those of the authors, and do not necessarily represent the views of Statistics Canada or Health Canada.

Figure 1: Survival curves for the Canadian populations by place of birth, 1991.

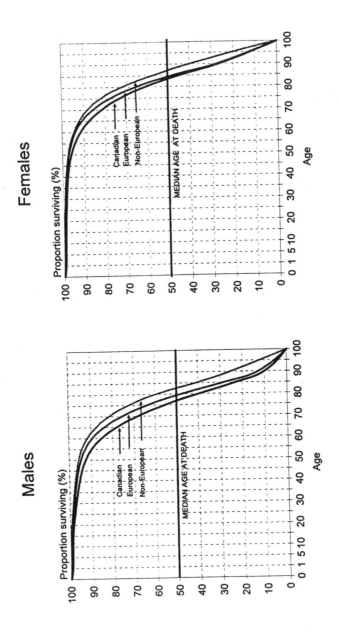

Table 1: Life expectancy by place of birth, Canada, 1986 and 1991 (in yrs)

Age	Males			Females		
Place of birth	1986	1991	Change	1986	1991	Change
At birth						
Canadian	72.3	73.6	1.3*	79.3	80.4	1.0*
European	75.6	76.3	0.8*	81.0	81.8	0.8*
Non-European	77.4	80.3	2.9*	83.4	85.7	2.3*
At age 65						
Canadian	14.6	15.3	0.8*	19.0	19.7	0.7*
European	15.7	16.2	0.5*	19.7	19.9	0.1*
Non-European	17.3	19.5	2.2*	21.5	23.8	2.3*

* Difference significant at 95% confidence.

Table 2: Age-adjusted prevalence of disability by severity and by place of birth, Canada, 1986 and 1991 (%)

Sex	Severe			Severe or moderate			Any disability		
Birthplace	1986	1991	Change	1986	1991	Change	1986	1991	Change
Males									
Canadian	2.7	2.7	0.0	7.2	7.4	0.2	14.2	16.5	2.3*
European	2.4	2.6	0.2	5.7	5.7	0.1	12.7	13.2	0.5
Non-Euro.	1.5	1.4	-0.1	3.3	2.8	-0.5	6.6	7.6	1.0
Females									
Canadian	3.3	3.3	-0.0	7.8	8.3	0.5*	13.7	16.2	2.5*
European	4.0	3.4	-0.5	8.4	7.9	-0.5	12.2	13.7	1.5
Non-Euro.	2.3	2.2	-0.1	5.6	4.8	-0.8	8.8	8.6	-0.2

a Rates are standardized based on the adjusted 1991 population of Canada.
Estimates are for the total population, including institutional residents.
* Difference significant at 95% confidence.

Table 3: Age-adjusted prevalence of dependency by place of birth, Canada, 1986 and 1991 (%)

Sex	Heavy			Heavy or moderate			Any dependency		
Birthplace	1986	1991	Change	1986	1991	Change	1986	1991	Change
Males									
Canadian	1.4	1.5	0.1	3.5	3.8	0.2	6.9	6.6	-0.3
European	1.5	1.6	0.1	3.1	3.4	0.3	5.5	5.5	0.0
Non-European	1.1	1.0	-0.1	2.3	3.6	1.3	3.3	4.5	1.2
Females									
Canadian	1.7	2.0	0.3*	4.2	4.9	0.6*	8.7	9.3	0.6*
European	2.3	1.7	-0.5*	5.0	4.8	-0.3	8.9	8.2	-0.8
Non-European	1.5	1.4	-0.2	4.2	4.1	-0.1	5.5	5.7	0.1

a Rates are standardized based on the adjusted 1991 population of Canada.
Estimates are for the total population, including institutional residents.
* Difference significant at 95% confidence.

Table 4: Health expectancy by level of disability and place of birth, Canada, 1991, and changes between 1986 and 1991 (in yrs)

Sex / Age Birthplace	Total Life expectancy		Free of severe disability		Free of severe or mod. disability		Free of any disability		Disability-adjusted life expectancy	
	1991	Change	1991	Change	1991	Change	1991	Change	1991	Change
Males										
At birth										
Cdn	73.60	1.30*	71.11	1.16*	66.94	0.82*	59.61	-0.98*	68.38	0.55
Euro.	76.30	0.75*	73.67	0.56	70.96	0.88	64.75	0.82	71.89	0.76
Non-Euro.	80.29	2.90*	78.57	2.82*	77.45	3.53*	71.89	0.98	77.18	2.35
At age 65										
Cdn	15.31	0.76*	13.37	0.56*	10.79	0.22	7.84	-0.27	12.32	0.37
Euro.	16.21	0.49*	14.34	0.71*	13.15	1.34*	10.76	1.98*	13.94	1.03*
Non-Euro.	19.48	2.23*	18.18	2.33*	18.06	3.29*	13.87	0.76	17.39	1.88
Females										
At birth										
Cdn	80.35	1.03*	76.27	0.88*	70.94	0.30	63.61	-1.62*	73.77	0.14
Euro.	81.81	0.80*	77.32	1.58*	72.37	1.62*	66.87	0.21	75.72	0.85
Non-Euro.	85.71	2.28*	82.51	2.40*	78.90	3.51*	74.43	2.72	81.09	2.49
At age 65										
Cdn	19.65	0.70*	16.20	0.46*	12.91	0.16	9.47	-0.91*	15.37	0.13
Euro.	19.85	0.14*	16.26	1.22*	13.35	1.67*	11.20	1.82*	16.04	0.98*
Non-Euro.	23.79	2.32*	21.18	2.68*	18.50	3.88*	15.90	3.49*	20.39	2.78

* Difference significant at 95% confidence.

Table 5. Health expectancy by degree of dependency and place of birth, Canada, 1991, and changes between 1986 and 1991 (in yrs)

Sex / Age Birthplace	Total Life expectancy		Free of heavy dependence		Free of heavy or mod. dependence		Free of any dependence		Disability-adjusted life expectancy	
	1991	Change	1991	Change	1991	Change	1991	Change	1991	Change
Males										
At birth										
Canadian	73.60	1.30*	72.28	1.20*	70.23	0.94*	67.62	1.23*	69.15	0.79*
European	76.30	0.75*	74.66	0.63*	72.92	0.47	71.02	0.81	72.45	0.74
Non-Euro.	80.29	2.90*	79.06	2.92*	76.02	1.09	75.22	1.21	77.07	2.01
At age 65										
Canadian	15.31	0.76*	14.29	0.78*	12.68	0.45*	10.79	0.15	12.57	0.41
European	16.21	0.49*	14.87	0.53*	13.70	0.61*	12.74	1.06*	14.06	0.92
Non-Euro.	19.48	2.23*	18.40	2.27*	16.12	0.87	16.00	1.07	17.23	1.58
Females										
At birth										
Canadian	80.35	1.03*	77.82	0.60*	74.49	0.15	69.81	0.06	74.08	0.19
European	81.81	0.80*	79.50	1.54*	75.81	1.42*	72.02	2.04*	76.06	1.07
Non-Euro.	85.71	2.28*	83.54	2.33*	79.35	1.60	77.47	1.18	80.97	2.10
At age 65										
Canadian	19.65	0.70*	17.29	0.30*	14.73	0.00	11.83	-0.31	15.35	0.08
European	19.85	0.14*	17.80	0.96*	15.10	1.26*	12.95	1.89*	16.08	1.02*
Non-Euro.	23.79	2.32*	21.81	2.34*	18.22	0.97	17.20	0.60	20.16	2.09

* Difference significant at 95% confidence.

Oscar E. Firbank

Stratégies de passage à la retraite et populations immigrantes

Abstract

The purpose of this article is to study the patterns of retirement followed by older immigrant workers in Canada, in comparison with those of the native-born population. The study consists of a secondary analysis of data from the Survey on Aging and Independence conducted by Statistics Canada in 1991. A sub-sample of the survey (n=3,171) provides data on Canadian of immigrant origin. The study shows that immigrants adopt distinctive pathways to exit the workforce, although differences among immigrants are as significant as between immigrants and the native population. Immigrants from the Third World, however, clearly stand out from other groups in the numerous challenges they appear to face in relation to retirement In conclusion, recommendations for policy are made to ameliorate the options available to this population, as well as improve their economic security.

Résumé

L'objet de cet article est d'étudier les modalités de passage à la retraite des travailleurs immigrants âgés au Canada en comparaison avec la population native. L'étude est faite à partir d'une analyse secondaire des données de l'Enquête sur le vieillissement et l'autonomie réalisée par Statistique Canada en 1991. Un sous-échantillon de l'enquête (n=3 171) est constitué d'individus d'origine immigrante. L'article montre que les immigrants empruntent des voies particulières pour quitter la vie active, mais que les différences parmi les groupes d'immigrants sont aussi importantes que celles entre les immigrants et la population native. Les immigrants des pays du Tiers Monde, cependant, se différencient clairement des autres groupes en raison des défis nombreux qu'ils ont à affronter face à la retraite. La conclusion en fin d'article formule une série de recommandations en matière de politiques sociales afin d'amé-liorer les choix et la sécurité économique des immigrants au Canada.

Introduction

Le passage de l'activité à la retraite des travailleurs et travailleuses âgés peut s'effectuer suivant des modalités fort différentes. La façon dont ce passage s'organise et, en particulier, la nature plus au moins volontaire de la décision de se retirer du marché de l'emploi, détermineront en grande partie le degré d'autonomie et de sécurité économique dont ces travailleurs et travailleuses seront en mesure de bénéficier une fois à la retraite.

Comprendre comment le processus qui mène à la retraite s'organise et quels facteurs entrent en jeu dans la décision de quitter le marché de l'emploi constitue une tâche complexe. Des caractéristiques socio-démographiques, telles que l'état de santé, le statut économique, la profession, l'expérience sur le marché du travail ou les qualifications, feront que les travailleurs et travailleuses pourront dans certains cas orienter leurs choix et avoir un contrôle relatif sur le moment de leur départ à la retraite. D'autres facteurs d'ordre structurel, cependant, tels que l'accès à des revenus de remplacement, la situation du marché de l'emploi ou les conditions entourant l'exercice d'un emploi restreindront la latitude d'action des individus. D'une façon générale, ces divers facteurs joueront sur le départ à la retraite soit en « poussant » les individus, soit en les « attirant » vers l'inactivité (Guillemard et Rein, 1993; Firbank, 1994; McDonald, 1994).

La population des travailleurs et travailleuses immigrants constitue un cas singulier en ce qui a trait à la retraite. Tout d'abord, ces travailleurs et travailleuses ont dans un grand nombre de cas des parcours de carrière différents de ceux des natifs. Étant donné que la plupart des immigrants sont de jeunes adultes au moment de leur arrivée au Canada, et qu'une période de transition en matière d'insertion professionnelle est souvent nécessaire pendant les premières années d'établissement, leur « carrière » commencera à un âge plus avancé que celle des Canadiens de naissance. Pour certains groupes immigrants, par ailleurs, l'insertion professionnelle a lieu dans des secteurs d'activité souvent à la périphérie du marché de l'emploi ou à l'intérieur de catégories socioprofessionnelles spécifiques. Ils seront donc particulièrement exposés au chômage et à des conditions d'emploi précaires (Côté, 1991; Raskin, 1993; Badets et Chui, 1994; Green, 1995).

L'accès à des régimes de retraite (publics et privés) et donc à des prestations de vieillesse est aussi fonction de leur expérience de travailleurs migrants. Sachant qu'il existe un lien direct entre secteur d'activité et accès à un régime complémentaire de retraite, la concentration importante de certains groupes immigrants dans des branches ayant une faible couverture implique que ces immigrants, une fois retraités, ne pourront compter que d'une façon assez restreinte sur ce type de pensions[1]. Dans le domaine des

régimes publics, certaines dispositions quant aux conditions d'accès à des prestations de vieillesse font aussi que les populations immigrantes sont désavantagées. Tout particulièrement, en ce qui concerne la Sécurité de la vieillesse, un immigrant ou une immigrante reçus de 65 ans et plus ont en principe droit à une pension maximale; pour ceux et celles arrivés au pays après l'âge de 18 ans, cependant, une pleine pension n'est accessible qu'après 40 ans de résidence au Canada. La possibilité de transférer des droits acquis par le fait d'avoir contribué à un régime de pensions dans leur pays d'origine est par ailleurs souvent inexistante ou limitée, ce qui augmente la vulnérabilité des immigrants confrontés à la décision de se retirer du marché de l'emploi.

Cet article vise à comprendre et à expliquer les modalités principales du passage de l'activité à la retraite des communautés immigrantes au Canada. Une première section fait le point sur l'état des connaissances en la matière et formule un certain nombre d'hypothèses à vérifier dans l'étude. Des aspects méthodologiques sont discutés dans une deuxième section, complétés, dans une troisième section, par une présentation du profil général de la population à l'étude. Les sections suivantes discutent tour à tour de la validité de chacune des hypothèses formulées à la lumière des données produites. La conclusion en fin d'article propose une synthèse des résultats de la recherche et examine la portée de ces derniers pour les programmes et politiques concernant la retraite et la sécurité du revenu des personnes âgées.

Recension des écrits et formulation des hypothèses

L'étude des liens entre l'appartenance à une communauté immigrante et le passage à la retraite n'a jusqu'à maintenant reçu qu'une attention très limitée. Les quelques recherches disponibles sont pour la plupart d'origine non canadienne et confondent souvent dans l'analyse groupes immigrés et minorités visibles ou ethniques nées au pays, des populations qui a priori connaissent des trajectoires professionnelles et individuelles dissemblables. Les enquêtes utilisées par ces recherches, par ailleurs, ne touchant aux questions de la retraite et du vieillissement que de façon très indirecte, disposent d'informations souvent peu détaillées à ce sujet.

La portée de ces études est variée. L'un des premiers aspects à avoir été exploré est le statut économique des retraités des groupes immigrants et leur vulnérabilité apparente (Gerber, 1983). Wanner et McDonald (1986), analysant les données du recensement de 1981, montrent que même si d'une façon générale l'appartenance à une communauté immigrante n'est pas un indicateur du statut économique des aînés canadiens, les sources de revenu des groupes provenant du Tiers-Monde et du sud de l'Europe sont claire-

ment différentes de celles d'autres groupes et des Canadiens natifs; les premiers sont beaucoup moins nombreux à recevoir des pensions de vieillesse et plus susceptibles de rester sur le marché de l'emploi jusqu'à un âge plus avancé. Analysant la situation des femmes habitant en région métropolitaine, Boyd (1989), pour sa part, souligne également la probabilité plus faible des immigrantes âgées de percevoir des prestations de vieillesse, mais démontre aussi que le statut économique est en lien direct avec la durée de leur résidence au pays. Wanner et McDonald ou Boyd ne souscrivent pas totalement au postulat théorique des désavantages cumulatifs des immigrants âgés (« multiple-jeopardy perspective ») selon lequel ces immigrants feraient face à des handicaps multiples affectant leur statut économique (statut minoritaire, âge, discrimination en matière d'emploi, ségrégation résidentielle) (Markides et Mindel, 1987; Penning, 1983), mais s'accordent pour reconnaître l'effet structurant du processus d'immigration à l'égard du départ à la retraite.

L'âge du départ à la retraite des communautés ethniques et immigrantes, ainsi que la continuité ou l'interruption involontaire de l'exercice d'une activité rémunérée sont aussi des sujets ayant été abordés par un certain nombre d'études. La tendance des immigrants âgés du Tiers-Monde à avoir un taux d'activité plus élevé que les Canadiens de naissance est un phénomène identifié par plusieurs auteurs (Gerber, 1983; Wanner et McDonald, 1986; Santerre, 1989). Pour Wanner et McDonald (1986) cette tendance s'explique par le manque d'accès à des pensions pleines et les difficultés que ces groupes ont à constituer des revenus de remplacement. Les différences entre communautés immigrantes peuvent cependant être importantes. Essayant d'interpréter les variations à propos de l'âge de départ à la retraite des communautés noire et hispanique aux États-Unis, certains auteurs ont avancé des explications un peu plus nuancées (Gibson, 1987, 1991 et 1993; Zsembik et Singer, 1990). D'une part, une proportion non négligeable des membres des communautés ethniques aurait tendance à se retirer du marché du travail d'une façon prématurée à la suite de problèmes d'invalidité dont l'incidence est plus fréquente que celle enregistrée pour les membres des communautés non ethniques. Ces individus ne s'identifieraient pas comme des retraités (Gibson les appelle des « non retraités-retraités ») (Gibson, 1991). D'autre part, en raison des parcours de carrière fréquemment interrompus, du manque de moyens financiers et de l'accès souvent limité à des prestations de vieillesse, ceux qui sont en mesure de travailler auraient tendance à rester plus longtemps sur le marché du travail. Le processus de retraite, donc, s'allongerait sur un nombre relativement important d'années, marqué par des périodes intermittentes d'activité rémunérée. Les recherches consultées permettent de dégager trois hypothèses :

Hypothèse 1a : Les modalités en fonction de l'âge du départ à la retraite des membres des communautés immigrantes (retraite anticipée, à 65 ans ou tardive) sont différentes de celles de la population née au pays.

Hypothèse 1b : Parmi les membres des communautés immigrantes, ceux qui partent à la retraite anticipée le font à un âge plus jeune en moyenne que l'ensemble de la population.

Hypothèse 1c : Les membres de ces mêmes communautés qui continuent à travailler au-delà de 65 ans, par contre, retardent leur passage à la retraite jusqu'à un âge plus avancé que celui des Canadiens d'origine.

Des recherches menées au Canada (Firbank, 1994; Schellenberg, 1994) et à l'étranger (Kohli *et al.*, 1991; Laczko et Phillipson, 1991) à propos de la réorganisation du passage de l'activité à la retraite au cours des vingt dernières années ont fait état d'un certain nombre de changements majeurs. Parmi les transformations identifiées par ces études, en rapport avec la tendance généralisée vers une réduction de l'âge de départ à la retraite, le premier phénomène qu'on remarque est celui de la multiplication des dispositifs assurant la transition de l'activité vers l'inactivité à la fin du cycle de vie. Les régimes publics de retraite, en particulier, traditionnellement les instruments par excellence réglant le passage à la retraite et assurant son financement, auraient graduellement cédé la place à une diversité de programmes à la fois publics (assurance invalidité, programmes pour chômeurs âgés de longue durée, aide sociale) et privés (retraites complémentaires, programmes d'incitation à la retraite).

Les changements enregistrés, cependant, n'auraient pas affecté les perpectives de carrière de toutes les catégories de travailleurs âgés de façon identique. Le positionnement spécifique de ces travailleurs sur le marché de l'emploi et leur stratification en fonction de la profession, des qualifications, du secteur d'activité ou du sexe conduiraient au développement de cheminements vers la retraite assez différents (Firbank, 1995; Carrière, 1995).

Hypothèse 2a : Les travailleurs migrants, étant donné la nature des trajectoires professionnelles qu'ils connaissent par suite de leur établissement dans le pays d'arrivée et de l'accès plus au moins restreint à des prestations de vieillesse, devraient aussi adopter des modalités de passage à la retraite reflétant leur expérience particulière.

Hypothèse 2b : Les raisons sous-jacentes à leur départ, par ailleurs, en lien avec ces mêmes facteurs, divergeraient à certains égards de celles déterminant le passage à l'inactivité des Canadiens de naissance.

Outre ce phénomène de diversification des voies de sortie de l'activité à la fin du cycle de vie, les recherches ont aussi fait ressortir que les frontières entre la vie active et la retraite seraient devenues moins stables (Kohli *et al.*, 1991), et que pour beaucoup de travailleurs âgés le passage à la retraite aurait pris la forme d'une transition graduelle (McDaniel *et al.*, 1993; Hayward *et al.*, 1994) modulée par une réduction du temps de travail et/ou l'occupation d'un emploi de type transitoire (« bridge jobs ») (Doeringer, 1990). Le statut de retraité, par ailleurs, aurait acquis un caractère moins définitif. Un nombre non négligeable d'individus, après avoir quitté le marché de l'emploi et être restés dans l'inactivité pendant une période de temps parfois importante, retourneraient au travail (The Commonwealth Fund, 1993; Firbank, 1996). Au Canada, les connaissances sur ce sujet sont relativement peu abondantes (Osberg, 1988); on peut toutefois penser que :

Hypothèse 3a : la retraite des travailleurs migrants, vu leur expérience sur le marché de l'emploi et leurs préférences particulières, adopterait un caractère plus ou moins définitif que celui des Canadiens d'origine; et que

Hypothèse 3b : dans l'éventualité d'un retour au marché de l'emploi, leur insertion devrait aussi suivre des modalités spécifiques.

Un certain nombre d'études, enfin, ont analysé la question de la préparation en vue du départ à la retraite et souligné son importance en tant que moyen susceptible d'assurer une meilleure stabilité économique et un plus haut degré d'autonomie financière des travailleurs âgés une fois inactifs (Ekerdt, 1993). Cette préparation passe par : la constitution d'un revenu d'épargne; le remboursement des dettes; la planification de la cessation partielle ou complète d'activité; etc. Les dispositions prises, par ailleurs, ont un lien avec les moyens à la portée des travailleurs et travailleuses et le contexte socio-économique dans lequel cette planification est faite. Dans la mesure où la cessation d'activité professionnelle ne peut pas être anticipée et, d'une façon plus générale, les ressources économiques ayant pu être accumulées au long de la vie active sont limitées, les préparatifs à la retraite seront peu nombreux ou inexistants. Les populations dites « vulnérables », en particulier, tels les chômeurs de longue durée âgés, les femmes

n'ayant pas pu accéder à des emplois stables et bien rémunérés ou ayant eu des parcours de carrière fréquemment interrompus, ainsi que certaines catégories d'immigrants ou des groupes ethniques auront plus de difficulté à organiser et planifier leur départ à la retraite. Pour beaucoup d'entre eux, le passage à la retraite se fera plus au moyen de « stratégies de survie » que des « stratégies de préparation » proprement dites.

Des études fondées sur des enquêtes récentes font état d'une amélioration considérable et généralisée des préparatifs que les travailleurs et travailleuses âgés font en prévision de leur retraite, le reflet surtout de meilleures conditions d'accès à des régimes de pension publics et privés (Crompton, 1993). Ces études, cependant, par le fait de traiter la population des travailleurs et travailleuses âgés et des retraités d'une façon assez homogène, n'attribuent que peu de poids aux particularismes propres à chaque sous-groupe de population.

Dans une étude portant sur le comportement des immigrants à l'égard de l'épargne en comparaison avec celui des Canadiens natifs, Shamsuddin (1995) conclut que les premiers sont plus enclins à faire des investissements au cours de leur vie active, mais aussi à les dépenser de façon accélérée lors de leur retraite. Le phénomène, selon Shamsuddin, constituerait une stratégie de compensation adoptée par les immigrants attribuable au fait qu'ils bénéficient moins souvent d'une pension de la Sécurité de la vieillesse.

Tenant compte des résultats des recherches, on peut à ce stade supposer :

Hypothèse 4a : qu'étant donné des parcours de carrière singuliers, et des préférences et besoins particuliers, la planification en vue de la retraite des immigrés ne comporterait pas les mêmes activités que celles des populations non immigrées; et que

Hypothèse 4b : dans la mesure où certaines communautés manqueraient plus que d'autres de ressources économiques ou de revenus de remplacement, le temps attribué à cette préparation par leurs membres serait moins important.

Méthodologie

L'étude repose sur une analyse secondaire des données de l'Enquête sur le vieillissement et l'autonomie menée par Statistique Canada en 1991. Cette enquête, portant sur 20 036 sujets âgés de 45 ans et plus, cherchait à examiner les différents facteurs contribuant à l'autonomie et à la qualité de vie des aînés d'aujourd'hui et de demain. L'enquête inclut donc une série de questions directement liées aux modalités de passage de l'activité à la retraite permettant d'effectuer des analyses relativement détaillées à ce sujet.

Un sous-échantillon des participants à l'enquête (n=3 171), en particulier, est constitué de sujets nés à l'étranger et ayant immigré au Canada à un moment non identifié de leur vie.

Malgré la richesse d'informations fournies par l'enquête, des limites sont à signaler. Tout d'abord, la taille et la nature du sous-échantillon des répondants nés hors du Canada ne permet pas d'effectuer des analyses très fines en fonction de la région d'origine. À cet effet, nous avons dû réunir les données en quatre catégories (Canada, États-Unis, Europe, et Tiers-Monde et autres) rassemblant parfois des immigrants originaires de pays de niveaux de développement économique assez disparates. La catégorie « Europe », par exemple, intègre des populations provenant d'Europe du Nord et des pays scandinaves (45 %), d'Europe de l'Ouest (21 %), et d'Europe de l'Est et du Sud (34 %); tandis que celle dénommée « Tiers-Monde et autres » regroupe des immigrants provenant en majorité de régions à faible développement économique (85 %), mais aussi de pays tels que l'Australie, l'Afrique du Sud, Hongkong, Israël, le Japon et la Corée (15 %). Ensuite, le même problème de taille limite parfois la possibilité d'effectuer des analyses comparant les hommes aux femmes, qui, on le sait, suivent des trajectoires de carrière et de passage à la retraite différentes. Enfin, l'absence d'informations au sujet de l'âge ou des conditions d'arrivée au Canada des répondants constitue une dernière faiblesse de l'enquête conditionnant le type d'interprétations possibles à partir des données disponibles. À cet égard, certaines recherches canadiennes portant sur le statut économique et la vitesse d'assimilation des immigrants ont fait état d'un effet de rattrapage de la part de ces derniers qui, en moyenne et toutes catégories confondues, devraient se rapprocher de la population native dans les 12 à 14 années suivant leur arrivée au pays (Chiswick et Miller, 1988; DeSilva, 1992; Fagnan, 1995). Étant donné l'âge relativement peu élevé auquel les immigrants arrivent au pays (l'âge médian était de 23,6 ans en 1991), on peut toutefois supposer qu'une majorité des répondants, surtout ceux appartenant aux cohortes âgées de 55 à 64 ans, et de 65 ans et plus, ont déjà dépassé ce seuil en années d'assimilation économique.

L'analyse se fera donc en fonction de trois catégories d'immigrants (États-Unis, Europe, et Tiers-Monde et autres), que nous comparerons à la population canadienne d'origine; et de trois cohortes (45 à 54 ans, 55 à 64 ans et 65 ans et plus). Des comparaisons hommes-femmes, en raison des limites imposées par la taille de l'échantillon, ne seront faites que de façon ponctuelle. Trois catégories de population définies en fonction du statut des répondants par rapport à l'emploi seront utilisées, ceci afin de disposer d'indicateurs à la fois objectifs et subjectifs du statut de retraité[2]. Les données seront exploitées au moyen de l'analyse exploratoire et descriptive.

Position face à l'emploi, limitations d'activité et statut économique des immigrés et des Canadiens natifs

Le tableau 1 fournit un profil détaillé et comparatif de trois cohortes de la population à l'étude établi en fonction d'une série d'indicateurs socio-économiques. Un certain nombre de tendances générales peuvent être identifiées.

Pour toutes les catégories d'âge, le taux d'activité des immigrants de la catégorie « Tiers-Monde et autres » est supérieur à celui des Canadiens d'origine. Le groupe d'immigrants nés en Europe suit la même tendance, tandis que celui des États-Unis, au contraire, a des taux d'activité inférieurs à ceux des autres catégories; la seule exception pour ces deux derniers groupes étant la cohorte des 65 ans et plus.

En ce qui concerne l'insertion des populations immigrées et non immigrées sur le marché de l'emploi, on note des différences importantes tant au niveau des professions que des secteurs d'activité. D'une façon générale, on ne peut pas parler d'une quelconque ségrégation occupationnelle des populations immigrantes qui, selon leur région d'origine, ont des modalités d'insertion très variées et aussi différentes que celles pouvant ressortir d'une comparaison avec la population canadienne. La seule situation « atypique » à signaler est, cependant, celle des immigrants du Tiers-Monde pour qui on dénote une tendance prononcée à travailler dans le secteur des industries de services (marchands) plutôt que celui des manufactures. Ce type particulier d'insertion déterminera en grande partie le degré d'accessibilité des membres de cette communauté à des programmes complémentaires de retraite et d'invalidité établis par les employeurs, affectant par cela même leurs modalités de passage à la retraite.

Par rapport aux limitations d'activité, les indicateurs subjectifs utilisés dans l'enquête font ressortir des différences intéressantes. Pour les trois cohortes, et tout particulièrement pour les plus jeunes (45 à 54 ans et 55 à 64 ans), les immigrants du Tiers-Monde s'écartent considérablement de la moyenne. Mais tandis qu'à l'intérieur du groupe des 45 à 54 ans une proportion importante de membres de cette communauté signalent ne pas avoir de limitations d'activité (6,3 % contre 18,6 %), à l'intérieur du groupe de 55 à 64 ans la situation est tout juste le contraire (42,9 % contre 27,4 %). Sans disposer d'informations plus détaillées sur le type de limitations et leur gravité[3], il est difficile d'avancer des explications solides sur les raisons amenant ces différences. Aux États-Unis, des études effectuées à propos des communautés noires et hispaniques ont permis d'affirmer qu'étant donné l'accessibilité réduite des membres de ces communautés à des programmes de retraite, le passage à la retraite anticipée est souvent financé au moyen

de pensions d'invalidité dont l'accès est fonction du statut de santé des prestataires; dans certains cas les membres de ces communautés auraient donc tendance à empirer l'évaluation subjective qu'ils font de leurs limitations d'activité. Quoique le statut de santé des immigrants au Canada ne puisse pas être assimilé à celui des minorités visibles aux États-Unis, il est toutefois possible de supposer que pour un nombre important d'immigrés provenant du Tiers-Monde, surtout ceux approchant l'âge de la retraite (55 à 64 ans), le même phénomène serait en jeu[4].

Les trois catégories suivantes du tableau 1 – revenu personnel, situation face au logement et existence d'une hypothèque – constituent des indicateurs du statut économique des populations à l'étude. Par rapport au revenu personnel (estimation personnelle), la situation des immigrés apparaît comparable à celle des non immigrés ou dans certains cas meilleure. La distribution des revenus, en particulier, semble être moins polarisée chez les immigrés que chez les non immigrés. Mais si l'on se concentre sur les immigrants du Tiers-Monde, et si l'on tient compte non seulement des niveaux de revenu mais aussi des taux d'activité en emploi à plein temps (beaucoup plus importants que ceux des autres groupes), on dénote que ces immigrants sont comparativement moins avantagés que les autres. Le taux inférieur d'accès à une propriété et la présence d'un prêt hypothécaire encore non payé parmi les membres de ce groupe viennent confirmer leur désavantage relatif.

Âge de départ à la retraite

Les données que nous avons fournies au tableau 1 ont déjà fait état du lien différent que les immigrants entretiennent avec le marché de l'emploi. Le taux d'activité des immigrants du Tiers-Monde, surtout en emploi à plein temps, est pour toutes les catégories d'âge beaucoup plus important que pour les immigrés des autres groupes et les Canadiens natifs. L'inactivité et la retraite anticipée, par ailleurs, sont beaucoup moins courantes pour ce groupe d'immigrants et pour les personnes nées en Europe que pour la population canadienne ou américaine.

Le tableau 2a, lequel fournit des informations sur la population retraitée en fonction des modalités de départ adoptées – retraite anticipée, à 65 ans, ou tardive –, vient compléter les indications du tableau précédent.

Toutes les catégories immigrantes manifestent une tendance à retarder leur départ à la retraite, ce qui se traduit, d'une part, par une moindre propension à prendre une retraite anticipée et, d'autre part, par une plus grande inclination à continuer à exercer une activité rémunérée au-delà de 65 ans.

En outre, l'âge moyen de départ à la retraite des immigrés est supérieur à celui des Canadiens d'origine (tableau 2b) – entre 1 et 2 ans selon

l'origine. Les immigrés du Tiers-Monde, cependant, partent à la retraite anticipée plus tôt que les autres catégories ou, s'ils continuent à travailler au-delà de 65 ans, le font en moyenne jusqu'à un âge plus avancé que les Canadiens de naissance et les autres groupes d'immigrés.

Les différences concernant le rapport à l'activité et l'âge de départ à la retraite semblent indiquer que les immigrés du Tiers-Monde sont contraints de quitter le marché de l'emploi à un âge moins avancé (probablement comme résultat de leur insertion professionnelle dans des secteurs d'activité où la sécurité de l'emploi est souvent absente); mais aussi, dans la mesure où ils peuvent continuer à exercer une activité rémunérée, ils le font jusqu'à un âge plus avancé que les autres (a priori afin de compenser pour les désavantages cumulatifs résultant de leur parcours professionnel).

Passage à la retraite – voies et raisons du départ vers l'inactivité

Si l'on se concentre maintenant sur les voies particulières empruntées par chaque communauté pour quitter le marché de l'emploi et que l'on identifie les sources de soutien qui sont disponibles aux travailleurs âgés, des différences sont aussi à noter.

Le tableau 3 décompose les sources de revenu des trois cohortes de population en fonction de leur statut d'activité et de leur origine régionale. Par rapport aux modalités de passage à la retraite, les comparaisons à première vue les plus intéressantes à établir à partir des données de ce tableau sont celles entre les différentes communautés d'origine, et entre la population active et la population inactive et retraitée des groupes d'âge de 55 à 64 ans et de 65 ans et plus (c'est-à-dire les catégories d'âge à l'intérieur desquelles la transition vers la retraite est plus courante). La taille par moments réduite du nombre de répondants par cellule ne permet malheureusement pas d'effectuer des analyses rigoureuses pour toutes les situations. Plusieurs observations sont toutefois possibles.

Si nous nous penchons d'abord sur les inactifs et les retraités appartenant à la cohorte de 65 ans et plus, il apparaît que la répartition des sources de revenu des communautés est assez dissemblable. Le groupe « Tiers-Monde et autres », encore une fois, se différencie clairement des autres : aussi bien les pensions publiques que privées occupent une place moins importante dans le revenu de ces populations et, au moins pour les inactifs, ce manque semble devoir être compensé par les revenus d'investissement ou l'apport financier d'autres membres de la famille.

Certains aspects de la répartition des sources de revenu du groupe précédent sont aussi observables dans le groupe des 55 à 64 ans. Les immigrés inactifs et retraités disposent, toutes catégories confondues, de revenus de

pensions publiques moins importants que les Canadiens d'origine et, dans le cas des retraités, de pensions privées qui occupent aussi une place moins significative dans leur revenu total. L'effet compensateur joué par les investissements et le soutien familial, d'autre part, est plus marqué que ce n'est le cas pour les membres de la catégorie d'âge précédente.

D'une façon générale, on peut donc affirmer que les voies empruntées par les communautés immigrantes pour quitter le marché de l'emploi et, éventuellement, partir à la retraite, sont différentes de celles des Canadiens d'origine. L'absence de ressources de remplacement, en particulier, résultat de l'accès parfois limité à de pleines pensions ou d'une couverture des régimes de retraite complémentaire moins importante[5], semble être à l'origine de cette différenciation. Des stratégies compensatrices, telles que le recours à des revenus d'investissement ou le soutien familial, doivent être utilisées par certains immigrés afin de combler les lacunes de la protection vieillesse publique et privée.

L'analyse des raisons ayant amené les communautés immigrantes à prendre la retraite fournit des informations supplémentaires sur les conditions entourant le départ à la retraite en lien avec les voies empruntées (tableau 4).

Indépendamment du lieu de naissance et de l'âge de départ à la retraite, plus de répondants déclarent avoir quitté le marché de l'emploi pour des raisons volontaires plutôt qu'involontaires; la nature volontaire de la retraite est cependant moins courante pour les immigrés de la catégorie « Tiers-Monde et autres ». Si on compare les raisons spécifiques invoquées par les personnes de cette catégorie ayant pris une retraite anticipée avec celles des natifs, on remarque qu'un nombre beaucoup moins important signalent avoir pris leur retraite en raison de leur revenu de pension, du régime de préretraite offert par l'employeur, ou de leur désir de cesser de travailler. Les membres de cette communauté manifestent, au contraire, être beaucoup plus affectés que les autres par l'absence d'emplois et la retraite obligatoire[6]. Les raisons avancées par les membres des différentes communautés ayant pris leur retraite à 65 ans ou plus tard sont en général assez comparables; on doit cependant noter que la santé, particulièrement pour les immigrés de la catégorie « Tiers-Monde et autres », est moins couramment citée que lorsqu'il s'agit de personnes précocement retraitées.

Organisation du départ à la retraite

Tout comme l'âge et les voies empruntées, l'organisation du départ à la retraite des immigrants semble se distinguer de celle des natifs et répondre à des expériences professionnelles et communautaires particulières. Le tableau 5 présente des informations à propos de la nature plus au moins

définitive du départ à la retraite et, dans le cas d'un retour à l'activité, des modalités suivies par les communautés immigrantes comparées à celles des Canadiens nés au pays.

Si l'on se concentre sur la population ayant pris une retraite précoce (avant 65 ans), d'abord, pour une minorité non négligeable, la transition vers la retraite s'accompagne d'un retour au travail; ce retour, cependant, est beaucoup plus courant pour les immigrés de la catégorie «Tiers-Monde et autres» que pour toutes les autres catégories (23,3 % des immigrés de cette catégorie contre 16,9 % des Canadiens d'origine). La réintégration au marché de l'emploi des retraités du groupe des 65 ans et plus appartenant à cette même catégorie touche toutefois un pourcentage assez réduit de personnes (3,4 %), surtout quand on le compare à celui des natifs (19,7 %).

Sans distinction des modalités de départ à la retraite adoptées (précoce, à 65 ans ou tardive), ceux qui retournent au travail le font dans la plupart des cas à temps partiel. Les immigrés, surtout ceux du groupe «Tiers-Monde et autres», cependant, font appel à ce type d'emploi de façon plus habituelle. La propension à exercer une activité salariée plutôt qu'à travailler à son compte est la norme parmi les retraités qui retournent au travail; immigrés et non-immigrés se différencient peu à cet égard.

Préparatifs en vue de la retraite

Les tableaux 6 et 7, enfin, fournissent des informations sur les préparatifs en vue du départ à la retraite effectués par les membres des différentes communautés en fonction de leur statut d'emploi et de leur groupe d'âge.

Une comparaison des populations immigrantes entre elles et avec les Canadiens de naissance démontre la diversité des situations et la difficulté à identifier des tendances spécifiques. Certaines analyses sont pourtant possibles.

Par rapport à nos hypothèses de départ, la proposition selon laquelle les immigrés, vu leur accessibilité limitée à des prestations de retraite, seraient plus prédisposés à épargner que les non-immigrés, ne peut être ni confirmée ni abandonnée. Si l'on regarde la population âgée de 65 ans et plus, les retraités aussi bien que les inactifs immigrés manifestent une disposition à contribuer à un REER, à accumuler des économies ou à faire d'autres placements comparable ou parfois moins importante que la population née au Canada. Les données recueillies à propos des répondants du groupe de 45 à 64 ans, par contre, surtout en ce qui concerne les immigrés de la catégorie « Tiers-Monde et autres », indiquent que la population immigrante a une propension à épargner plus forte que la population native.

D'autre part, l'hypothèse voulant que les populations immigrantes aient des stratégies de préparation de départ à la retraite ne ressemblant pas à celles

des Canadiens natifs semble être fondée. Face à la retraite, les communautés immigrantes sont, par exemple, moins enclines à modifier leur régime de travail ou à recueillir des renseignements à ce sujet. La variabilité *entre* communautés à propos du genre de préparatifs entrepris est cependant importante.

Le nombre d'années de planification active avant de prendre la retraite confirme que les immigrés adoptent des modalités particulières. En moyenne, ces derniers semblent être moins disposés ou moins en mesure de se préparer à la retraite : proportionnellement plus d'immigrés que de Canadiens natifs signalent ne pas se préparer (48,4 % des derniers contre 53,3 % des premiers). Mais même quand préparation il y a, le nombre d'années investies est généralement moins important pour les immigrés (surtout ceux provenant du Tiers-Monde et autres) que pour les personnes nées au pays. Peu de différences significatives existent entre ceux ayant pris une retraite anticipée et ceux ayant quitté le marché de l'emploi à 65 ans ou plus, si ce n'est le fait que ces derniers sont concentrés dans la catégorie « trois à quatre années » plutôt que celle « une à deux années ».

Conclusion

L'analyse que nous avons effectuée démontre que l'appartenance à une communauté immigrante joue un rôle important dans la définition du processus qui mène de l'activité à la retraite. Ce processus n'est pas identique pour toutes les catégories d'immigrants et dépend de diverses circonstances. La rupture créée par l'événement migratoire dans l'itinéraire professionnel des travailleurs ainsi que les possibles difficultés de réinsertion rencontrées dans le pays d'accueil sont des facteurs qui affectent le parcours professionnel des immigrés et font que leur retraite se différencie de celle des non-immigrés.

Par rapport à nos hypothèses de départ, il a pu être constaté que la tendance vers un départ à la retraite anticipée caractéristique de ces vingt dernières années a davantage affecté les travailleurs natifs que les travailleurs immigrés. Pour le groupe d'immigrés qui partent à la retraite anticipée, cependant, ce départ intervient à un âge moins avancé, surtout s'il s'agit d'immigrants du Tiers-Monde (fort probablement comme résultat d'une plus grande vulnérabilité face à l'emploi). L'activité au-delà de 65 ans est aussi plus courante pour les immigrants et s'allonge jusqu'à un âge plus avancé que pour les Canadiens d'origine. Ce dernier phénomène est à première vue l'expression d'une stratégie de compensation face à l'insertion « accidentée » de ces travailleurs et, pour certains, à un accès restreint à des pensions de retraite.

La place moins importante occupée par les pensions de retraite publiques et privées dans le revenu des immigrés laisse supposer que ces derniers

empruntent des voies différentes pour quitter l'activité. Par ailleurs, plus d'immigrants en provenance du Tiers-Monde que d'Europe ou des États-Unis prennent la retraite de façon involontaire et, quoique les raisons motivant leur départ soient semblables, l'absence d'emploi et la retraite obligatoire affectent le premier groupe davantage que les autres.

Une minorité non négligeable de travailleurs âgés, immigrés ou non, retournent à la vie active après leur passage à la retraite par le biais d'emplois à temps partiel. Les retraités originaires du Tiers-Monde ayant quitté l'activité de façon anticipée sont plus nombreux que les autres, cependant, à suivre ce parcours de carrière. La « retraite partielle » de ce groupe de population semble être en relation avec leur départ involontaire du marché de l'emploi et leur accès plus limité à des revenus de remplacement suffisamment importants pour ne pas avoir à retourner en activité.

Nos données ne permettent pas de valider ou d'invalider la proposition selon laquelle les immigrés auraient une propension à épargner plus importante que les natifs afin de corriger les effets créés par l'accessibilité limitée à des revenus de pension. Les immigrés, néanmoins, sont nettement moins nombreux à se préparer en vue de la retraite; les modalités adoptées sont par ailleurs différentes de celles des Canadiens nés au pays.

D'une façon générale, on ne peut pas parler des immigrants comme d'une population « globalement vulnérable » face à la retraite, nécessitant une attention particulière de la part des pouvoirs publics. Le statut économique et les ressources à la disposition de certaines catégories de travailleurs immigrés âgés sont comparables à ceux des travailleurs natifs moyens, parfois même meilleurs. Notre étude a toutefois fait ressortir l'existence de catégories d'immigrants qui, confrontés à la retraite, semblent avoir à faire face à plus de difficultés et à une latitude décisionnelle moindre. La situation des immigrants provenant des régions « non traditionnelles », en particulier, mérite d'être soulignée par le fait qu'il s'agit non seulement du groupe le plus désavantagé, mais aussi celui qui, compte tenu des tendances démographiques récentes, risque d'augmenter de façon importante.

Dans une perspective de politique publique, il serait sans doute difficile de concevoir des instruments d'intervention ciblant des populations en fonction de leur seule origine nationale. Les interventions les plus efficaces, par ailleurs, seraient celles qui visent à corriger les désavantages subis par certains groupes tout au long de leur carrière plutôt qu'à la fin. Des mesures susceptibles à la fois d'élargir les options à la portée des communautés immigrantes face à la retraite et d'améliorer leur statut économique une fois inactifs sont cependant envisageables.

Tout d'abord, dans la mesure où les travailleurs immigrés âgés souhaitent ou ont besoin de retarder le moment du départ à la retraite, souvent

au-delà de 65 ans, les politiques de retraite obligatoire encore en vigueur dans la plupart des provinces constituent un obstacle qui s'ajoute à leurs difficultés d'emploi. Presque 68 % des répondants de l'Enquête sur la vieillesse et l'autonomie résidaient dans ces provinces. L'abolition légale de la retraite obligatoire, suivant l'exemple du fédéral et de trois provinces (Québec, Manitoba et Nouveau-Brunswick), pourrait favoriser l'activité de certaines catégories de travailleurs âgés immigrés.

C'est cependant le critère d'admissibilité au régime de Sécurité de la vieillesse, ainsi que, parfois, l'absence de mécanismes permettant de transférer les cotisations aux régimes de retraite effectuées dans leur pays d'origine, qui affaiblit le plus le statut économique des immigrés âgés. Le « rattrapage » économique des immigrés pendant leur vie active au Canada ne semble pas compenser pour ces désavantages. La couverture offerte par les régimes complémentaires de retraite, aux immigrés comme aux nationaux, est par ailleurs assez limitée. Il serait sans doute souhaitable que les conditions d'admissibilité des immigrés au régime de Sécurité de la vieillesse soient élargies, surtout en ce qui concerne les personnes ayant un revenu au-dessous du seuil de pauvreté. Les revenus de pensions provenant des cotisations aux régimes de vieillesse faites par les immigrés avant leur établissement au Canada pourraient aussi ne pas être comptabilisés dans le calcul des prestations du Supplément de revenu garanti. Des initiatives, aussi bien à l'échelon fédéral qu'à celui du Québec, visant à étendre les accords avec d'autres pays à propos du transfert des droits à une pension, enfin, constitueraient un pas en vue de soulager les tensions économiques vécues par beaucoup d'immigrants dans leur transition vers la retraite.

Notes

1. D'après les données du dernier recensement, 23 % travaillaient dans l'industrie manufacturière, 16 % dans le commerce et 13 % dans les services (Badets et Chui, 1994)
2. Une différenciation nette des répondants en retraités et non-retraités est sans doute problématique. À cet effet il a été suggéré que la retraite est à la fois un statut objectif (défini essentiellement par l'âge, l'abandon total ou partiel d'un emploi de carrière et l'importance des pensions dans le revenu des travailleurs) et subjectif (déterminé par la reconnaissance de la part des individus de leur situation de retraité). Pour les populations immigrées ou les minorités ethniques, cependant, la signification même du concept de retraite est problématique, et il semble valable de se demander jusqu'à quel point des codes culturels distincts, assignant un sens et une valeur particulière au « travail rémunéré », aux « loisirs », ou à « l'inactivité », n'invalident pas la pertinence des catégories analytiques créées à partir de l'expérience

des travailleurs américains et canadiens moyens (Santerre, 1989). Les indicateurs de la retraite que nous retenons donc sont à certains égards imparfaits; ils expriment toutefois cette coupure entre activité rémunérée et inactivité à la fin du cycle de vie qu'il est convenu d'appeler retraite.

3. Les variables « limitations d'activités en emploi » ou « capacité de faire face à une limitation », dû au taux de réponse très bas des sujets participant à l'enquête, ne fournissent pas des informations fiables à cet égard.

4. Parmi les raisons invoquées par les immigrés pour expliquer leur départ à la retraite, la santé a une importance de premier ordre. La proportion d'immigrés attribuant leur retraite anticipée à des problèmes de santé, cependant, est comparable à celle des non immigrés (se référer au tableau 4).

5. Parmi les retraités du groupe de 45 à 64 ans, par exemple, 59,9 % des Canadiens d'origine signalaient avoir été couverts par un régime complémentaire de retraite contre 22,2 % des personnes appartenant à la catégorie Tiers-Monde et autres. La situation pour les inactifs âgés de 65 et plus est semblable (12,0 % contre 6,3 %) mais assez comparable pour les actifs et les retraités.

6. Étant donné que la majorité des répondants de ce groupe avaient moins de 65 ans au moment de prendre leur retraite et que la retraite obligatoire en dessous de cet âge est peu courante, on soupçonne que l'identification du point « la politique en matière de retraite obligatoire » comme étant l'un des facteurs ayant motivé leur départ à la retraite fait référence plutôt aux conditions générales les « obligeant » à quitter leur emploi qu'aux « politiques de retraite obligatoire » proprement dites.

Références

Badets, J. et T.W.L. Chui (1994) *Évolution de la population immigrante au Canada*, Ottawa, Prentice Hall et Statistique Canada.

Boyd, M. (1989) « Immigration and income security policies in Canada: Implications for elderly immigrant women », *Population Research and Policy Review*, 8: 5-24.

Carrière, Y. (1995) « Le dualisme économique et les inégalités face à la retraite », dans A.-M. Guillemard, J. Légaré et P. Ansart (dir.), *Entre travail, retraite et vieillesse. Le grand écart*, Paris, L'Harmattan.

Chiswick, B.R. et P.W. Miller (1988) « Earnings in Canada: The Role of Immigrant Generation, French Ethnicity, and Language », dans *Research in Population Economics*, Greenwich, Conn., JAI Press.

The Commonwealth Fund (1993) *The Untapped Resource. The Final Report of The Americans Over 55 at Work Program*, New York, Author.

Côté, M.G. (1991) « Minorités visibles dans la population active au Canada », *Perspectives sur le revenu et l'emploi*, (Été), p. 17-26.

Crompton, S. (1993) « À l'approche de la retraite », *L'emploi et le revenu en perspective*, 5(1): 35-43.

Oscar E. Firbank

DeSilva, A. (1992) *Les gains des immigrants*, Ottawa, Conseil économique du Canada.

Doeringer, P.B. (dir.) *Bridges to Retirement: Older Workers in a Changing Labour Market*, Ithaka, N.Y., I.L.R. Press.

Ekerdt, D.J. (1993) « Retirement Preparation », *Annual Review of Gerontology and Geriatrics*, 14, 321-356.

Firbank, O.E. (1994) *Reversing the Trend Toward Early Retirement? The Effect of Social Policy and Labour Markets*, Montréal, Université de Montréal.

Firbank, O.E. (1995) « Les 'Baby-boomers' à la retraite : nouveaux riches ou nouveaux pauvres ? », *Le Gérontophile*, Numéro spécial « Émergence de nouvelles vieillesses : Enjeu de l'an 2000 », 17 (2), 13-17.

Firbank, O.E. (1996) « Renverser le mouvement vers la préretraite ? L'effet des politiques sociales et du marché du travail », dans Bourbonnais, R. et L. Mercier (dir.) *Le travail aujourd'hui : discontinuités et opportunités*, Ste-Foy, PUQ.

Gerber, L.M. (1983) « Ethnicity Still Matters: Socio-Demographic Profiles of the Ethnic Elderly in Ontario », *Canadian Ethnic Studies*, 15 (3), 60-80.

Gibson, R.C. (1987) « Reconceptualizing Retirement for Black Americans », *The Gerontologist*, 27 (6), 691-698.

Gibson, R.C (1991) « The Subjective Retirement of Black Americans », *Journal of Gerontology: Social Sciences*, 46 (4), S204-209.

Gibson, R.C. (1993) « The Black American Retirement Experience », Jackson, J.S., L.M. Chatters et R.J. Taylor (dir.) *Aging in Black America*, Newbury Park, Cal., Sage.

Green, D.A. (1995) « Intended and Actual Occupations of Immigrants », dans D.J. DeVoretz (dir.), *Diminishing Returns. The Economics of Canada's Recent Immigration Policy*, Winnipeg, Hignell Printing Limited.

Guillemard, A. M. et M. Rein (1993) « Comparative patterns of retirement: Recent trends in developed societies », *Annual Review of Sociology*, 19, 469-503.

Hayward, M.D., E.M. Crimmins et L.A. Wray (1994) « The relationship between retirement, life cycle changes and older men's labour force participation rates », *Journal of Gerontology: Social Sciences*, 49 (5), S219-S230.

Kohli, M., M. Rein, A-M. Guillemard et H. van Gunsteren (dir.) (1991) *Time for Retirement: Comparative Studies of Early Exit from the Work Force*, New York, Cambridge University Press.

Laczko, F. et Phillipson, C. (1991) *Changing Work and Retirement: Social Policy and the Older Worker*, Philadelphia, Open University Press.

Markides, K.S. et Ch.H. Mindel (1987) *Aging and Ethnicity*, Newbury Park, Cal., Sage.

McDaniel, S., N.M. Lalu et H. Krahn (1993) « Labour force transitions of older Canadian women: A multistate life table approach », communication présentée à la Population Association of America, Cincinnati, Ohio, avril.

McDonald, L. (1994) *Retirement Revisited. A Secondary Data Analysis*, Toronto, The Canadian Aging Research Network.

Osberg, L. (1988) *Is it Retirement or Unemployment? The Constrained Labour Supply of Older Canadians*, Ottawa, Santé et Bien-Être social.

Penning, M. (1983) « Multiple jeopardy: Age, sex and ethnic variations », *Canadian Ethnic Studies*, 15, 81-105.

Raskin, C. (1993) *International Migration for Employment. De facto discrimination, immigrant workers and ethnic minorities: A Canadian overview*, Genève, Bureau International du Travail.

Santerre, R. (1989) « Ethnicité et vieillesses québécoises », dans R. Santerre et G. Letourneau (dir.) *Vieillir à travers le monde*, Québec, Les Presses de l'Université Laval.

Schellenberg, G. (1994) *La retraite : les changements démographiques et économiques des dernières années*, Ottawa, Conseil canadien de développement social.

Shamsuddin, A.F.M. (1995) « Asset Demand of Immigrants and Canadian-Born Households », dans D.J. DeVoretz (dir.), *op. cit.*

Wanner, R.A. et P.L. McDonald (1986) « The Vertical Mosaic in Later Life: Ethnicity and Retirement in Canada », *Journal of Gerontology*, 41 (5), 662-671.

Zsembik, B.A. et A. Singer (1990) « The problem of Defining Retirement Among Minorities: The Mexican Americans », *The Gerontologist*, 30 (6), 749-757.

Tableau 1 : Répartition de la population en fonction de certaines variables socio-économiques, par groupe d'âge et lieu de naissance, Canada 1991.

en %	45 à 54 ans				55 à 64 ans				65 ans et plus			
	Can.	É.U.	Europe	Tiers-Monde & autres	Can.	É.U.	Europe	Tiers-Monde & autres	Can.	É.U.	Europe	Tiers-Monde & autres
STATUT SUR LE MARCHÉ DU TRAVAIL												
Actifs	84,8	81,7	88,6	90,9	51,7	43,6	62,4	71,6	6,1	7,3	5,5	6,5
Travail à temps plein	67,1	66,7	71,6	76,7	38,9	34,5	46,5	56,8	3,6	2,3	2,7	5,4
Travail à temps partiel	10,6	10,0	10,3	5,0	7,7	7,3	9,6	9,5	2,5	5,0	2,8	1,1
Au chômage	7,1	5,0	6,7	9,2	5,1	1,8	6,3	5,3	0,0	0,0	0,0	0,0
Inactifs	13,4	16,7	10,3	8,3	28,7	27,3	22,5	20,0	37,0	37,3	32,5	34,8
Retraités	1,9	1,7	1,2	0,8	19,7	29,1	15,1	8,4	56,9	55,5	62,0	58,7
PROFESSIONS												
Professionnels	9,8	26,4	12,8	9,6	7,2	17,9	9,6	16,7	7,0	9,6	6,5	9,7
Cadres supérieurs	11,7	11,3	11,7	7,0	10,6	10,3	11,5	9,5	9,2	13,2	9,5	12,9
Semi-professionnels	2,6	5,7	2,9	3,5	2,8	0,0	3,9	3,6	2,3	2,9	2,9	3,2
Techniciens	5,0	9,4	6,0	11,4	4,1	5,1	1,5	6,0	4,2	4,4	3,6	8,1
Cadres moyens	9,3	7,5	12,5	11,4	8,9	17,9	13,0	11,9	8,2	10,3	8,9	6,5
Travailleurs qualifiés et semiqualifiés	41,0	35,8	34,7	36,8	46,4	30,8	41,7	34,5	46,4	46,3	45,2	40,3
Travailleurs non qualifiés	20,6	3,8	19,3	20,2	20,1	17,9	18,9	17,9	22,6	13,2	23,5	19,4
BRANCHE D'ACTIVITÉ												
Production de biens	32,9	18,9	34,7	24,6	32,5	33,3	39,5	21,4	37,7	34,8	39,8	21,0
Production de services	67,1	81,1	65,3	75,4	67,5	66,7	60,5	78,6	62,3	65,2	60,3	79,0
LIMITATIONS D'ACTIVITÉ												
Oui	18,6	14,8	16,6	6,3	27,4	21,7	24,7	42,9	35,9	36,2	35,8	33,3
Non	81,4	85,2	83,4	93,7	72,6	78,3	75,3	57,1	64,1	63,8	64,2	66,7
REVENU PERSONNEL												
Moins de 20 000 $	39,0	42,6	31,8	34,8	54,7	59,1	48,4	47,1	78,0	71,6	75,1	81,5
20 000 $ à 39 999 $	32,4	17,0	31,8	33,7	30,2	22,7	30,7	26,5	17,9	19,4	20,5	13,6
40 000 $ à 59 999 $	18,5	17,0	23,9	16,9	9,4	13,6	12,8	13,2	2,7	6,5	3,3	2,5
60 000 $ et plus	10,1	23,4	12,4	14,6	5,6	4,5	8,2	13,2	1,4	2,6	1,0	2,5
LOGEMENT												
Propriétaire	82,5	78,7	83,7	74,8	80,3	70,0	84,1	68,6	71,6	72,5	73,9	59,5
Locataire	17,5	21,3	16,3	25,1	19,7	30,0	15,9	31,4	28,4	27,5	26,1	40,5
HYPOTHÈQUE												
Payée	58,7	53,2	47,0	45,3	80,3	85,0	71,1	55,1	93,6	95,9	94,9	81,3
Non payée	41,3	46,8	53,0	54,7	19,7	15,0	28,9	44,9	6,4	4,1	5,1	18,8

Source : Enquête sur le vieillissement et l'autonomie, août 1991, Statistique Canada.

Tableau 2a : Modalités de départ à la retraite en fonction du lieu de naissance, Canada 1991.

en %	Canada	États-Unis	Europe	Tiers-Monde & autres
Retraite anticipée	58,54	54,29	52,28	49,18
Retraite à 65 ans	26,41	26,43	30,33	21,31
Retraite tardive	15,05	19,28	17,39	29,51

Source : Enquête sur le vieillissement et l'autonomie, août 1991, Statistique Canada.

Tableau 2b : Âge de départ à la retraite en fonction des modalités et du lieu de naissance, Canada 1991.

	Total				Retraite anticipée				Retraite tardive			
	Canada	États-Unis	Europe	Tiers-Monde et autres	Canada	États-Unis	Europe	Tiers-Monde et autres	Canada	États-Unis	Europe	Tiers-Monde & autres
Âge moyen	61,57	62,88	62,41	63,13	58,01	59,37	58,54	57,93	69,41	69,85	69,52	70,44
Écart-type	6,55	5,48	6,64	7,65	6,04	4,36	6,54	6,92	3,48	3,60	4,15	4,23

Source : Enquête sur le vieillissement et l'autonomie, août 1991, Statistique Canada.

Tableau 3 : Répartition de la population en fonction des sources de revenu et du statut par rapport à l'emploi, par groupe d'âge et lieu de naissance, Canada 1991.

	45 à 54 ans				55 à 64 ans				65 ans et plus			
	Canada	États-Unis	Europe	Tiers-Monde et autres	Canada	États-Unis	Europe	Tiers-Monde et autres	Canada	États-Unis	Europe	Tiers-Monde & autres
ACTIFS												
Emploi	89,0	95,7	91,7	87,4	84,5	77,3	86,3	83,9	49,1	54,5*	56,5	83,3*
Pensions d'entreprise	0,4	0,0	0,3	0,0	3,3	13,6	1,4	1,6	3,4	0,0	1,6	0,0
Pensions publiques	0,4	0,0	0,6	0,0	2,4	0,0	0,7	1,6	38,3	18,2*	33,9	16,7*
Autres prestations publiques	6,9	4,3	5,0	5,8	5,9	0,0	6,0	8,1	1,2	0,0	0,0	0,0
Investissements	1,4	0,0	0,6	4,9	2,5	4,5	4,2	3,2	7,6	27,3*	8,1	0,0
Membres de la famille	1,5	0,0	1,5	1,0	0,7	0,0	1,1	1,6	0,0	0,0	0,0	0,0
Autres sources	0,4	0,0	0,3	1,0	0,7	4,5	0,4	0,0	0,2	0,0	0,0	0,0
INACTIFS												
Emploi	5,8	12,5	3,2	0,0	1,2	0,0	3,3	12,5	0,2	0,0	0,0	0,0
Pensions d'entreprise	3,8	0,0	6,5	0,0	10,9	7,7	13,3	12,5	6,9	11,0	5,8	3,2
Pensions publiques	11,4	0,0	0,0	0,0	32,8	23,1	23,3	0,0	83,7	74,4	83,8	71,0
Autres prestations publiques	51,0	50,0	61,3	30,0	32,5	46,2	21,1	37,5	1,1	1,2	1,9	3,2
Investissements	15,7	0,0	12,9	50,0	15,0	0,0	21,1	25,0	6,7	11,0	7,2	9,7
Membres de la famille	9,6	37,5	9,7	20,0	4,9	7,7	14,4	12,5	0,7	1,2	0,6	6,5
Autres sources	2,6	0,0	6,5	0,0	2,7	15,4	3,3	0,0	0,6	1,2	0,6	6,5
RETRAITÉS												
Emploi	3,2	0,0	25,0*	.	3,3	0,0	5,5	0,0	0,5	0,0	0,9	0,0
Pensions d'entreprise	34,9	100,0*	50,0*	.	49,2	50,0*	46,6	16,7*	23,2	25,4	24,3	19,6
Pensions publiques	17,5	0,0	0,0	.	18,7	28,6*	16,4	0,0	66,0	55,3	64,5	64,7
Autres prestations publiques	14,3	0,0	0,0	.	9,3	0,0	8,2	0,0	1,4	0,9	1,6	5,9
Investissements	25,4	0,0	0,0	.	16,8	7,1*	16,4	50,0*	8,4	16,7	7,5	7,8
Membres de la famille	3,2	0,0	25,0*	.	1,8	0,0	1,4	16,7*	0,2	0,9	0,9	0,0
Autres sources	1,6	0,0	0,0	.	1,0	14,3*	5,5	16,7*	0,3	0,9	0,4	2,0

Note : * N < 15

Source : *Enquête sur le vieillissement et l'autonomie, août 1991, Statistique Canada.*

Tableau 4 : Conditions et raison(s) ayant amené à prendre la retraite en fonction des modalités de départ et du lieu de naissance, Canada 1991.

	Retraite anticipée				Retraite à 65 ans ou plus tard			
	Canada	États-Unis	Europe	Tiers-Monde et autres	Canada	États-Unis	Europe	Tiers-Monde et autres
CONDITIONS								
Volontaire	73,0	80,3	74,8	73,3	72,9	79,7	77,8	67,7
Involontaire	27,0	19,7	25,2	26,7	27,1	20,3	22,2	32,3
RAISONS								
Santé	38,1	39,5	37,0	36,7	21,9	19,7	20,8	16,1
Soins à un proche	10,2	13,5	14,5	10,0	7,1	9,8	6,4	9,7
Revenu	35,7	53,4	32,8	13,3	27,0	34,4	26,9	25,8
Retraite obligatoire	5,0	4,1	6,5	13,8	36,3	30,6	39,4	35,5
Incitation au départ	16,6	16,2	13,1	13,3	1,8	1,6	1,3	3,2
Manque d'emploi	6,1	5,5	9,1	10,0	3,7	6,6	4,0	3,2
Pression des collègues	2,0	0,0	1,7	3,3	2,0	0,0	2,1	6,5
Voulait cesser de travailler	53,5	60,0	54,8	46,7	53,9	61,3	55,3	61,3

Source : *Enquête sur le veillissement et l'autonomie, août 1991, Statistique Canada.*

Tableau 5 : Population retraitée qui retourne au travail en fonction des modalités de départ et du lieu de naissance, Canada 1991.

	Retraite anticipée				Retraite à 65 ans ou plus tard			
	Canada	États-Unis	Europe	Tiers-Monde et autres	Canada	États-Unis	Europe	Tiers-Monde et autres
% retournant au travail	16,9	18,4	14,6	23,3	19,7	18,8	23,3	3,4
TYPE D'EMPLOI								
Travail à temps plein	22,3	28,6*	18,3	14,3*	21,1	18,2*	19,2	20,0*
Travail à temps partiel	77,7	71,4*	81,7	85,7*	78,9	81,8*	80,8	80,0*
MODALITÉS D'EMPLOI								
Travailleur à son compte	19,6	21,4*	14,5	0,0	21,9	18,2*	19,2	20,0*
Travailleur salarié	80,4	78,6*	85,5	100,0*	78,1	81,8*	80,8	80,0*

Note : * N < 15

Source : Enquête sur le vieillissement et l'autonomie, août 1991, Statistique Canada.

Tableau 6 : Types de préparatifs en vue de la retraite en fonction du statut par rapport à l'emploi, par groupe d'âge et lieu de naissance. Canada 1991.

en %	45 à 54 ans				55 à 64 ans				65 ans et plus			
	Canada	États-Unis	Europe	Tiers-Monde et autres	Canada	États-Unis	Europe	Tiers-Monde et autres	Canada	États-Unis	Europe	Tiers-Monde & autres
ACTIFS												
Modifié régime de travail	14,0	15,6*	13,8	4,3*	18,0	0,0	12,3	10,6*	42,3	50,0	38,5	66,7
Recueilli des renseignements	25,4	34,7	26,9	25,2	29,5	25,0*	25,6	20,9*	20,1	31,3	23,4	33,3
Cotisé à un RÉER	57,8	63,3	63,2	59,6	58,8	58,3*	61,1	64,7	46,5	31,3	47,6	33,3
Accumulé des économies	52,4	53,1	56,6	63,9	58,7	82,6	61,3	58,8	69,2	62,5	81,0	33,3
Fait d'autres placements	33,2	59,2	36,2	37,4	26,9	45,8	29,7	27,9	26,9	31,1	31,7	33,3
Remboursé ou évité de faire des dettes	64,1	65,3	61,4	51,9	71,0	69,6	69,2	57,4	71,4	37,5	87,7	100,0
INACTIFS												
Modifié régime de travail	18,2	0,0	0,0	50,0*	8,9*		0,0	33,3*	17,9	0,0	0,0	
Recueilli des renseignements	14,2	30,0*	14,3*	30,0*	17,4	20,0*	20,9	16,7*	10,2	10,0	9,8	6,3
Cotisé à un RÉER	30,4	30,0*	30,2*	50,0*	32,7	40,0*	38,6	50,0*	17,3	14,8	20,5	12,5
Accumulé des économies	35,8	30,0*	44,2	70,0*	44,7	33,3*	50,0	55,6*	55,2	73,8	60,2	31,3
Fait d'autres placements	17,6	30,0*	18,6*	30,0*	15,8	26,7*	20,2	16,7*	15,9	25,3	16,4	18,8
Remboursé ou évité de faire des dettes	61,1	70,0*	53,5	70,0*	65,9	73,3*	68,4	66,7*	66,5	75,3	68,9	71,9
RETRAITÉS												
Modifié régime de travail	13,0*	0,0	40,0*	100,0*	13,7	12,5*	15,8*	25,0*	14,2	14,0	15,1	15,1
Recueilli des renseignements	19,4	0,0	40,0*	0,0	33,7	31,3*	34,2	12,5*	17,3	17,2	19,5	13,2
Cotisé à un RÉER	40,8	100,0*	60,0*	100,0*	61,0	50,0*	73,7	25,0*	33,3	27,9	34,6	39,6
Accumulé des économies	40,8	100,0*	60,0*	100,0*	61,3	62,5*	69,7	75,0*	63,6	75,2	62,7	45,3
Fait d'autres placements	27,1	100,0*	20,0*	0,0	29,3	43,8*	29,3	12,5*	21,8	32,0	22,9	24,5
Remboursé ou évité de faire des dettes	53,5	100,0*	80,0*	100,0*	63,3	62,5*	59,2	62,5*	61,2	63,3	58,4	47,2

Note : * N < 15

Source : Enquête sur le vieillissement et l'autonomie, août 1991, Statistique Canada.

Tableau 7 : Nombre d'années de préparation en vue de la retraite en fonction des modalités de départ et du lieu de naissance, Canada 1991.

en %	Retraite anticipée				Retraite à 65 ans ou plus tard			
	Canada	États-Unis	Europe	Tiers-Monde et autres	Canada	États-Unis	Europe	Tiers-Monde et autres
Une à deux années	23,3	24,0	21,0	26,7	19,7	18,8	23,3	3,4
Trois à quatre années	11,2	14,7	6,4	6,7	10,5	9,4	10,6	17,2
Six à dix années	6,3	5,3	6,4	6,7	5,8	9,4	4,7	6,9
Plus de dix années	10,8	10,7	12,1	6,7	11,9	14,1	10,3	10,3
Pas de préparation	48,4	45,3	54,1	53,3	52,1	48,4	51,2	62,1

Source : *Enquête sur le veillissement et l'autonomie, août 1991, Statistique Canada.*

Alexander Freund and Laura Quilici

Using Oral History to Explore Subjectivity in the Narratives of German and Italian Women in Vancouver, 1947-1961[1]

Abstract

This essay uses what the authors call the New Oral History (i.e., the emphasis on subjective experience) to draw upon two cases studies about the working lives of German immigrant domestic servants and Italian immigrant housewives with boarders in post World War II Vancouver.

The case studies are based upon personal interviews conducted by the authors. The first case study, on German immigrant women, was conducted and written by Alexander Freund. The second case study, on Italian immigrant women, was conducted and written by Laura Quilici. Both authors collaborated on the preparation of the introduction and conclusion of the paper.

Résumé

Cet essai utilise ce que les auteurs appellent la nouvelle histoire orale (c'est-à-dire l'importance accordée à l'expérience subjective) pour exa-miner deux histoires de cas, soit celle d'immigrantes allemandes qui travaillaient comme domestiques et celle d'immigrantes italiennes qui hébergeaient des pensionnaires à Vancouver après la Deuxième Guerre mondiale.

Les études de cas sont basées sur des entrevues personnelles réali-sées par les auteurs. La première étude, sur les immigrantes allemandes, a été réalisée et rédigée par Alexander Freund. La seconde, sur les immigrantes italiennes, a été réalisée et rédigée par Laura Quilici. L'introduction et la conclusion de cet article ont été préparées en colla-boration par les deux auteurs.

Historians have in the past used oral history to shed light on the lives of immigrants. Although the scope of oral history has been broadened since then, revealing its complexities, Canadian immigration historians have not taken advantage of newly refined methods. Most scholars still see oral history merely as a way to gain objective information about ethnic groups;

this information might include the conditions immigrants encountered in their settlement, or their roles in, and contributions to, Canadian society. Scholars including Raphael Samuel, Paul Thompson, and Luisa Passerini in Europe, and Ronald Grele, Daphne Patai, and Sherna Berger Gluck[2] in the United States, have challenged such conventional ways of using oral history. These scholars have argued that, "as soon as we recognize the value of the subjective in individual testimonies, we challenge the accepted categories of history. We reintroduce the emotionality, the fears and the fantasies carried by the metaphors of memory, which historians have been so anxious to write out of the formal accounts."[3]

In order to elaborate the usefulness of what we call the New Oral History (i.e., the emphasis on subjective experience) on Canadian immigration studies, this paper will draw upon two case studies about the working lives of German immigrant domestic servants and Italian immigrant housewives with boarders in post-World War Two Vancouver.[4] Unlike recent studies in women's immigration historiography, which document women's *roles* in the migration process,[5] our work treats *perception* and *subjectivity* as legitimate tools for the historian; it assumes that the meanings historical actors attach to events in their lives are as important as the events themselves. As historians, we must also place this "making sense" – i.e., construction of identity – into its larger historical context. What power structures are forged, reinforced, or contested through subjectivity? How do narrative forms and social discourses structure identity formation?

The immigration process is a disruptive force in people's lives – particularly in how they perceive themselves in gendered terms. Simply making the decision to emigrate abroad forces people to re-imagine ways of seeing themselves. Women, for example, may have a predominant image of themselves (buttressed, no doubt, by dominant ideologies) as being passive, submissive, or dependent. Once they decide to emigrate, however, they may associate the move with independence, adventure, and travel – concepts which initially seem antithetical to their traditional "nature." Through the migration process and the confrontation with a new culture – complete with its own codes of womanly behaviours – women are forced to realign themselves to their changing circumstances. The disruption caused by immigration exposes the volatile nature of gender identities. Our two case studies examine how German and Italian women altered their feminine identity models to suit their new circumstances in Canada.

German Immigrant Women: Meanings and Politics of Identity

In 1993, I interviewed ten women who, along with 25,000 other women in the 1950s, had left Germany and come to Canada to work as domestic serv-

ants.[6] All of them had immigrated as single women, often by themselves but sometimes with a girl-friend or a relative. The women I interviewed were between twenty and thirty years old when they arrived in Vancouver, where they immediately began to work and live as maids in the households of the middle and upper classes. After an average of ten months, the women left their live-in positions and went into other menial jobs such as cleaning or factory work. All of the women married, an average of two years after their arrival in Canada.

The women had left Germany for many reasons. It was, however, the search for adventure, freedom, travel, and independence that the German women mentioned most often when they explained why they emigrated. This association of emigration with adventure, freedom, travel, and independence motivated the women to leave behind family and friends, quit jobs and apartments, and abandon a familiar culture and society. The women were willing to take these risks in order to fulfill their dreams.[7] Heidi Schute, who was twenty-nine years old when she left her German hometown, explained: "I was always fascinated by travel and wanting to go to foreign countries... I wanted to go and see the world... I was going to work till I had enough money to buy a car and then pack things up and go and travel to South America, to – I wanted to see the whole world and that was just it."[8] Heidi Schute's narrative, as well as those of the other women, make clear that their identities as immigrants were forming before they left Germany. Moreover, they had no diffculty integrating this concept of themselves as immigrants into their identities as women. Women, they argued, could be both adventurous and independent.

The German women, however, arrived in Vancouver not only as immigrants, but also as domestic servants, often on government contracts[9] that obliged them to work in a household for one year. Expectations, images, hopes, and wishes were hit by reality. Brigitte Rabe remembered how disappointed she was when her dreams of becoming a famous dress-maker were shattered by her having to "go in a household and... work for a pittance."[10] Doris Schulz was "shocked" when, instead of fulfilling her dreams of establishing her own pottery-shop, she had to wear a uniform and clean out other people's fireplaces.[11] Other women felt humiliated when their employers ignored them or called them with a bell. Mirroring the experiences of other immigrant women, the German women found themselves in a conflicting, often frustrating, situation. How did they make sense of this experience? How did they reconcile this contradiction between their immigrant dreams and their work and living realities?

They did so by shifting the focus of their identity as both women and immigrants. Slowly, the women removed adventurousness and independ-

ence off of their immigrant identities and chose new focal points, such as the ability to assimilate and to do domestic tasks. Being an immigrant no longer meant being an adventurous traveller but assimilating quickly and thoroughly. And in the case of being a maid, the women argued that assimilation was best achieved through domestic service. To most of the German women, domestic service was not work around which they could establish a work identity; rather, domestic service became a means through which they could maintain their identities as immigrants. The women had invested too much in their immigrant identity to just replace it with a worker identity. Instead, the women considered domestic service a "learning experience," a "first stepping stone," or "a start" in their lives as immigrants. The women saw it as a good, if not the best, way to assimilate and integrate into Canadian society. By ascribing these meanings to domestic service, the women constructed the occupation as an integral part of successful immigration. Thus, within the constraints of their situation, the immigrant women – at least temporarily – invented new meanings for their identities.

At the same time, domestic service served as a way to shift the meanings of their identities as women. A prevalent notion in postwar Canadian society was that after women had "helped out" in the paid labour force during the war, they should now return home to kitchen and kids.[12] Many Canadians, as well as many immigrants, felt that female immigrants could best assimilate by apprenticing in the craft of good middle- and upper-class Canadian housewifery. For many German women, then, domestic service would be a "stepping stone," not into better occupations or towards the fulfilment of their dreams, but into the destination of women in the 1950s – marriage and family. When asked what she had learned, what she had gotten out of domestic service, Christel Meisinger explained that it had prepared her "maybe for marriage, with all those kids. Having those kids around me."[13] And Margot Buchwald felt that "from then on I kind of liked housework."[14] Thus, the women's focus began to shift from adventure and independence to traditional notions of femininity and domesticity so that they could better adapt and sustain their identities as immigrants and women.

This shift in the meanings of their identities allowed the women to better deal with the daily stress and frustration that accompanied domestic service, as well as the overall life experience, in their new country. The women's belief that being a maid would pay off in the end helped them to deny the occupation's exploitative and degrading character as well as to mask the hierarchical relationship between them and their employers. Thus, each task that was added to the women's work routines was not seen as a form of exploitation. Rather, they described their work routines as "a good way to get to know the Canadian way of life."[15] This went so far that some women

voluntarily worked more than was expected of them, and did not protest against not being paid extra for doing extra work. This mystification of domestic service as a useful means of integration into Canadian society had two consequences. On an individual and psychological level, the women could – at least momentarily – suppress the memory of their shattered dreams of travelling and being adventurous. The corollary was that on a social level, the German women sustained and reinforced a hierarchical and exploitative relationship between worker and employer as well as the broader social and gender hierarchies.

At the same time, however, the women asserted or reclaimed some of their earlier notions of being an immigrant and a woman. They used these older notions of independence, freedom, and adventure to contest the dominant discourses of femininity and foreignness to which they were urged to conform. Public discourses both in Germany and in Canada claimed that independence, adventure, and woman were mutually exclusive concepts, which, if confounded, would result in delinquency, disease, and disruption. Against such ideas, the German women held that women could be both adventurous and independent, and that they themselves were the best proof of that. In order to legitimize their independence, however, the women framed their independent status within the concept of the independent immigrant, and not of the socially unaccepted concept of the independent woman. Thus, while to a certain degree the women transgressed gender boundaries, they masked and legitimized this transgression by representing themselves as independent immigrants.

This masking was most apparent in the women's struggle to retain their independence when it was threatened. Margot Buchwald told about her work as a cook in a private hospital in West Vancouver, run by an Austrian man who did not want her to cook so well for the old people ("'because it was too expensive'"), and how she, together with her female German co-workers, organized a protest: "We talked to each other about it, it's not right the way he treated us and he didn't like the idea, but [after we quit] he had to do his own work for a while. Because I said to him: 'You're not [any] more in Germany where you get treated like [by] a Nazi. We're in Canada, we're freer.'"[16] Margot Buchwald's independence – the area of autonomy and resistance she had carved out in her job by cooking meals that were better than the boss wanted to afford, and her sense that people should be treated in a certain way by their superiors – was threatened. Her response to this threat was informed by her status as an immigrant and as a German, as much as it was by her gender. Margot Buchwald could have claimed that she should not be suppressed as a woman, a worker, or a human being. But instead of arguing from such "feminist," "Marxist," or "humanist" perspectives, she

invoked the "common" past experiences in the Third Reich ("You're not more in Germany where you get treated like [by] a Nazi."). She also identified with the good, democratic Canadian host-society (*"we're* in Canada, *we're* freer") and depicts her boss as the "troublemaker," the German-speaking immigrant who still has not adjusted to living in Canada (*"You're* not more in Germany"). By constructing defiance within the framework of her immigrant identity, Margot Buchwald could justify in socially acceptable terms why she did not submit to her employer's practices, as immigrants and women were expected to in postwar Canada.

Femininity Redefined: The Issue of Women's Community

Much of our work explores the relationship between work, ethnicity, and femininity. What meanings did German and Italian immigrant women attach to their work in Canada? How did their work as domestic workers and housewives with boarders contribute to the construction of their identities as women in Canada? Were conceptions of femininity altered through the migration process? In order to answer these questions adequately, we must first examine what femininity meant prior to immigration. The eight women I interviewed for this study all came from northern Italian peasant backgrounds. Many worked on family plots of land prior to emigration, while others whose families were too poor to own land either worked as seamstresses or were sent away to live as domestic workers in families with greater means. In northern Italy, woman meant not only idealized female subordination to idealized male dominance, but simultaneously the recognition of female physical and moral strength.[17] Women displayed this strength through their ability to provide household care and by working alongside their husbands in the fields.[18] Two predominant aspects of a northern Italian peasant woman's identity were marriage and motherhood, with limited opportunities for women who chose not to marry or bear children. But another, perhaps less well documented, part of women's identity in northern Italy had been a sense of kinship with other, often unrelated, women. In Italian peasant society, love and solidarity meant helping each other to survive; it entailed working and helping others work.[19] As Anna Bravo has noted, "the identification of women with the needs of other women, intertwined with a generic feeling of religious pity for those who suffered, was an expression of a deep internalization of their role as women."[20]

Women's work in Italy was often performed in the company of other women in the community. Because most peasants lived in what Donna Gabaccia called "agrotowns" – densely populated rural settlements – the *cortile* was the main focus for community activity. Throughout agrotowns in both southern and northern Italy, streets opened onto hundreds of small

cortili. These semi-enclosed courtyards were usually surrounded by six or eight attached houses.[21] Whether or not women of the *cortile* belonged to the same extended family, they often worked together. Tasks within the household were defined by gender, which meant that women gathered together and performed their work with other women. They would often sit together in the *cortile* as they sewed, peeled vegetables, or made clogs.

A woman's *cortile* neighbours constituted a stable group that shared gossip as well as labour. As Gabaccia noted, "this exchange of information was both the basis for social relationships and the means of evaluating them."[22] By participating in an ongoing exchange of neighbourhood gossip, women were able to exert some influence in maintaining social and moral stability. A young woman knew that if she was seen in the *piazza* with a boy, news would quickly spread to the women of her *cortile* and, most likely, to her mother. This was often enough to stop young women from attempting to engage in surreptitious rendezvous with members of the opposite sex. Because the worst imaginable situation for a woman was to be seduced and subsequently abandoned, mothers carefully monitored the actions of their daughters. Mrs. Tonetti recalled that while she was a teenager, her mother closely monitored her actions. When she sent her on an errand – to the bakery to buy bread, for example – Mrs. Tonetti's mother would say, "I'm going to spit on the floor. And you better make sure that you get back before the spit dries up. Because if you come later, tonight it's *botte* !" Mrs. Tonetti continued, "So I had to run and if she sent me to a store and there was a line up, well, I used to get [a] stomach upset because I knew that spit was drying up. It's true, I'm not kidding. This is how it was."[23]

Once in Canada, however, female identities had to be redefined because social and economic conditions were different than they had been in rural northern Italy. Concepts such as female community, for example, which had formed an integral part of women's self-definition in northern Italy, did not carry the same meanings once women immigrated to Canada. The women I interviewed immigrated to Canada after 1949 and came either with their parents, if they were single, or with their husbands. They began to take between three to seven young, single, Italian men into their homes as boarders, not only to contribute to the family income, but also out of a sense of obligation to these men who had no mothers or wives in Canada to look after them.

Housewives with boarders in Vancouver were isolated from other women who performed similar work. In Italy, women were accustomed to working with other women of their *cortile* but this option did not exist for Italian women who kept boarders in Canada. Because women maintained

boarders in their own homes, they had little opportunity to interact with other women. Consider the following interview excerpt with Mrs. Torturo:

> *Q: How much contact did you have with other families that were keeping boarders? Did you know a lot of them?*
>
> A: Well, not really, no. Well, because all the people that had boarders were lots older than me. Maybe 8, 9, 10 years older than me. So I was not really close to these people. I knew them if I walked on the street and I see them I say "hi" but not really close like friends.[24]

Other interviewees agreed with Mrs. Torturo. Few of the women I interviewed had close friends who also kept boarders in their homes.

Many women felt threatened by other women who kept boarders. Perhaps because women regarded the boarding arrangement partly as a business, they felt that other women were potential competitors for profits. In addition to being a business, however, the boarding arrangement was an obligation to measure up to the ideal of womanhood women carried with them from Italy. (You will recall that in Italy, motherhood was one of the pillars upon which a woman's identity rested. Upon immigration, women who maintained boarders expanded this role to include not only their own children, but also the men in their homes.) Thus, women may have been competing not only for profits, but also to keep their sense of womanhood intact. The comments of Mrs. Peluso may clarify this point. She commented, "You know, I did everything for my boarders. The other women who kept boarders didn't sew for them, they didn't give them very much to eat, they didn't help them out. I was the only one. This is why the boys liked me and liked staying here."[25] Like Mrs. Peluso, many housewives with boarders viewed other women who did this type of work as rivals. Often in the interviews, the women spoke disdainfully of other boardinghouse keepers. Even when these women were friends, they viewed each other as competitors. Mrs. Torturo had a friend, Mrs. Schiavelli, who was a well known boarding-house keeper in Vancouver. Once when the two women were talking, Mrs. Schiavelli told Mrs. Torturo, "You're young, you don't have [many boarders]. Look at how many I have in here!" Mrs. Torturo countered, however. She told me,

> But she had a lot of help from [her daughter] because she was a pretty big girl at that time and her mother and father helped a lot. You know, but I was just by myself with my husband. We had small kids, you know, that's all. It was harder for me. I don't

think Schiavelli did the laundry too. She kept the beds clean
and everything in the room clean but I don't think she did the
laundry for the guys.[26]

Women who maintained boarders worked in isolation from other
women who did similar work. This occurred partly because the work itself
was solitary; it took place within the confines of a family home which is
usually regarded as private space. Even the women of the Italian *cortile*
typically worked outside the home in a common courtyard. Housewives
with boarders remained isolated because they viewed other women who did
this work as competitors. They did not compete for "business" so much as
they felt their womanliness was being put to the test. Women who "took
better care" of their boarders, cooked tastier and larger meals, and did extra
work such as laundry or clothes mending, saw themselves as conforming
more fully to their image of femininity than women who did not perform
these other services.

Conclusion

Listening to the meanings the Italian and German women ascribed to their
work, and to their ethnic, immigrant, and gender identities, allowed us to
glimpse how they dealt with the constraints imposed on their quest for their
immigrant dreams and expectations. We could see how the women partially
accepted and thus reinforced the power relations that had denied them the
fulfilment of their wishes and fantasies. At the same time, a potential and
actual dissent inherent in the women's consent to authority was also
visible.[27] Thus, through an analysis of how historical actors narrate,
contextualize, and give meaning to their working lives, we can gain a richer
understanding of how history is shaped both by events and emotions.

Notes

1. An earlier version of this paper was presented at the "BC and Beyond:
   Gender Histories" conference in Victoria, BC, 16-18 June 1994. An expanded version will appear in *BC Studies* in Spring/Summer, 1995.
2. Raphael Samuel and Paul Thompson (eds), *The Myths We Live By* (London
   and New York: Routledge, 1990); Luisa Passerini, "Work-Ideology and Consensus under Italian Fascism," *History Workshop Journal*, 8 (1979): 82-108,
   and "Mythbiography in Oral History," in Samuel and Thompson (eds), *Myths
   We Live By*, 49-60; Ronald Grele, "Listen To Their Voices: Two Case Studies in the Interpretation of Oral History Interviews," *Oral History* 7:1 (1979),
   33-42; Sherna Berger Gluck and Daphne Patai (eds), *Women's Words: The
   Feminist Practice of Oral History* (New York and London: Routledge, 1991).

3. Samuel and Thompson (eds), *Myths We Live By*, 2.
4. These case studies are based on our MA theses. See Alexander Freund, "Identity and Immigration: Self-Conceptualization and Myth in the Narratives of German Immigrant Women in Vancouver, BC, 1950-1960" (MA thesis, Simon Fraser University, 1994), and Laura Quilici, "'I Was a Strong Lady': Italian Housewives with Boarders in Vancouver, 1947-1961" (MA thesis, Simon Fraser University, April 1995).
5. See for example, Varpu Lindström-Best, *Defiant Sisters: A Social History of Finnish Immigrant Women in Canada* (Toronto: Multicultural History Society of Ontario, 1988); Franca Iacovetta, *Such Hardworking People: Italian Immigrants in Postwar Toronto* (Kingston and Montreal: McGill-Queen's University Press, 1992); Ruth A. Frager, *Sweatshop Strife: Class, Ethnicity, and Gender in the Jewish Labour Movement of Toronto, 1900-1939* (Toronto: University of Toronto Press, 1992); Frances Swyripa, *Wedded to the Cause: Ukrainian-Canadian Women and Ethnic Identity, 1891-1991* (Toronto: University of Toronto Press, 1993).
6. For statistics, see Department of Citizenship and Immigration, Statistics Section, Ottawa, *Immigration Statistics*, 1951-1961; see also Marilyn Barber, *Immigrant Domestic Servants in Canada*, Canada's Ethnic Groups, Booklet No. 16 (Ottawa: Canadian Historical Association, 1991), 2. The interviewees were contacted through notices in British Columbia newspapers as well as through visits to two German-Canadian churches in Vancouver. All interviews save one were conducted in English rather than German. The names of the interviewees were changed to secure anonymity.
7. A comparison of the reasons for e/immigration between Italian, Lithuanian, and German women is problematic. Iacovetta focused on married women, but has shown that the decision to immigrate was not solely made by the men. Italian women came to Canada with their own dreams of "America" and a better life. Many Lithuanian displaced persons came to Canada with the dream of returning to Lithuania one day. But not unlike the many German refugees, Lithuanians left a country (Germany) that was hostile towards them.
8. Heidi Schute, interview with author, 30 November and 6 December 1993, Surrey, BC, audio tape. The names of all the narrators are pseudonyms. All recordings are in the possession of the author.
9. In February 1951, Canada adopted the Assisted Passage Loan Scheme "for the purpose of assisting immigrants from Europe whose services were urgently required here in Canada and who were unable to finance their transportation costs." Single women who were between eighteen and forty-five years old and had no children could apply for this loan but had in turn to sign a contract that required them to work in domestic service for one year. *Canada Year Book, 1952-53*, 164.
10. Brigitte Rabe, interview with author, 14 September 1993, Burnaby, BC, audio tape.

11. Doris Schulz, interview with author, 22 September 1993, Richmond, BC, audio tape.
12. See Veronica Strong-Boag, "Home Dreams: Women and the Suburban Experiment in Canada, 1945-60," *Canadian Historical Review*, 72:4 (1991): 471-504; Yvonne Matthew-Klein, "How They Saw Us: Images of Women in National Film Board Films of the 1940's and 1950's," *Atlantis. A Women's Studies Journal*, 4:2 (Spring 1979), 20-33; Gertrude Joch Robinson, "The Media and Social Change: Thirty Years of Magazine Coverage of Women and Work (1950-1977)," *Atlantis. A Women's Studies Journal*, 8:2 (Spring 1983), 87-111; M. Susan Bland, "Henrietta the Homemaker, and 'Rosie the Riveter': Images of Women in Advertising in *Maclean's* Magazine, 1939-1950," *Atlantis. A Women's Studies Journal*, 8:2 (Spring 1983); reprint in Laurel Sefton MacDowell and Ian Radforth (eds), *Canadian Working Class History. Selected Readings* (Toronto: Canadian Scholars' Press, 1992), 595-622.
13. Christel Meisinger, interview with author, 1 December 1993, Burnaby, BC, audio tape.
14. Margot Buchwald, interview with author, 27 September 1993, Aldergrove, BC, audio tape.
15. *Ibid.*
16. *Ibid.*
17. Anna Bravo, "Solidarity and Loneliness: Piedmontese Peasant Women at the Turn of the Century," *International Journal of Oral History*, 3, 2 (1982), 82.
18. Donna R. Gabaccia, *From Sicily to Elizabeth Street: Housing and Social Change Among Italian Immigrants, 1880-1930* (Albany: State University of New York, 1984), 44-51.
19. Bravo, "Solidarity and Loneliness," 83.
20. *Ibid.*, 80.
21. Gabaccia, *Sicily to Elizabeth Street*, 16.
22. *Ibid.*, 48.
23. A beating.
24. S. Torturo, interview with the author, 10 September 1993, North Vancouver, BC, audio tape.
25. M. Peluso, interview with the author, 16 August 1994, Burnaby, BC, audio tape in Italian.
26. S. Torturo.
27. Passerini, "Working Class Ideology and Working Class Attitudes to Fascism," 58, 75.

Serge Jaumain et Matteo Sanfilippo

L'immigration belge et l'Église catholique au Canada et aux États-Unis avant la Première Guerre mondiale[1]

Résumé

Avant la Première Guerre mondiale, les Belges ne représentent qu'une faible proportion de l'immigration européenne en Amérique du Nord. On note cependant trois grandes vagues migratoires qui, de 1850 à 1914, conduisent un nombre croissant d'entre eux à s'établir aux États-Unis puis au Canada. Après avoir présenté une synthèse des connaissances sur la présence belge en Amérique du Nord, cet article fait état de recherches récentes dans les archives du Vatican qui ont révélé l'existence de nombreuses sources inexploitées : statistiques concernant les fidèles diocèse par diocèse, plaintes des groupes ethniques de religion catholique, rapports des fonctionnaires du Vatican sur l'émigration catholique en Amérique du Nord. Elles permettent aujourd'hui de reconstituer la géographie des établissements belges aux États-Unis et au Canada avant la Première Guerre mondiale, ainsi que d'analyser l'intégration socio-religieuse des Wallons et des Flamands dans la société nord-américaine.

Abstract

Prior to World War I, Belgian emigration to North America was not significant. Nonetheless, it is possible to distinguish three waves from 1840 to 1914, each of them bringing an increasing number of Belgians to the United States and, later, to Canada. After addressing the state of current scholarship on Belgian migration to North America, this paper presents new research based on unexplored sources of information on Belgian communities in the U.S. and Canada found in the Vatican archives. This wealth of information includes: statistics on the ethnic origins of Catholics in each North American diocese; complaints made by different ethnic groups against their bishops; and reports by the Vatican bureaucracy on Catholic emigration to North America. By exploiting these sources, it is possible to draw together the geography of North American Belgian communities before World War I, and to analyse the socio-religious integration in North American society of Wallon and Flemish migrants.

L'immigration belge en Amérique du Nord est bien connue. Des deux côtés de l'Atlantique les historiens ont souligné les grandes caractéristiques de ces mouvements de population qui conduisirent, dès le milieu du XIXe siècle, un nombre croissant de Belges à franchir l'océan. Leurs travaux n'ont toutefois pas toujours été très attentifs au rôle tenu par l'Église dans ces migrations. L'ouverture de nouvelles archives romaines permet aujourd'hui de mieux cerner les structures de contrôle mises en place par les autorités religieuses d'Amérique du Nord et de montrer l'intérêt du Vatican pour les populations catholiques du Nouveau Monde. Nous nous proposons donc de présenter ici une brève synthèse des travaux réalisés sur l'immigration belge aux États-Unis et au Canada tout en démontrant, dans une seconde partie, l'intérêt que recèlent les documents conservés dans les archives du Vatican et de la Congrégation « de Propaganda Fide[2] », pour une analyse approfondie du processus d'intégration religieuse des immigrés belges.

L'immigration belge en Amérique du Nord. Survol historique (1865-1914)

La faiblesse du mouvement migratoire

« Il n'y a rien au monde de plus incrusté dans son foyer et de moins accessible à la fièvre de l'exode que le Belge d'aujourd'hui », écrit en 1887 le vice-recteur de l'Université catholique de Louvain, Mgr Cartuyvels[3]. Si l'on considère l'ensemble du XIXe siècle, il est exact que les Belges ne semblent guère attirés par l'émigration lointaine. En 1900, ils sont à peine 29 000 aux États-Unis contre 94 000 Hollandais, 115 000 Suisses, 153 000 Danois. Même le Grand-Duché de Luxembourg, qui n'a jamais atteint le vingtième de la population belge au cours de la seconde moitié du XIXe siècle, envoie à lui seul, entre 1840 et 1900, près de 40 000 personnes aux États-Unis[4]. Quant à l'émigration belge vers le Canada, elle constitue un phénomène plus marginal encore, du moins avant 1900.

Les raisons de ce faible mouvement migratoire sont intimement liées à la situation politico-économique du petit royaume. Depuis son indépendance, acquise en 1830, la Belgique forme un pays aux ressources naturelles nombreuses et diversifiées (charbon, minerais, matériaux de construction, vastes forêts...). Sa superficie limitée et le développement rapide des réseaux routier, fluvial et ferroviaire facilitent grandement l'exploitation de ses richesses et la bourgeoisie industrielle peut en outre profiter d'une main-d'oeuvre abondante (la population belge est passée de 3 700 000 habitants en 1830 à 7 400 000 en 1910) et à bon marché. Ces éléments favorisent une telle croissance que dans le troisième quart du XIXe siècle, la Belgique sera considérée comme le pays le plus industrialisé du monde après l'Angleterre[5].

À ces éléments qui n'incitent guère au départ s'ajoute une Constitution très libérale qui garantit les grandes libertés (libertés de presse, d'enseignement, de culte, d'association...), ce qui explique pourquoi, avant 1914, le pays ne connaît pratiquement pas d'émigration à caractère religieux ou politique[6].

Il faut également souligner l'absence de « politique d'émigration ». Au milieu du XIXᵉ siècle, il y eut bien des essais d'implantation, aux États-Unis notamment, de colonies agricoles où l'on envoya quelques centaines de mendiants et de condamnés libérés, mais l'expérience fit long feu. Elle fut abandonnée à la suite de protestations du gouvernement américain[7], et à partir de 1856, les autorités belges choisirent de ne plus intervenir en matière d'émigration. Elles veillèrent tout au plus à protéger les candidats au départ contre certaines malversations en luttant contre les agents d'émigration malhonnêtes et en cherchant à améliorer les conditions de voyage.

Une organisation catholique, la Société Saint-Raphaël[8], se charge pour sa part « non d'encourager l'émigration mais de la diriger et de protéger les émigrants contre les dangers auxquels ils vont s'exposer, au point de vue moral et religieux[9] ». Inspirée du modèle allemand, elle vise surtout à combattre les pratiques malhonnêtes de certains agents recruteurs « en plaçant à proximité des amateurs d'émigration un homme capable de les conseiller et éclairer[10] ». Grâce à un réseau de délégués régionaux, elle répond aux interrogations des candidats au départ et les dirige vers les destinations où leurs chances de réussite semblent les plus grandes. Son travail ne se limite pas à conseiller les futurs émigrants, il tend aussi à les encadrer lors de leur voyage et même à les accueillir à l'arrivée. Elle fait encore pression sur les armateurs pour que les conditions de transport soient les plus décentes possible au point de vue de l'hygiène, de la nourriture et de la morale. La Société Saint-Raphaël espère ainsi maintenir les émigrants dans un contexte catholique et éviter qu'une fois outre-mer ils ne négligent leurs devoirs religieux. Quant aux organisations socialistes, sans s'opposer au mouvement migratoire, elles attirent, elles aussi, l'attention des candidats au départ sur les tromperies dont sont trop souvent victimes les ouvriers qui découvrent parfois, dans leur nouvelle patrie, des conditions de travail beaucoup moins favorables qu'en Belgique[11].

L'action du gouvernement conjuguée à celle de ces diverses associations catholiques et socialistes tempère l'ardeur des émigrants potentiels. Elle constitue une sorte de contrepoids au discours et à la propagande[12] diffusés par les agents d'émigration. Mais le facteur fondamental de la faiblesse de l'émigration vers l'Amérique du Nord est ailleurs. Comme le montre le professeur Stengers, « cette émigration ne s'est pas révélée indispensable parce que, l'emploi manquant ou ses ressources étant insuffisantes,

le Belge a trouvé le moyen d'améliorer son sort, en se déplaçant sans doute, mais moins loin, en changeant beaucoup moins de milieu[13] ». On assiste en effet avant la Première Guerre mondiale à d'importantes migrations internes vers les régions industrialisées de Wallonie ou vers un État voisin : la France[14]. Si l'on possède peu de chiffres sur ces déplacements de population, on peut raisonnablement penser qu'ils ont largement contribué à diminuer le nombre d'émigrants outre-Atlantique. Il faut donc relativiser l'image d'un Belge sédentaire et hostile à toute forme de migration. Les freins à l'expatriation vers des pays lointains n'empêchent d'ailleurs ni le départ de nombreux prêtres belges, ni celui de vagues de travailleurs industriels et agricoles, notamment dans les premières années du XXe siècle, à destination des États-Unis et, dans une moindre mesure, du Canada[15].

Première destination : les États-Unis

Comme l'écrit C.C. Qualey, « The United States was by far the most promising under-developed area in the world in the nineteenth century until World War I[16] ». C'est donc tout naturellement vers ce pays que se dirigent des millions d'émigrants européens qui profitent de l'amélioration des transports maritimes et terrestres pour gagner les ports d'Europe et traverser l'Atlantique. Ils réalisent ainsi « perhaps the greatest folk migration in the known history of mankind[17] ». Si, pour les raisons exposées plus haut, la Belgique prend une part modeste dans ce vaste mouvement de population, Jean Stengers montre qu'avant la Première Guerre mondiale on peut dégager trois grandes vagues d'émigration belge vers les États-Unis et le Canada qui ont chacune leurs caractéristiques propres et concernent des catégories bien particulières de la population.

1) 1850-1856

Outre les tentatives avortées d'établir des colonies agricoles pour les mendiants, les vagabonds et les condamnés libérés, cette période est surtout marquée par le départ, en 1855-1856, de plusieurs milliers d'agriculteurs belges originaires du Brabant wallon. Ce mouvement soudain et très localisé mais qui, par son ampleur, inquiète les pouvoirs publics[18], s'arrête aussi subitement qu'il a commencé, en 1857-1858. Il semble avoir eu pour origine la correspondance échangée entre des familles de la région de Wavre (notamment de Grez-Doiceau) installées en 1853 dans les environs de Green Bay (Wisconsin[19]) et leurs amis restés au pays. Mais deux éléments amplifient le mouvement de départ : une conjoncture économique défavorable et l'action des agents d'émigration (les compagnies maritimes d'Anvers, flairant la bonne affaire, envoient des agents recruteurs dans les campagnes brabançonnes[20]). Le mouvement s'arrête à la faveur d'une légère reprise

économique, à cause des difficultés rencontrées par de nombreux émigrants victimes des pratiques frauduleuses des agents recruteurs et qui dénoncent les mauvaises conditions de voyage[21] ou les pièges que réserve l'établissement aux États-Unis. Les enquêtes sur la vie des émigrants belges menées sur place par les consuls freinent elles aussi le mouvement.

Cette émigration, qui est surtout le fait de familles entières, permet la formation d'une petite communauté d'agriculteurs wallons dans la région de Green Bay. Restée très unie, elle forme aujourd'hui encore un des principaux points d'ancrage wallon aux États-Unis[22] et a suscité une abondante littérature[23].

Il faut encore souligner qu'au milieu du XIXe siècle, un certain nombre de Wallons se dirigent vers la Pennsylvanie tandis que les États du Michigan et de l'Indiana accueillent une importante immigration flamande.

2) 1880-1893

Cette fois, ce sont surtout des ouvriers originaires des régions industrielles du Hainaut, touchés par les graves difficultés économiques, qui décident de s'expatrier. On note, entre autres, le départ de nombreux ouvriers verriers de la région de Charleroi. Après une grève très dure en 1884, leur syndicat, l'Union verrière, reçoit en effet le soutien des « Knights of Labor » de Pittsburgh qui offrent de payer le voyage de quelques centaines de souffleurs pour occuper des places vacantes aux États-Unis[24]. Nombreux sont aussi les ouvriers qui se dirigent vers les villes de l'Illinois (comme Moline) et du Michigan (notamment Detroit), où ils forment des communautés très actives. On leur doit notamment deux journaux flamands, la *Gazette van Moline*[25] publiée de 1907 à 1940 et la *Gazette van Detroit* apparue en 1914 et qui existe toujours. Autre caractéristique de cette émigration, les travailleurs conservent souvent des liens avec le mouvement ouvrier belge et continuent à exprimer leur soutien aux luttes menées dans leur pays d'origine[26].

3) 1901-1913

Cette troisième grande période d'émigration a été bien analysée par le professeur G. Kurgan[27] qui a mis en évidence l'existence de deux courants migratoires distincts :

1) 60% des émigrants sont originaires des Flandres[28], il s'agit la plupart du temps d'hommes jeunes, cultivateurs ou journaliers, aux ressources très limitées et qui, cette fois, partent seuls vers le Nord Midwest des États-Unis où ils rejoignent souvent des petites colonies belges déjà existantes. Ils espèrent améliorer leurs conditions

de vie même si cela les oblige à choisir une activité professionnelle différente de celle exercée en Belgique.

2) À l'opposé, 15% d'émigrés partent du Hainaut (notamment de la région de Charleroi). La plupart de temps, il s'agit d'ouvriers, surtout de mineurs, attirés par les salaires plus élevés et les meilleures conditions de travail offertes aux États-Unis. Ils emmènent avec eux leur famille et se dirigent notamment vers la Pennsylvanie[29]. À la différence des agriculteurs flamands, ces ouvriers disposent généralement de ressources financières plus importantes et, une fois sur place, ils ont tendance à se disperser davantage.

L'immigration belge au Canada

Des habitants des territoires qui formeront plus tard la Belgique sont présents au Canada depuis le XVIIe siècle. Plusieurs missionnaires belges jouent même un rôle de premier plan dans l'évangélisation des populations amérindiennes mais l'immigration proprement dite est beaucoup plus tardive[30]. Si au XIXe siècle ce sont surtout les États-Unis qui attirent les Belges, le Canada n'est cependant pas absent des statistiques, mais c'est surtout au début du siècle qu'un nombre croissant de Belges optent pour cette destination. Ils sont 2 312 de 1900 à 1904, 2 883 de 1905 à 1909, et 8 940 de 1910 à 1914[31]. Cette première période[32] sera suivie dans les années 20 par une seconde vague d'émigrants, originaires surtout des régions flamandes, puis par une troisième, au lendemain de la Seconde Guerre mondiale.

À la différence des États-Unis, l'intérêt des Belges pour le Canada est en partie lié à la politique des gouvernements de ce pays : les autorités canadiennes mais aussi celles du Québec et du Manitoba orchestrent très tôt de grandes campagnes de recrutement pour encourager les Belges à s'installer sur leur territoire[33]. Le Canada envoie dès 1869 un agent en Belgique et le Québec ne tarde pas à faire de même. Dans le troisième quart du XIXe siècle, de petites implantations d'agriculteurs belges voient ainsi le jour au Québec (notamment à Namur – dans l'Outaouais – et dans les Cantons de l'Est) et au Manitoba (à Saint-Boniface et dans ses environs, à Saint-Alphonse, à Bruxelles, à Swan Lake, à Mariapolis et à Somerset) mais aussi en Saskatchewan (au sud-est de Saskatoon) et en Alberta (au nord d'Edmonton[34]).

Dans les dernières années du XIXe siècle, le gouvernement canadien intensifie son action de propagande. Il ouvre à Anvers, en 1898, un bureau spécial pour l'immigration dirigé par le Belge Tréau de Coeli qui fait imprimer de multiples brochures dans les deux langues nationales et même des documents pour les écoles[35]. Ces publications ainsi que de nombreux

articles publiés dans la presse et les périodiques présentent le Canada comme une terre d'avenir pour les travailleurs entreprenants. Attirés par cette publicité, de nombreux agriculteurs se dirigent vers les provinces de l'Ouest canadien et tout particulièrement le Manitoba[36]. D'autres, souvent originaires de Wallonie, choisissent le Québec où la communauté de langue avec la population locale accélère le processus d'intégration : on trouve peu de traces de groupements « belges » dans la province francophone[37].

On note aussi, dès le début du siècle, une importante émigration de travailleurs flamands, anciens ouvriers saisonniers employés dans les champs de betteraves du Nord de la France et qui partent cultiver ceux du Sud-Ouest de l'Ontario[38]. La province anglophone verra encore arriver, dans les années 20, de nombreux agriculteurs venus cultiver ses champs de tabac et qui y créeront une petite communauté flamande[39]. Il faut enfin souligner l'émigration de groupes d'ouvriers, le plus souvent attirés par une publicité mensongère sur les conditions de travail et les salaires offerts. Fin XIXe, début XXe siècle, des équipes de mineurs wallons arrivent ainsi en Nouvelle-Écosse, au Nouveau-Brunswick et même en Alberta et sur l'île de Vancouver[40]. Les emplois offerts se révèlent souvent beaucoup moins rémunérateurs que promis, ce qui provoque plusieurs scandales. De nombreux ouvriers trompés cherchent à revenir en Belgique ou se dirigent vers les États-Unis[41]; quant à ceux qui choisissent de rester, l'expérience syndicale et la tradition socialiste acquises en Belgique les conduisent souvent à s'afficher parmi les plus actifs lors des conflits sociaux. Ils continuent en Amérique les luttes entreprises dans leur pays d'origine en faveur de meilleures conditions de travail et jouent parfois un rôle de premier plan dans le mouvement syndical canadien[42].

L'intégration religieuse des immigrés belges

La plupart des groupes ethniques catholiques installés en Amérique du Nord ont laissé dans les archives du Vatican des témoignages de leurs problèmes[43]. Très tôt les immigrés écrivent à Rome pour protester contre des évêques qui refusent de leur porter assistance. Les évêques, eux, se plaignent des difficultés rencontrées dans l'administration de diocèses multi-ethniques. Rome est informée de ces problèmes dès la fin du XVIIIe siècle[44]. Dans la première moitié du siècle suivant, ses dossiers sur l'Amérique du Nord grossissent à vue d'œil (en raison des querelles entre les immigrés irlandais et un clergé qui parle surtout le français[45]) mais c'est dans la deuxième moitié du XIXe siècle que la situation devient réellement préoccupante : l'Église catholique des États-Unis et plus tard du Canada doit répondre aux requêtes de dizaines de groupes ethniques originaires d'Europe, d'Asie et d'Amérique latine.

Face à ces mouvements de mécontentement, les autorités romaines sont bien obligées de reconnaître le principe des « paroisses ethniques[46] ». L'épiscopat local éprouve cependant les plus grandes difficultés à trouver des prêtres pour tous ces groupes[47] et, dans plusieurs cas, il tente de ralentir le processus en prônant, sans grand succès, l'américanisation immédiate des immigrants[48]. Comme il est impossible de satisfaire les requêtes de chaque communauté d'immigrants, des groupes apparentés sont rassemblés dans une même paroisse. On réunit les Français, les Québécois, les Acadiens, les Suisses romands et les Wallons[49], on mélange Flamands et Hollandais, parfois même on rassemble des immigrants en fonction de leur origine géographique. Dans la province ecclésiastique de Saint-Boniface au Manitoba, des Polonais de langue polonaise sont ainsi desservis par un clergé polonais, mais de langue allemande[50], tandis que dans la paroisse St. Charles de Detroit, un clergé hollandais et flamand prend en charge une communauté composée de Hollandais, de Flamands et de Wallons[51].

Dans ce contexte, les Belges qui, pour les raisons évoquées plus haut, ne sont déjà pas très nombreux en Amérique du Nord peuvent difficilement espérer former un grand nombre de paroisses autonomes. Dans le diocèse de Green Bay, on voit par exemple qu'entre 1875 et 1900 il y a seulement deux paroisses franco-wallonnes et une flamando-hollandaise[52]. En 1920, il n'y a toujours que neuf paroisses belges pour l'ensemble des États-Unis[53].

Il faut souligner que les immigrés qui sont ainsi réunis par les évêques en groupes linguistiques, nationaux ou géographiques hétérogènes n'apprécient guère les prêtres n'appartenant pas à leur propre sous-groupe : aux États-Unis, les Franco-Canadiens refusent les prêtres français ou belges[54] et on constate un phénomène comparable dans bon nombre de paroisses wallonnes-flamandes-hollandaises. Même dans les diocèses où l'on n'enregistre aucun différend d'ordre ethnique, les évêques signalent dans leurs rapports la présence de groupes minoritaires et la possibilité de problèmes futurs.

En comparaison avec la faiblesse de l'immigration belge, le clergé originaire de ce pays et officiant aux États-Unis, comme au Canada, est toutefois fort nombreux et particulièrement actif. Prêtres et religieux belges sont présents depuis le XVIIe siècle en Amérique du Nord où ils ont desservi les premières paroisses coloniales et assuré les missions auprès des autochtones. Un Liégeois, Pierre-Herman Dosquet, devient même évêque de Québec en 1733[55]. Dans la deuxième moitié du XIXe siècle, cette présence du clergé wallon et flamand en Amérique du Nord connaît un nouvel essor : de nombreux missionnaires belges sont envoyés chez les Indiens de la côte Pacifique, dans les paroisses francophones de la Louisiane et auprès des nouveaux immigrants originaires d'Europe[56]. On peut parler d'une

véritable petite émigration cléricale belge stimulée par la fondation, en 1857, du Collège Américain de Louvain. De 1857 à 1870, celui-ci envoie aux États-Unis et au Canada 170 prêtres, dont cinq sont désignés comme évêques et appellent à leur tour d'autres compatriotes[57]. En outre, en 1879, des Rédemptoristes belges sont envoyés au Québec pour administrer la paroisse de Sainte-Anne de Beaupré[58], d'autres s'établissent à Montréal en 1883[59] et quinze ans plus tard, l'archevêque de Saint-Boniface au Manitoba confie toujours à des Rédemptoristes belges les immigrés ukrainiens de son diocèse[60].

Lorenzo Caratelli signale encore dans sa *Relatio (abreviata) Archidiocesis Sanctae Fidei in Novo Mexico* qu'en 1892 les catholiques mexicains de ce diocèse sont assistés par des prêtres belges[61]. Dans le diocèse de Vancouver, sept prêtres belges et quatre hollandais s'occupent des pionniers anglophones et des communautés indiennes[62]. Dans le diocèse de Grand Rapids, Michigan, où résidaient douze familles belges (dont onze dans la paroisse mixte de St. Jacob de Montagne) on relève également la présence de deux prêtres belges qui, toutefois, ne travaillent pas avec leurs compatriotes[63].

Les paroissiens nord-américains desservis par ce clergé belge s'en plaignent à maintes occasions. Les colons américains et canadiens refusent les curés wallons[64], les Ukrainiens n'apprécient guère les Rédemptoristes belges[65] et les prêtres belges eux-mêmes (surtout ceux d'origine flamande) ne sympathisent pas facilement avec leurs collègues de langue française. Dans le diocèse de Natchitoches, Louisiane, il y eut ainsi des querelles entre ecclésiastiques français et belges[66]. Michel Letellier, missionnaire chez les Canadiens français immigrés aux États-Unis, proteste le 22 avril 1899 auprès du cardinal Ledochowski, préfet de la Congrégation « de Propaganda Fide » : « Les Belges, qui, écrit-il, n'ont qu'un petit nombre de leurs coreligionnaires dans ce pays, comptent cinq évêques[67] ». En 1903, Paul Bruchési, archevêque de Montréal, demande au même Ledochowski de ne plus lui envoyer de Rédemptoristes belges parce que son clergé ne s'entend pas avec ses confrères français et belges[68]. Il faut enfin signaler que les prêtres belges éprouvent aussi quelques difficultés avec les évêques de langue anglaise, par exemple dans le diocèse de Victoria, Colombie-Britannique[69].

Dans l'ensemble, la présence belge aux États-Unis et au Canada reste toutefois limitée et elle ne débouche pas sur des querelles semblables à celles engendrées par les Franco-Américains. D'une certaine façon les Belges sont protégés par le nombre de prélats nord-américains nés en Belgique ou qui ont étudié à Louvain. C'est seulement là où ces prélats manquent que naissent parfois quelques problèmes d'ordre linguistique lorsque l'on assimile les Belges aux Hollandais.

Le 17 novembre 1906, des habitants de la colonie belge du Wisconsin écrivent ainsi au Saint-Père pour demander des prêtres de la même nationalité. Desservis par des Norbertins hollandais qui ne comprennent pas leur langue, ils les accusent de les traiter comme des « cannibales[70] ». Les fonctionnaires de la Propagande ne prennent pas cet appel en considération et, l'année suivante, quatre immigrés belges résidant dans le village de Luxembourg écrivent à nouveau au délégué apostolique à Washington, Diomede Falconio, pour lui demander de régler le problème[71]. Falconio se renseigne auprès de P.J. Lochman, vicaire général du diocèse de Green Bay, qui défend les Norbertins et souligne qu'un des signataires de la protestation a appartenu à l'Église schismatique de Joseph René Vilatte[72].

En 1908, les Belges de Luxembourg reviennent à la charge : ils accusent les Norbertins de leur enlever « la foi, nos églises, notre langue maternel [sic], notre argent ». Cette fois, le délégué apostolique écrit à l'évêque de Green Bay et demande des renseignements. Mgr Fox conteste ces allégations et répond que les immigrés wallons dans la péninsule située entre le lac Michigan et Green Bay « were very weak in the faith when they emigrated from Belgium, owing to a lack of instruction, and the most of them could neither read nor write ». Il estime, par conséquent, que l'on ne doit pas porter attention à ces accusations d'autant que les Prémontrés parlent très bien le français et ont fait beaucoup pour leur paroisse. Aux yeux de l'évêque, ils ont en plus le mérite d'avoir obligé Vilatte à abandonner la partie[73]. Fox convainc Falconio de ne pas répondre aux signataires, mais ceux-ci écrivent à nouveau l'année suivante. Ils qualifient les Norbertins de « brigands de la Hollande », « des vrais franc maçons et anarchistes », « qui font du businesse [sic] avec la religion ». Le délégué ne répond toujours pas et après plusieurs lettres, écrites de juin 1909 à août 1910, les Belges du village de Luxembourg, Wisconsin, cessent leurs plaintes. Il s'agit très probablement d'une renonciation définitive, puisque la dernière lettre fut envoyée de Bruxelles, le 19 août 1910, et signée « Un groupe de Belges revenu d'Amérique ».

Les dossiers du Vatican sur les Belges installés au Canada sont beaucoup moins nombreux. Les seules véritables communautés catholiques belges sont situées dans l'Ouest du pays, plus particulièrement au Manitoba[74]. En 1896, l'abbé Hubert Heynen devient par exemple membre du clergé de Saint-Boniface et les catholiques belges de Boissevain et d'autres établissements de l'archidiocèse lui sont confiés. Trois ans plus tard, il est désigné comme curé de la paroisse de Bruxelles, Manitoba, où, en 1905, il déclare desservir environ 200 fidèles de langue française et 150 de langue flamande[75]. En 1911, le journal du diocèse note qu'une paroisse flamande va bientôt voir le jour à Saint-Boniface[76], et deux ans plus tard, l'archevêque

de Saint-Boniface, Adélard Langevin, dit à Francesco Pellegrino Stagni, délégué apostolique à Ottawa, qu'il y a trois paroisses rurales flamandes dans son diocèse[77]. La même année, Langevin répond à une enquête de la Congrégation consistoriale sur l'immigration catholique au Canada qu'il y a deux prêtres flamands pour 600 immigrés « ex Flandria belgica » et il précise « Flandrii sunt in parochiis Bruxelles, Sti-Alphonsi, Swan Lake, et Sti-Bonifacii, Stae-Amaliae ». Il souligne enfin que « ...Flandrii, generatim loquendo, fideliter missae aliisque sacris functionibus adsunt » et qu'ils envoient leurs enfants dans les écoles catholiques[78].

Les renseignements donnés par Langevin contrastent nettement avec ceux de deux autres évêques qui répondent à la même enquête. James Morrison, ordinaire d'Antigonish, Nouveau-Brunswick, révèle la présence de 137 Belges et 97 Français dans son diocèse mais il ajoute : « Inter Belgos et Gallos adsunt plures socialistae qui spiritum anticlericalismi fovere invenientur[79] ». Pour sa part, Alex MacDonald note que, dans le diocèse de de Victoria, Colombie-Britannique, il y a 50 Français et 100 Belges qui, sauf quelques exceptions, ne fréquentent pas la messe[80].

Ces divergences s'expliquent aisément : les immigrés belges du Manitoba et ceux du Nouveau-Brunswick et de la Colombie-Britannique ne proviennent pas des mêmes groupes socio-professionnels. Les premiers sont surtout des agriculteurs flamands, les seconds des ouvriers wallons. Cornelius Jaenen a bien mis en évidence la tradition socialiste et anticléricale des mineurs belges émigrés en Colombie-Britannique et dans les Maritimes[81]. Cette tradition était par contre tout à fait étrangère à la plupart de ceux qui émigrèrent dans les Plaines où, entre 1890 et 1910, l'Église catholique avait mis en place un véritable réseau d'agents d'émigration qui y emmenaient prioritairement les « bons catholiques »[82]. L'arrivée des Belges fut organisée par le diocèse de Saint-Boniface avec le concours de la Société Saint-Raphaël, du Chapitre général des oblats et d'un certain nombre d'ecclésiastiques et de journalistes canadiens-français et belges, parmi lesquels il faut citer Louis Hacault[83] qui ne fut pas seulement un propagandiste de la colonisation catholique du Manitoba en Belgique, mais qui y émigra pour devenir l'un des maîtres-à-penser du catholicisme franco-manitobain[84].

Conclusions

Cette brève étude montre donc que l'émigration vers l'Amérique du Nord reste un thème peu abordé par les historiens belges. Si l'on excepte l'ouvrage de synthèse de Jean Stengers, l'article très fouillé de Ginette Kurgan sur l'émigration au début du XXe siècle, les travaux de Cornelius Jaenen sur le Canada, le récent article de Marc Debuisson et Nathalie Tousignant[85], et

quelques mémoires[86], le sujet n'a guère fait l'objet d'une approche globale[87]. Par contre, on découvre de nombreuses petites contributions qui portent notamment sur l'établissement des Belges dans la région de Green Bay au milieu du XIXe siècle et sur le départ de groupes de villageois flamands au début du XXe siècle.

Ces divers travaux, auxquels s'ajoutent les dossiers du Vatican, montrent que l'émigration belge se caractérise par sa faible amplitude (même s'il y eut quelques périodes de pointe), son absence de caractère politique ou religieux (sauf quelques exceptions) et l'attitude très réservée des autorités politiques, religieuses et même du mouvement socialiste, qui mirent en garde les candidats au départ contre les pièges de la propagande sans toutefois déconseiller formellement l'expatriation.

Peu nombreux par rapport aux vastes mouvements de population auxquels on assiste dans les autres pays européens, les émigrants belges auront tendance à s'éparpiller dans le Midwest américain et les diverses provinces du Canada. Souvent trop disséminés pour former une véritable communauté ethnique, ils se fondirent dans la population. On découvre néanmoins quelques points d'ancrage comme la région de Green Bay, les villes de Detroit et Moline, Saint-Boniface dans la banlieue de Winnipeg et plusieurs régions de l'Ontario où d'importantes communautés belges virent le jour au XXe siècle et subsistent toujours aujourd'hui. Cette « survivance » belge est surtout le fait des travailleurs de la terre, les ouvriers s'étant quant à eux mélangés plus rapidement avec la population locale. Il y a d'ailleurs une intéressante littérature qui souligne la capacité des Belges à être absorbés dans le *melting pot* nord-américain[88]. Toutefois, les dossiers du Vatican montrent que ce processus ne fut « pacifique » que là où l'immigration belge était protégée par des prélats belges. Dans d'autres situations, les Wallons montrèrent soit un esprit anticlérical fort développé, soit une tendance à refuser le rassemblement avec les Flamands.

On note aussi que malgré le maintien d'une certaine identité wallonne dans les environs de Green Bay, les immigrants flamands (souvent des agriculteurs) semblent avoir formé plus fréquemment des groupes ethniques distincts; les deux seuls journaux belges publiés en Amérique du Nord avant 1914 sont d'ailleurs de langue flamande. La religion n'est sans doute pas tout à fait étrangère à ce phénomène : les émigrants belges d'origine rurale qui provenaient souvent des régions flamandes, étaient profondément catholiques et ce sentiment religieux (qui se traduira par la mise en place d'églises et d'écoles catholiques) semble avoir facilité le maintien d'une certaine identité culturelle. À l'inverse, les ouvriers belges originaires de Wallonie et marqués par une tradition socialiste et anticléricale ne pourront, eux, utiliser le sentiment religieux comme ciment de leur groupe ethnique.

L'immigration belge et l'Église catholique au Canada et aux États-Unis
avant la Première Guerre mondiale

Il semble au contraire que les idées internationales véhiculées par les doctrines socialistes facilitèrent leur intégration dans les syndicats américains qui, d'une certaine manière, constitueront un instrument d'assimilation. Les ouvriers belges n'auront guère tendance à constituer des groupes ethniques fermés.

Notes

1. Une première version de cette étude ne portant que sur les États-Unis et intitulée « Migrants, Bishops and the Vatican : Belgian Immigration in the United States before World War I », a été publiée dans *Studi Emigrazione/ Études Migrations*, XXVIII, 103 (1991), p. 393-406.
2. Pour une présentation des séries archivistiques utilisées, cf. M. Benoit et M. Sanfilippo, « Sources romaines pour l'histoire de l'Église catholique du Canada : le pontificat de Léon XIII (1878-1903) », *Revue d'histoire de l'Amérique française*, 44, 1 (1990), p. 85-96.
3. Mgr Cartuyvels, « De l'émigration belge en Amérique », dans *Congrès des oeuvres sociales à Liège. Deuxième session 5-7 septembre 1887*, Liège, 1887, p. 512.
4. J. Stengers, *Émigration et immigration en Belgique au XIXe et au XXe siècles*, Bruxelles, Académie royale des Sciences d'Outremer, 1978, p. 53. Cet ouvrage reste encore aujourd'hui la meilleure synthèse sur l'émigration belge avant 1914.
5. B.S. Chlepner, *Cent ans d'histoire sociale en Belgique*, Bruxelles, éd. de l'Université de Bruxelles, 1972 (1ère éd. 1956), p. 48.
6. Dans son étude « Quelques témoignages sur l'immigration hennuyère, 1884-1889 » (*Bulletin de l'Académie royale des Sciences d'Outre-Mer*, 3 (1973), p. 443-463, Jean Puissant montre que l'émigration de certains leaders ouvriers, à la fin des années 1880, a bien un aspect politique; il ne s'agit cependant pas là de la principale motivation des milliers d'ouvriers qui quittent la Belgique à la même époque.
7. Cf. A. Desmet, « L'émigration belge aux États-Unis pendant le 19ème siècle jusqu'à la guerre civile », dans *Album Antoine De Smet*, Bruxelles, 1974, p. 450-455 (ce texte a d'abord été publié dans les *Annales de la XXXIIe session de la Fédération archéologique et historique de Belgique*, 1947, p. 188-208) et R. Boumans, « Een onbekend Aspect van de Belgische Uitwijking naar Amerika : de gesubsidieerde Emigratie van Bedelaars en oud-gevangenen (1850-1856) », *Bulletin des séances de l'académie royale d'outre-mer*, XI, 2 (1965), p. 354-393.
8. Le *Bulletin de la société belge de l'archange Raphaël* dénonce régulièrement les pratiques des agents recruteurs.
9. F. Waldbott de Bassenheim, « La protection de l'émigrant », dans *Congrès des oeuvres sociales à Liège. Troisième session 7-10 septembre 1890*, Liège, 1890, p. 8.

10. *Ibid.*, p. 9.
11. Cf. J. Puissant, « Quelques témoignages... »
12. Sur cette propagande voir V. Van Coillie, *Propaganda en voorlichting met betrekking tot de Belgische overzeese emigratie, 1880-1914*, mémoire de licence en Histoire, Rijksuniversiteit Gent, 1980.
13. J. Stengers, *Emigration...*, p. 59.
14. Cf. V. Aelbrecht, « L'immigration ouvrière belge à Tourlaing durant le Second Empire », *Revue Belge d'histoire contemporarine*, XXI, 3-4i (1990), p. 351-381. L. Schepens, *Van Vlaskuter tot Franschman. Bijdrage tot de geschiedenis van de Westvlaamse plattenlandsbewolking in de negentiende eeuw*, Bruges, 1973.
15. Pour une bibliographie récente sur l'émigration belge, voir M. Dumoulin et E. Stols, *La Belgique et l'étranger aux XIXᵉ et XXᵉ siècles*, Bruxelles-Louvain-la-Neuve, 1987.
16. C.C. Qualey, « Immigration to the United States since 1815 », dans *Les migrations internationales de la fin du XVIIIᵉ siècle à nos jours*, Paris, Éditions du CNRS, 1980, p. 37. Sur l'image des États-Unis en Belgique à la fin du XIXᵉ siècle, voir N. Lubelski-Bernard, « Images du Nouveau Monde ramenées par quelques voyageurs belges à la fin du XIXᵉ siècle et au début du XXᵉ siècle », dans M. Dumoulin et E. Stols, *La Belgique et l'étranger...*, p. 127-146.
17. C.C. Qualey, « Immigration to the United States... », p. 36.
18. Les gouverneurs de province diffuseront une mise en garde contre les agissements de certains agents d'émigration. J. Stengers, *Émigration...*, p. 37.
19. A. De Smet a montré que parmi ces premières familles d'émigrants plusieurs d'entre elles étaient de religion protestante. A. De Smet, « La communauté belge du nord-est du Wisconsin. Ses origines, son évolution jusque vers 1900 », dans *Album Antoine De Smet*, p. 463-464 (paru une première fois en 1957) et *id.* « Antécédents et aspects peu connus de l'émigration belge dans le nord-est du Wisconsin », *Wavriensia*, II (1953), p. 17-39.
20. Sur la motivation de ces départs et leurs conséquences voir la très bonne étude de Th. Eggerickx et M. Poulain, « Le contexte et les conséquences démographiques de l'émigration des Brabançons vers les États-Unis au milieu du XIXᵉ siècle », *Annales de démographie historique*, 1987, p. 313-336. Voir aussi M. A. Defnet, J. Ducat, Th. Eggerickx et M. Poulain, *From Grez-Doiceau to Wisconsin. Contribution à l'étude de l'émigration wallonne vers les États-Unis d'Amérique au XIXᵉ siècle*, Bruxelles, 1986.
21. Sur ce sujet, cf. E. Spelkens, « Antwerp as a port of Emigration 1843-1913 », dans G. Kurgan et E. Spelkens, *Two Studies on Emigration through Antwerp to the New World*, Bruxelles, 1976, p. 87.
22. Sur les associations belges dans le Midwest américain, au début des années 1960, voir F. Standaert, *Belgian immigrants in the Midwest of the U.S.A.*, Evanston, 1963. Ces régions agricoles attireront aussi des immigrants fla-

mands, cf. G.C.P. Linssen « Limburgers naar Noord Amerika » *Maasgauw*, 93, 1974, col. 39-54; J. et L. Rentmeester, *Flemisch in Wisconsin*, s.l., 1985.

23. Sur l'installation des Belges au Wisconsin on se référera notamment à deux ouvrages américains : H.R. Holand, *Wisconsin's Belgian Community*, Sturgeon Bay, 1933, et Tlachac Math S., *The History of the Belgian Settlement in Door, Kewaunee and Brown Counties*, Algoma, s.d. (réimprimé en 1974 par le *Peninsula Belgian American Club*). Voir aussi, A. De Smet, « La communauté belge... »; F. Lempereur, *Les Wallons d'Amérique du Nord*, Gembloux, 1976; C. Pansaets, *Belgian emigration to the United States of America and more in particular to the state of Wisconsin (1850-1914) : The Pierquet Mathieu Family*, mémoire de licence en Histoire, Katholieke Universiteit Leuven, 1987; J. Ducat, « Nouveau Bruxelles (Brussels) en Amérique. Une création brabançonne », *Wavriensia*, XXXV, 1986, p. 79-84; *id.*, « Des Dionnais aux Amériques » *Wavriensia*, XXXVI, 1987, p. 107-119; *id.*, « Les Brabançons au Far-West. Jay Township. Une colonie grézienne au Minnesota »,*Wavriensia*, XXXVI, 1987, p. 121-128. J.J. Gaziaux, « Feuillets d'émigration. À la recherche de Constant Fortemps (1856-1929) », *Wavriensia*, XXXVIII (1989), p. 33-64 et 65-104; E. Racette, *L'émigration brabançonne vers les États-Unis au milieu du XIXe siècle. Le cas de Beauvechain, Tourinne-la-Grosse (1855-1856)*, mémoire de licence en Histoire, Université catholique de Louvain, 1989. On trouvera une bibliographie et diverses indications sur les sources disponibles au Wisconsin à propos de ce mouvement migratoire dans D.L. Heinrich et L.C. Mc Auley, *Belgian American Research Materials : A Selected Bibliography*, Green Bay, University of Wisconsin, 1976. Pour l'état d'avancement des recherches sur les communautés wallonnes du Midwest américain voir J. Ducat, « L'émigration hesbignonne du XIXe siècle », *Bulletin du Cercle Art et Histoire de Gembloux et environs*, II, 28 (1986), p. 449-459. Voir aussi Jean Ducat, *Arlonais fondateurs de Belgium-Wisconsin*, Biesme-Mettet, chez l'auteur, 1993 et *id.*, *Namurois dans le Nouveau Monde*, Biesme-Mettet, chez l'auteur, 1995.

24. Cf. J. Puissant, « Quelques témoignages... », p. 444; F. Poty et J.-L. Delaet, *Charleroi, pays verrier*, Charleroi, 1986, p. 75-77; J. Ducat, « Migration massive de souffleurs de verre carolorégiens vers l'Amérique en 1889 », *Bulletin trimestriel de la société royale d'archéologie de Charleroi*, 3-4 (1987), p. 2-3.

25. Sur l'histoire de ce périodique flamand d'Amérique, voir G.P. Baert, « Witwijking naar Amerika vijftig jaar geleden » *Bijdrage tot de geschiedenis der stad Deinze*, 22 (1955), p. 42-59.

26. Les lettres d'émigrants hennuyers entre 1884 et 1889 publiées par Jean Puissant sont à cet égard très révélatrices : J. Puissant, « Quelques témoignages... ».

27. G. Kurgan-van Hentenryk, « Belgian Emigration to the United States and Other Overseas Countries at the Beginning of the Twentieth Century », dans

G. Kurgan et E. Spelkens, *Two Studies on Emigration through Antwerp to the New World*, Bruxelles, 1976, p. 9-49

28. Cette émigration flamande a fait l'objet de plusieurs études locales. Voir notamment, P. Dewitte et F. Depoorter, « Op zoek naar het beloofde land. Het wel en wee van streekgenoten in Amerika », *De Roede van Tielt*, XII, 2-3 (octobre 1981), p. 3-104; P. Dewitte, « Dagelijkse realiteit van prijzen en lonen. Hun invloed op de emigratie naar Noord-Amerika uit de streek van Tielt (1840-1914) », *De Roede van Tielt*, XIII, 2 (juin 1982), p. 71-88; E. De Smet, « Eekloose uitwijkelingen naar Amerika (XIXe-XXe eeuw) », *Appeltjes van het Meetjesland*, XXVIII (1977), p. 5-105; P.G. Baert, « Uitwijking naar Amerika », *Het land van Nevele*, IX (1978), p. 113-138.

29. G. Kurgan-van Hentenryk, « Belgian emigration... », p. 43.

30. On trouvera dans les notes de la seconde partie du texte, une bibliographie complète sur le rôle de ces missionnaires. Pour une bonne synthèse sur l'immigration belge au Canada, voir Cornelius Jaenen, *Les Belges au Canada*, série « Les groupes ethniques du Canada », brochure n° 20, Ottawa, Société historique du Canada, 1991, p. 7. Cette petite brochure constitue aujoud'hui la meilleure synthèse sur l'immigration belge au Canada. Il faut la compléter par deux autres articles : la notice « Belgians » rédigée pour *The Peoples of Canada : An Encyclopedia for the Country* (à paraître) et « De Belgische aanwezigheid in Canada » dans Leen d'Haenens (dir.), *Het Land van de Ahorn. Visies of Canada : Politiek, Cultuur, Economie*, Gand, Academia Press, 1995, p. 131-157.

31. Cf. C.J. Jaenen, « Le contexte socio-économique de l'immigration belge au Canada, 1880-1960 » dans G. Kurgan-van Hentenryk, *La question sociale en Belgique et au Canada, XIXe-XXe siècles*, Bruxelles, éd. de l'Université de Bruxelles, 1988, p. 166.

32. Cette première période correspond aussi à la première vague d'investissements belges au Canada. Cf. G. Kurgan-van Hentenryk et J. Laureyssens, *Un siècle d'investissements belges au Canada*, Bruxelles, éd. de l'Université de Bruxelles, 1984, p. 14-31; et A. Vermeirre, « Un aspect de l'émigration belge au début du XXe siècle : Hubert Biermans, pionnier et philanthrope », *Canadian Journal of Netherlandic Studies*, IV-V (1983), p. 14-19.

33. La première loi sur l'immigration au Canada, votée en 1864, comprenait une courte liste de pays dont il fallai attirer les nationaux; la Belgique en faisait partie. Voir C. Jaenen, *Les Belges...*, p. 7.

34. C. Jaenen, *Les Belges...*, p. 8-10; L. Trépanier, « La colonie franco-belge de Namur. 1871-1881 », *Asticou*, 18 (1977), p. 14-32; K. Wilson et J. Wyndels, *The Belgians in Manitoba*, Winnipeg, Peguis Publishers, 1976; J. Delmelle, « Les Brabançons de la montagne Pembina (Manitoba/Canada) », *Le Folklore brabançon*, 214 (1977), p. 129-137.

35. Cf. M. Journee, *De Lokroep van een nieuwe frontier. Belgische emigratie in Kanada 1880-1940*, mémoire de licence, KUL, 1981 p. 44 et *id.*,

« Algemeen achtergronden, profiel, feiten en aspecten van de Belgische emigratie naar Noord Amerika », *De Vlaamse Stam*, XXIII (1987), p. 61-72. Plusieurs Belges avaient déjà publié des ouvrages encourageant leurs compatriotes (surtout les agriculteurs possédant quelques capitaux) à se rendre au Québec ou dans les prairies. Cf. L. Hacault, *Les colonies belges et françaises du Manitoba. Notes de voyages au Canada en 1890*, Bruxelles, Alfred Vromant, 1892; G. Vekeman, *Eene reis in Canada*, Sherbrooke, 1882; *id.*, *Lettres d'un émigrant ou voyage au Canada. Suivi d'un appendice sur la Manitoba*, Bruxelles, Loge, 1883; *id.*, *Le Canada. Notes d'un colon*, Sherbrooke, Société typographique des Cantons de l'Est, 1884; *id.*, *Guide des émigrants au Canada et spécialement dans les cantons de l'Est*, Bruxelles, 1890 (sur Vekeman voir Jeanne Vekeman-Masson, *Grandmaman raconte La Grosse Île*, Ottawa, Corporation pour la mise en valeur de la Grosse Île Inc., 1993 (5e tirage); J. Herreboudt, *Le Canada au point de vue de l'émigration*, Bruges, 1890; *id.*, *De l'avenir de nos relations commerciales avec le Canada*, Bruxelles, 1892; A. Robert, « Au Canada. La province de Québec », *Revue sociale catholique*, XI (1906-1907), p. 140-155; G. Willems, *Les Belges au Manitoba. Lettres authentiques*, Ottawa, 1894.

36. C.J. Jaenen, « Le contexte... », p. 153. Voir aussi, K. Wilson et J.B. Wyndels, *The Belgians in Manitoba*, Winnipeg, 1976 et J. Delmelle, « Les Brabançons de la montagne Pembina (Manitoba/Canada) » *Le Folklore brabançon*, 214 (juin 1977), p. 129-137.

37. Voir A. Vermeirre, « Un ciel de pluie contre des arpents de neige », *Cahiers d'Histoire*, Montréal, 1984, p. 61-69.

38. J. Magee, *The Belgians in Ontario. An History*, Toronto, 1987, p. 25-38. Ce livre doit être utilisé avec prudence. Voir notre compte rendu dans « Le Bulletin d'Histoire de Belgique (1986-1987) » de la *Revue du Nord*, LXX, 278, (1988), p. 611-612.

39. En 1987, ils formaient toujours une petite communauté ethnique, très catholique dont les membres déclaraient encore avoir une très bonne connaissance du néerlandais. (J. Magee, *The Belgians in Ontario*, p. 186 et 197).

40. C.J. Jaenen, « Le contexte... », p. 157-162.

41. M. Journee, *De Lokroep...*, p. 52-53.

42. *Ibid.*, p. 54. C'est un immigrant belge, Gustave Franq, qui est considéré comme le père des Unions internationales au Canada (cf. J. Rouillard, « Francq, Gustave » *Canadian Encyclopedia*, p. 689). D'une manière générale, on s'accorde d'ailleurs à reconnaître que les émigrants d'Europe occidentale eurent un impact déterminant sur l'évolution du mouvement ouvrier canadien. Cf. L. Hertzman, « L'immigration au Canada avant et après la confédération » dans *Les migrations internationales...*, p. 85-86.

43. Cf. M. Sanfilippo, « La question canadienne-française dans les diocèses de la Nouvelle-Angleterre, 1892-1922 : les sources documentaires romaines », dans *Canada ieri e oggi 2*, II, *Sezione storica e geografica*, Selva di Fasano,

Schena Editore, 1990, p. 55-76.

44. Cf. V.J. Fecher, *A Study of the Movement for German National Parishes in Philadelphia and Baltimore (1787-1802)*, Romae, Apud Aedes Universitatis Gregorianae, 1955.

45. Cf. L. Codignola, « Conflict or Consensus? Catholics in Canada and in the United States, 1780-1820 », The Canadian Catholic Historical Association, *Historical Studies* (dorénavant CCHA), 55 (1988), p. 43-59.

46. Archivio della Sacra Congregazione di Propaganda Fide, Rome (dorénavant APFR), *Acta* (1887), f. 215.

47. APFR, *Nuova Serie* (dorénavant NS), vol. 333 (1905), ff. 552-563.

48. Cf. Ph. Gleason, « Immigrant Past, Ethnic Present », dans *id.*, *Keeping the Faith. American Catholicism Past and Present*, Notre Dame, University of Notre Dame Press, 1987, p. 35-57.

49. APFR, NS, vol. 145 (1898), ff. 471-493 : rapport de Sebastian Messmer sur le diocèse de Green Bay.

50. Archivio Segreto Vaticano (dorénavant ASV), *Delegazione Apostolica Canada* (dorénavant DAC), boîte 75, dossier 10/2, Lewis Drummond, s.j., to Donato Sbarretti, délégué apostolique au Canada, 10.2.1905, non folioté.

51. APFR, NS, vol 169 (1899), ff. 553-95. Les Belges étaient nombreux à Detroit dès l'érection du diocèse en 1833. Ils s'étaient réunis dans la paroisse de Sainte-Anne. Cf. Ph.D. Sabbe et L. Buyse, *Belgians in America*, Tielt, 1960, p. 63-64.

52. Cf. J. Olson, *Catholic Immigrants in America*, Chicago, Nelson-Hall, 1987, p. 105.

53. *Ibid.*, p. 122.

54. Cf. M. Sanfilippo, « The French Canadian Question in the Dioceses of New England, 1895-1912. Preliminary Resarch in the Vatican Archives », *Storia Nordamerica*, IV, 1-2 (1987), p. 205-22.

55. Cf. J.-G. Pelletier, « Dosquet, Pierre-Herman », *Dictionary of Canadian Biography*, IV, Toronto, University of Toronto Press, 1979, p. 220-222.

56. Cf. J.A. Griffin, *The Contribution of Belgium to the Catholic Church in America (1523-1857)*, Washington, Catholic University of America, 1932; A. Vermeirre et C.J. Jaenen, *Les Belges au Canada*, chapitre sur la vie religieuse, à paraître. Voir aussi, J. Stengers, « Hennepin et la découverte du Mississippi », *Bulletin de la Société Royale Belge de Géographie d'Anvers* (1945), p. 61-82; A. Louant, « Le P. Louis Hennepin, Nouveaux jalons pour sa biographie », *Revue d'histoire ecclésiastique*, XLV (1950), p. 186-211; J.-R. Rioux, « Hennepin, Louis », *Dictionary of Canadian Biography*, III, Toronto, University of Toronto Press, 1969, p. 277-82; « Selections from the diary and gazette of Father Pierre Potier, S.J. (1708-1781) », *Mid-America*, 18 (1936), p. 199-207; P.J. De Smet, *Oregon Missions and Travels over the Rocky Mountains*, New York, 1947; A.J. Brabant, *Mission to Nootka 1874-1900. Reminiscences of the West Coast of Vancouver Island*, Ch. Lillard (dir.), Sydney, BC, Gray Publishing, Ltd., 1977; B.M.

Gough, « Father Brabant, and the Hesquiat of Vancouver Island », CCHA, *Study Sessions*, 50 (1983), p. 553-68; J.M. Hill, « Archbishop Seghers, Pacific Coast Missionary », CCHA, *Report*, 18 (1950-51), p. 13-23.

57. Cf. J. Van der Heyden, *Life and Letters of Father Brabant, A Flemish Missionary Hero*, Louvain, J. Wouters-Ickx, 1920; J. Sauter, *History of the American College of Louvain, 1857-1898*, Louvain, 1959. Voir aussi, *American College Bulletin* (Louvain), One Hundredth Centenary Issue, XXXVI (June 1957).

58. Cf. J.-P. Asselin, *Les Rédemptoristes au Canada*, Montréal, Bellarmin, 1981, p. 29-38.

59. *Ibid.*, p. 68-74.

60. Une maison fut fondée à Brandon, Manitoba, en 1898, une autre à Yorkton, Saskatchewan en 1904. *Ibid.*, p. 120-123. Voir aussi, E. Tremblay, *Le père Delaere et l'Église ukrainienne du Canada*, Ottawa, Bernard, 1961.

61. APFR, NS, vol. 27 (1893), ff. 269-270.

62. *Ibid.*, ff. 590-93.

63. *Ibid.*, ff. 448-49.

64. Voir les protestations dans le diocèse de Vancouver. ASV, *Délégation Apostolique États-Unis* (dorénavant DASU), IV, 34, ff. 4-5.

65. ASV, DAC, boîte 150 et 184.

66. APFR, NS, vol. 295 (1904), ff. 792-794v.

67. APFR, NS, vol. 169 (1899), ff. 757-759.

68. APFR, NS, vol. 265 (1903), ff. 9-14.

69. ASV, DAC, boîte 97.

70. APFR, NS, vol. 362 (1906), ff. 563-566.

71. Toutes les lettres des Belges de Green Bay à Falconio se trouvent dans le dossier ASV, DASU, IX, Green Bay, 37.

72. Originaire de Paris, Joseph René Vilatte avait étudié à Rome et au Canada français. Il s'était ensuite rendu au Wisconsin, où l'évêque épiscopalien l'avait autorisé à prêcher aux Belges de la région. En 1891, Vilatte se fit consacrer archevêque de l'Église des Vieux-Catholiques d'Amérique contre la volonté des épiscopaliens. Il fut excommunié l'année suivante par l'Église épiscopalienne et essaya alors de rentrer dans l'Église catholique. L'évêque de Green Bay refusa et appela les Prémontrés de l'abbaye de Berne, dans les Pays Bas – c'est-à-dire les Norbertins hollandais dont parlent les protestations des Belges de Luxembourg – pour combattre l'influence de Vilatte dans les communautés belges du diocèse. En 1894, les fidèles belges de Vilatte étaient réduits à une cinquantaine de familles et quatre ans plus tard, il dut abandonner la partie (Vilatte finit par se rendre à Rome et se réconcilia avec l'Église catholique). Toutefois, ses disciples ne se rendirent pas. C'est dans la communauté belge du Wisconsin qu'a été formée la première congrégation américaine des Vieux Catholiques ainsi qu'une Église presbytérienne et une secte spiritualiste. Voir ASV, DASU, IX, Green Bay, 2 et 3,. et A. De Smet, « La communauté belge du nord-est

du Wisconsin », dans *Album De Smet*, p. 495-497

73. Entre les lignes de la lettre de Fox on comprend que pour lui ces protestations sont liées à la défaite des Vieux Catholiques, mais le différend entre
les fidèles et les Prémontrés semble surtout provenir de la décision de
l'évêque d'élever le salaire de ces derniers en demandant une forte contribution à la congrégation paroissiale.

74. En 1911, il y avait 9 593 Belges au Canada, dont 938 en Colombie-Britannique, 1 269 en Alberta, 1 538 en Saskatchewan et 2 453 au Manitoba. Cf.
Bulletin XIII, Fifth Census of Canada, Ottawa, 1911.

75. Cf. le chapitre sur la vie religieuse dans l'ouvrage de C. Jaenen et
A. Vermeire relatif à l'histoire de l'émigration belge (à paraître).

76. « Paroisse flamande à Saint-Boniface », *Les Cloches de Saint-Boniface*,
(15 mars 1911), p. 82.

77. ASV, DAC, boîte 77, dossier 14, s.d., [Langevin], adresse à Stagni, non
folioté.

78. ASV, DAC, boîte 131, dossier 2/3, ff. 187-199.

79. *Ibid.*, ff. 166-170.

80. *Ibid.*, ff. 210-212.

81. Cf. C.J. Jaenen, « Le contexte socio-économique de l'immigration belge
au Canada, 1880-1960 », dans *La question sociale en Belgique et au Canada*, éd. par G. Kurgan-van Hentenryk, Bruxelles, Éditions de l'Université
de Bruxelles, 1988, p. 158-161.

82. Cf. R. Painchaud, *Un rêve français dans le peuplement de la Prairie*, Saint-
Boniface, Éditions des Plaines, 1987, p. 165-202.

83. Cf. S. Jaumain, « Un regard belge sur la question sociale au Canada (1880-
1940) », dans *La question sociale en Belgique et au Canada*, p. 205-206.

84. Hacault était très apprécié par Mgr Langevin (ASV, DAC, boîte 75, dossier
16, Langevin à Sbarretti, 8.3.1908; voir aussi, *Les Cloches de Saint-
Boniface* (15 février 1909), p. 47) et était tenu en haute considération par la
Délégation apostolique d'Ottawa (ASV, DAC, boîte 52, dossier 10/2, Alfred A. Sinnott to Lewis Drummond, s.j., 16.12.1907). Son catholicisme
était ultramontain et se traduisait par un antisémitisme virulent, doublé par
la peur de la franc-maçonnerie et du socialisme. Cf. M. Sanfilippo, « Una
lettera dal Manitoba sulle elezioni romane del 1907 », *Archivio della Società
Romana di Storia Patria*, 109 , 1986, p. 239-50.

85. Marc Debuisson et Nathalie Tousignant, « L'émigration belge vers le
Québec au XXe siècle, ou l'histoire de l'émigration de Belgique vers le
Canada », dans *Les chemins de la migration en Belgique au Québec : XVIIe-
XXe siècles*, sous la direction de Yves Landry *et al.*, Beauport (Québec),
MNH, 1995, p. 247-257.

86. M. Journee, *De Lokroep...*; G. Verrijken, *Aspecten van de emigratie naar
Amerika, inzonderheid de Verenigde Statten, vanuit Antwerpen (1856-1914)*,
Katholieke Universiteit Leuven, 1984; F. Van de Pitte, *Belgische immi-
granten in de Verenigde Staten, 1850-1920*, Rijksuniversiteit Gent, 1987.

87. Cf. D.C. Skemer, *American History in Belgium and Luxembourg : A Bibliography*, Bruxelles, 1975.
88. « Belgians have integrated easily into the Canadian population, probably because they are few in number, widely dispersed and culturally very similar to French and English Canadians. » (A. Vermeirre, « Belgians », *Canadian Encyclopedia*, I, Edmonton, Hurtig Publishers, 1985, p. 159).

Fernando Mata

Birthplace and Economic Similarities in the Labour Force: An Analysis of Toronto's Census Microdata

Abstract

This paper uses four microdata samples from the 1981 and 1991 censuses of Canada to examine the similarities in labour force attributes among workers of different birthplace and gender residing in the Metropolitan Toronto area. Nine selected economic indicators were used as a basis for the comparison of groups. Labour force indicators were analyzed to: (1) explore the nature of the economic domains underlying the data; (2) determine how stable these domains were between 1981 and 1991; (3) assess changes in the positions of birthplace groups within the economic hierarchy; and, (4) determine how similar or dissimilar the groups were in their labour force characteristics at the two census periods.

The multivariate analysis of the census microdata suggests that Toronto's labour force continues to be stratified along ethnic and nationality lines. There are three basic domains which characterize the economic life of the labour force in Metro Toronto. Despite minor variations, these economic domains appeared to be relatively stable between 1981 and 1991. The positions that birthplace groups occupied within the domains also did not change much during the decade. Immigrants from the U.S., U.K. and some European countries had the greatest advantages in the economic domains while individuals born in Poland, Latin America and the Caribbean had the greatest disadvantages. Socio-demographic characteristics were found to have different impacts on the groups' positions depending on the economic dimension being examined.

Résumé

Cet article utilise quatre échantillons de micro-données tirés des recensements canadiens de 1981 et 1991 pour examiner les similarités des activités sur le marché du travail des travailleurs d'origines et de sexes différents résidant dans la région métropolitaine de Toronto. Les groupes ont été comparés en fonction de neuf indicateurs économiques, qui ont été analysés pour : (1) examiner la nature des domaines économiques sous-jacents aux données, (2) déterminer le degré de stabilité de ces domaines entre 1981 et 1991, (3) évaluer les changements survenus

dans la position des groupes de différentes origines dans la hiérarchie économique et (4) déterminer dans quelle mesure ces groupes étaient similaires ou non sur le plan de leurs activités sur le marché du travail lors des deux périodes de recensement.

L'analyse multivariable des micro-données de recensements indique que la population active de Toronto continue à être stratifiée en fonction de l'origine ethnique et de la nationalité. Trois domaines de base caractérisent la vie économique de la main-d'oeuvre dans la région torontoise. Malgré certaines variations mineures, ces domaines économiques sont demeurés relativement stables entre 1981 et 1991. La position occupée dans ces domaines par les groupes de différentes origines ethniques n'a pas beaucoup changé non plus au cours de cette décennie. Les immigrants originaires des États-Unis, du Royaume-Uni et de certains pays européens étaient les plus avantagés dans les domaines économiques, tandis que les immigrants originaires de Pologne, d'Amérique latine et des Antilles étaient les plus désavantagés. Selon la dimension économique examinée, les caractéristiques socio-démographiques avaient des incidences différentes sur la position des groupes.

Introduction

Toronto is the centre of gravity for immigration to Canada. One out of three of Canada's immigrants resided in Metropolitan Toronto in 1991. Throughout the years, continuous immigration from all world regions has contributed to Toronto's demographic primacy as well as its ethnic and cultural diversity. Early immigrants to Toronto came primarily from Britain, the U.S. and Europe. During the latter half of the 1980s and early 90s, the number of immigrants originating from Asian, African, Caribbean and Latin American countries destined for Toronto rose significantly. The more recent immigrants are members of visible minority groups.

Between 1981 and 1991, the immigrant population of Toronto increased from 1.1 to 1.5 million. During this period of extraordinary growth, new workers entered the economic system into different echelons of the occupational hierarchy. Past studies undertaken in the Toronto area have shown that ethnicity persists as a basis for social and economic differentiation in the labour force. One of the most likely outcomes of this process is that some immigrant groups may become increasingly similar in terms of their labour force characteristics. Studying these similarities is important. It illustrates the ethnic stratification process taking place in an urban context such as Toronto. It also helps to understand how immigrants are adjusting to their new socio-economic milieu and their relative success (or failure) in doing so.

Birthplace and Economic Similarities in the Labour Force:
An Analysis of Toronto's Census Microdata

Using four samples drawn from the census microdata of 1981 and 1991, the purpose of this paper is fourfold: (1) to explore the nature of the economic domains underlying Toronto's labour force data; (2) to determine how stable these domains were between 1981 and 1991; (3) to assess changes in the positions of birthplace groups within the economic hierarchy; and, (4) to determine how similar or dissimilar the groups were in their labour force characteristics at the two census periods.

It should be noted that the major thrust of this paper is to identify patterns of economic similarity rather than systematically attempt to explain them. In this sense, this work is descriptive in nature. It could, however, produce valuable background information for undertaking more comprehensive studies of Toronto's labour force.

Birthplace and Economic Similarities

The similarities in labour force attributes which exist between foreign-born segments of the labour force are the result of complex factors. These factors include, among others, differences in human capital, occupational segregation processes, and immigration regulations in force (Pendakur 1995). Several sociological models of the economic adaptation of immigrants agree in asserting that, due to their skills, education, and patterns of adjustment to the urban economy, many immigrants end up being concentrated in specific economic sectors (Beaujot 1988, 11). For instance, in Toronto, immigrants from the U.K., U.S., Northern and Central Europe are more likely to work in white collar occupational "niches" than Southern Europeans and/or Third World immigrants who are found in blue collar ones. (Reitz *et al.* 1981; Reitz 1982).

"Entrance status" theory offers a rationale for birthplace being a strong predictor of economic status. A change in the position of a specific immigrant group in the economic hierarchy is seen as a function of the degree to which the group has moved away from, or remained closer to its original "entrance status" to the labour market (Porter 1985; Lautard and Guppy 1990). Some individuals tend to enter white collar or professional jobs while others tend to enter blue collar jobs of a skilled or unskilled nature. Over time, this process leads to the stratification of the labour force and the concentration of workers in particular occupations, branches of industry and even earning brackets. Occupational mobility "traps" impede the workers' movement from their original economic positions in the labour market (Darroch 1979).

Another theoretical view emphasizes the role of ethnic networks as important factors in the ethnic stratification process (Breton 1984). Some immigrant communities attain a high degree of "institutional completeness"

which, in turn, affects the economic adaptation of the immigrants within communities. In Toronto, institutional completeness is expressed in various aspects of community life such as business, media, welfare organizations, churches, and schools. All of these institutions and networks can be used by immigrant workers as "resources" or "opportunity structures," that is, as channels for social mobility within certain segments of the labour market (Sullivan 1978; Driedger 1989).

From a longitudinal perspective, there are two questions pertaining to the ethnic stratification process that are relevant. How persistent over time are the economic positions that different birthplace groups occupy within the economic hierarchy? As a consequence of this stratification process, for instance, are birthplace groups in Toronto becoming indistinguishable in their labour force attributes? To address these research questions, four general hypotheses were explored in relation to Toronto's 1981 and 1991 census microdata. Succinctly, these hypotheses stated that:

(a) the labour force characteristics of workers from different countries living in Metropolitan Toronto may be described in terms of a few interrelated economic domains;

(b) these domains did not change significantly between 1981 and 1991 (i.e., no new domains had emerged);

(c) the positions that birthplace groups occupy within the economic domains had not fundamentally changed during this period;

(d) birthplace groups formed distinctive clusters of similarity in terms of their economic and occupational attributes.

Data, Indicators and Methodology

In the absence of adequate longitudinal data (panel studies or otherwise), cross-sectional samples from the population censuses constitute rich data sources to study the changes in the ethnic composition of Toronto's labour force over time. The data for this analysis were drawn from the individual files of the Public Use Sample Tapes (PUST) of the 1981 Census of Canada and the Public Use Microdata Files (PUMF) of the 1991 Census of Canada. The 1981 PUST and 1991 PUMF samples contain data based on 2 per cent and 3 per cent, respectively, of the population enumerated in the census in these years.

Four samples were studied: males 1981 (N=15,213), males 1991 (N=28,996), females 1981 (N=11,495) and females 1991 (N=24,286). The samples comprised members of the Toronto Census Metropolitan Area (CMA) labour force aged 15-65 who were not school attenders at least nine months prior to the census dates (June 3, 1981 and June 4, 1991 respectively).

The PUST 1981 and PUMF 1991 census microdata files defined the countries of birth according to the boundaries set at the time of their respective census dates. The aggregation of birthplace in the microdata files has not been uniform across census periods. In 1981, the birthplace variable focused mostly on European groups but did not provide sufficient detail on the geographical origins of immigrants coming from Asia, Africa, Central America, South America, and the Caribbean. In 1991, although more geographical detail of these regions became available, aggregations present in the counts made it impossible to undertake individual country comparisons. Some of the birthplaces were, in fact, world regions which comprise several nationalities. The reader should keep this fact in mind while reading the results from this analysis.

Due to limitations present in the microdata, the analysis is restricted to the following birthplace origins:

(1) Canada
(2) United Kingdom
(3) United States
(4) Germany
(5) Italy
(6) Portugal
(7) Poland
(8) USSR
(9) Other European Countries
(10) Asia
(11) Africa
(12) Central America, South America, and the Caribbean
(13) Other Countries (residual category)

The domain of the economic life of the labour force was approximated using indicators of labour market access, economic performance, employment status, occupational status, income and wages, and home ownership.[1] These represent factors which have been found to be important in prior research (Richmond and Rhyne 1982; DeVries 1988; Thomas 1992). Indicators were chosen to avoid typical problems of "multicollinearity" and "closure" in multivariate analysis of the data. In total, nine indications were selected. The number of weeks worked during the year and full-time, unemployment, and self-employment status were used as proxies for market access and performance. Managerial, professional, manual, and social service work (the industry branch where "white collar" tends to be more commonly found) provided information on the basic occupational characteristics of workers. The income measure chosen was the total income product from all sources

(governmental and non-governmental). Home ownership was included as an indicator which reveals, to some degree, wealth and ownership status in the labour force.

The indicators used were interval and binary types of variables. Binary variables measured the presence (value=1) or absence (value=0) of a specific economic characteristic in an individual worker. The indicators were given the following values:

FUL=1 if the person worked mostly full-time during the previous year; =0 otherwise.

SER=1 if the person was working in social service industries such as educational, health, social, or federal government sectors during the census reference week; =0 otherwise.

PRO=1 if the person was working in occupations involving managerial or professional work during the census reference week (1980 SOC groups: 11, 21, 23, 27, 31, and 33); =0 otherwise.

MAN=1 if the person was working in occupations involving manual type of work during the census reference week (1980 SOC groups: 71, 73, 75, 77, 81, 83, 85, 87, and 91); =0 otherwise.

OWN=1 if the person lived in and owned a home; =0 otherwise.

SEL=1 if the person was self-employed during the census reference week; =0 otherwise.

INC= the total non-zero annual income product from all sources.

UNP=1 if the person reported unemployment status during the census reference week; =0 otherwise.

WKS= the number of weeks worked in the previous year.

Principal Components Analysis (PC) was chosen as the main multivariate analysis technique.[2] In the first stage of analysis, principal components were extracted from the four correlation matrices: males 1981, males 1991, females 1981, and females 1991. Based on the information contained in the component loadings associated to each indicator, component scores were calculated for each individual in the four samples. Due to the mathematical property of "orthogonality" (at right angles) present in the principal components, the 13 birthplace groups were then located on PC "space" based on the prior knowledge of their average component scores. Changes in labour force characteristics that occurred between 1981 and 1991 were assessed by undertaking paired samples t tests on the component scores.

The final stage of the analysis produced distance matrices between birthplace groups. "Mahalanobis" distances allowed the identification of the patterns of economic similarity present in the sample data. As a way of

summarizing the findings, hierarchical clustering analysis was applied to the distance matrices to determine possible changes in the cluster memberships occurring between 1981 and 1991.

The Samples

The breakdown of the four samples by birthplace is presented in Table 1. The PUMF 1991 contained almost double the number of observations available in the PUST 1981. Canadian-born males and females made up about half of the sample populations. In 1981, Europeans dominated. There were several times as many immigrants born in Europe as there were immigrants born in Asia, Africa, and Latin America combined. By 1991, however, the percentages were roughly equal.

The length of residence of the immigrant population in the samples is shown in Table 2. In the 1981 sample, most males and females of the European groups (with the exception of Portugal) had longer periods of residence in Canada. Conversely, those born in Portugal, the U.S., Asia, Africa, and Latin America, had relatively shorter lengths of residence. In the 1991 sample, Asian, African, Latin American, and Polish workers arranged shorter periods of residence in Canada. The rest of the European groups and the U.S.-born had longer periods of residence in the country. There were, however, two noticeable differences for those who were born in the U.S. and in Poland. The U.S.-born sampled in 1991 had longer periods of residence (53 per cent over 21 years in Canada) compared to those sampled in 1981 (38 per cent over 21 years in Canada). The opposite is true for Polish-born immigrants, who in 1991 had a shorter period of residence (67 per cent less than 11 years in Canada) than those sampled in 1981 (46 per cent less than 11 years in Canada).

Table 3 presents detailed labour force characteristics by the 13 birthplace groups. As expected, males earned substantially more than females at both census periods. Unemployment levels were higher in the 1991 sample than in 1981. Individuals born in Poland, Asia, Africa, and Latin America were the most affected.

Data Analysis

Principal Components Analysis

Table 4 shows the correlation matrices for the economic indicators corresponding to the 1981 and 1991 samples. Correlations between indicators did not change substantially between the census periods. PC analysis extracted three major components from each of the four correlation matrices (see Table 5). The three principal components displayed an eigenvalue or

latent root greater than 1. As a whole, they accounted for more than half of the variation in the four sets of data. Varimax rotated component loadings, which are obtained by maximizing column differences in the factor matrix, are presented in Table 5.

The first component tapped an economic domain of overall work performance. The number of weeks worked (WKS) and full-time work (FUL) loaded highly and positively with this component while unemployment status (UNP) did so negatively. The second factor contrasted white- and blue-collar workers. Professional and managerial jobs (PRO) and social service sector work (SER) loaded positively with this second component, while manual jobs (MAN) did so negatively. The third component, the smallest one, contrasted individuals who were self-employed and lived in an owned home to tenants and paid workers. Total income (INC) loaded positively on all three components suggesting that individuals who have high standings in any of these domains are also likely to earn higher incomes.

Component Scores

Males

In Tables 6 and 7, average component scores are contrasted by birthplace for the male and female samples.[3] WP, WC and OS are used here as acronyms for identifying *work performance, white-collar,* and *ownership* and *self-employment* component scores. The high WP scores for males born in the U.S., U.K. and Germany indicate that these workers were performing better than the rest of groups at both census periods. They worked more, were more likely to be employed full-time and earned more. Workers born in Canada and other European countries were close to average levels. Asians performed below average. The sign reversal of the WP component scores (+.088 to -.328) for Poland and USSR (-.013 to -.211) suggest that workers from these countries sampled in 1991 were relatively more disadvantaged in the labour force compared to those sampled in 1981. Asians and Latin Americans displayed negative WP scores at both census periods.

Inspection of the WC component scores revealed the presence of two typical segments of workers: a white collar "pole" made up by workers from the U.S., U.K. and African countries and a blue-collar "pole" made up of Italians, Portuguese, Poles, and Latin Americans. When groups were contrasted in terms of their OS scores, Italians and Germans ranked at top levels while individuals born in Central and South America and the Caribbean ranked at bottom levels. To assess if there were any significant differences in the sample means occurring between 1981 and 1991, t-tests for paired samples were

used. The low and nonsignificant t-values (below the 1.96 mark) suggests that, overall, scores for males were similar across census periods and the observed fluctuations were mostly attributable to sample error.

Females

Table 7 shows the average component scores for the female samples of 1981 and 1991. Here, a different picture emerged. Distinctions in WP scores were almost "invisible" (all groups converged to average values). Distinctions by WC scores, however, were apparent. Women born in Canada and in the U.S. were found mostly in managerial and professional jobs or in the social service sector. In contrast, Italian, Portuguese, and Asian women were more likely to be found in manual jobs. With respect to the OS scores, women born in Italy, Germany, and other European countries ranked at top levels in this economic dimension while women from Latin America and the Caribbean ranked at bottom levels. Like males, the paired sample t-tests also failed to identify any significant changes in the mean scores across censuses.

Distance Matrices

The mathematical property of orthogonality (at right angles or zero correlation), which is established between the principal components, allows for the treatment of the average component scores as approximate geometrical positions in a three-dimensional "space" (spanned by the WP, WC and OS axes). Euclidean distances between groups may be readily calculated in this "space." A small Euclidean distance calculated between one group and another is used as an indicator of resemblance in labour force attributes between these two groups. Mahalanobis distances (Euclidean distances in PC "space") between the 13 birthplace groups of male and female samples are presented in Tables 9 and 10.

Males

In 1981, the characteristics of the Canadian-born group closely resembled the characteristics of the U.S., U.K., Asian, and African groups (see Table 8). Germans, Poles, Soviets and those born in the other European countires resembled each other. The large distances between U.S.-Italy, U.S.-Portugal, Portugal-Africa and Italy-Africa reflected the large differences in WC and OS scores found between these groups. In general, the 1991 distance matrix had a close resemblance to the 1981 distance matrix with two notable exceptions. First, there was great dissimilarity between the U.S. and other groups. Secondly, there was a greater similarity among workers born in Poland, Latin America, and the Caribbean.

Females

The Mahalanobis distance matrices for the female samples revealed that, compared to 1981, the birthplace groups were more uniform in terms of their labour force characteristics (see Table 9). The only outstanding large Mahalanobis distances (d >1.0000) were those observed between the U.S. and the typical "blue-collar" groups (Italy and Portugal) and between Italy and the residual birthplace category. Like males, Polish women very closely resembled the labour force characteristics of Asian, Central and South American, and Caribbean women.

Inter-matrix correlations of Mahalanobis distances are useful to illustrate the consistency of the similarity patterns found in the data (i.e., if larger distances between a particular pair of birthplaces in sample 1 is associated with larger distances for the same pair in sample 2, etc.). Product moment correlation coefficients were used as estimators of the degree of the match between pairs of distances in the matrices. Inter-matrix correlation coefficients are presented in Table 10. All correlations were significant and of a magnitude = or > .65, suggesting that the patterns of similarity were fairly consistent across the samples. Correlations were stronger for synchronic (same census date, different genders) than for diachronic (different census dates, same gender) comparisons. Table 10 also shows the means and standard deviations of the Mahalanobis distances in each of the samples. The highest average dissimilarity was found in the male sample of 1981 and the lowest in the female sample of 1991.

Cluster Analysis

To summarize the patterns of similarity present in the data a hierarchical method of cluster analysis was applied to the datasets. This method was the average linkage between groups.[4] A 4-cluster solution was deemed as the most appropriate for its simplicity and interpretability of results. Cluster memberships obtained from this taxonomic procedure are presented in Table 11. Agglomeration coefficients (synthetic measures of the point at which all groups converge into one cluster) revealed that, for males, there was a slight increase in average dissimilarity present in the 1991 sample compared to 1981 (.68 to .61). For females, confirming previous observations, the average dissimilarity between groups in 1991 was much lower than that observed in 1981 (.61 to .72).

Males

The clustering procedure assigned those born in Canada, the U.K., Asia and Africa to the first cluster at both census periods (cluster 1). Workers born in

the U.S. were assigned to cluster 1 in 1981, but in 1991 they constituted their own cluster (cluster 2). Cluster 3, the blue-collar one, comprised workers born in Italy and Portugal. Workers from Latin America and the Caribbean were assigned to cluster 4. This latter cluster is a cluster of "disadvantage" in the Toronto labour market. Workers from Poland, who were originally clustered with the other European groups in 1981, were also assigned to cluster 4 in 1991.

Females

The predicted cluster memberships of 1981 and 1991 reflect a homogenization in terms of labour force characteristics. Cluster 1, the largest, comprised eight out of the 13 birthplace groups in 1991. Females born in the U.S. were assigned to cluster 2 at both census periods. Like their male counterparts, women born in Poland were assigned to cluster 4 with Latin Americans in 1991. Clustering results confirmed that the Latin American and Caribbean women sampled in 1991 were relatively worse off than those sampled in 1981.

Socio-Demographic Predictors of Component Scores

At the final stage of the multivariate analysis it became relevant to explore how the social demography of workers affected their economic and occupational standings. Using the individual observations in the four microdata samples, multiple regression models using selected socio-demographic characteristics as predictor variables of the component scores were tested across four segments of workers: Canadian-born males, foreign-born males, Canadian-born females, and foreign-born females. The predictor variables were: age (years), family size (number of members in census family), married status (binary: 1=yes, 0=no), and the possession of a university degree (binary: 1=yes, 0=no). The regression model for females contained an extra explanatory variable: the presence of children under 6 years of age in the census family (binary: 1=yes, 0=no). Results of the testing of these regression models are shown in Table 12.

Standardized regression (beta) coefficients established the relative importance of predictors within each economic domain.[5] Controlling for other socio-demographic predictors, being married produced about a .25 change in the standard deviation in the WP scores of Canadian-born males in 1981 and 1991. This suggests that workers who were married were more likely to work full time, work more and earn more during the year. The impacts of marital status on the WP scores were less noticeable for foreign-born males. They were almost negligible for both Canadian-born and foreign-born females. The possession of a university degree was the most reliable predictor of standing

93

in the white collar work domain, particularly for foreign-born males (beta coefficients = or >+ .30). Age and family size were found to be the most significant predictors of the OS scores. In short, multiple regression analysis suggests that the importance of each socio-demographic predictor varies according to the economic domain being examined.

Conclusion

The brief empirical analysis undertaken here allowed a closer look at the way in which workers of different national origins are accessing and sharing the economic rewards of the Toronto labour market.

Rather than being at odds with the previous research, the major findings of this study complement those of past reports about Toronto's immigrants. There were three basic domains (performance, type of work and some measure of wealth and ownership) which currently characterize the economic life of the labour force of Metropolitan Toronto, and these economic domains were relatively stable between 1981 and 1991. Due to numerous factors which require further study, the positions occupied by members of different nationality groups in the economic hierarchy also tended to remain stable over the period examined.

Toronto's labour force continues to be stratified along ethnic and nationality lines. Immigrants born in the U.S. were the most advantaged group in the three domains and constituted a unique cluster of workers. Individuals born in the U.K., Germany, the Soviet Union, and Canada occupied inter-mediate positions. Workers from Italy and Portugal constituted a "typical" blue-collar segment of workers, although the former group had an economic advantage over the latter. Workers from Latin America and Poland occupied the bottom positions within the three basic economic domains.

Findings on immigrants from Africa and Asia are less certain. Immigrants from Africa were found to be closer to the white-collar "pole" while Asians were found performing at slightly below average levels at both censuses. Data aggregation present in the microdata has in all likelihood "masked" significant intra-group variations in the economic standings of the groups. An inspection of the component scores of the Asian groups (available only in the 1991 microdata) revealed significant variations in average component scores by nationalities. For instance, individuals born in Vietnam, South East Asia, and the People's Republic of China were more disadvantaged in the labour force than immigrants born in Hong Kong or South Asia. The former were mostly blue-collar workers who experienced more unemployment and earned very low incomes. Similar intra-group vari-

ations are also likely to be found among African-born groups (e.g., South Africans vs. North Africans).

The economic situation of immigrants born in Latin America and the Caribbean is of some concern. Individuals from these countries are experiencing the most serious integration problems and risk being confined to the lower strata of Toronto's economic hierarchy. Unlike the Poles (who were recent arrivals to Canada in 1991), their lower standings in all three economic domains may not be entirely attributable to a shorter length of stay in the country. Past research has shown that immigrants from Latin America and the Caribbean have, on average, larger human capital endowments than Southern European groups, and skills and educational levels comparable to those of immigrants from West, Central, and Eastern Europe. However, integration "liabilities" are heavy for these groups. These may range from problems related to the recognition of their educational credentials to plain racial discrimination practised by employers. Further research has to be undertaken on how these and other factors affect immigrant integration into Toronto's labour market.

Notes

1. For more detailed inofrmation on the indicators and other measures available in the microdata files readers should consult the documents "1981 PUST-User Documentation" (catalogue 8-1200-609) and "1991 PUMF of Individuals-Data Documentation" (Service 48-039E) of the 1981 and 1991 Census of Canada.

2. Principal Components Analysis is a type of factor analysis. It reduces data to a number of variables (components) which progressively explain the total variation in the data.

3. Component scores are specific values of a component calculated for a particular sampling unit and is formed by a weighted sum of the values of standardized variables for that sampling unit. As variables, component scores are standardized measures (mean=0 and standard deviation=1). A positive component score for a group indicates that members of this group are above average with respect to work performance, white collar work or home ownership and self employment. Negative scores indicate the opposite.

4. This method uses a Sokal-Michener algorithm which groups observations considered to be similar in accordance with the average distance between pairs of units, one from each two clusters.

5. A standardized regression coefficient expresses the impact of a particular independent variable in terms of the change in the standard deviation of the dependent variable controlling for other independent variables present in the model.

References

Beaujot, R. "The Relative Economic Situation of Immigrants in Canada: Review of Past Studies and Multivariate Analysis of the 1981 Data," report prepared to the Review of Demography and Its Implications for Economic and Social Policy, Health and Welfare Canada, 1986.

Breton, R. "Institutional Completeness of Ethnic Communities and Personal Relations to Immigrants," *American Journal of Sociology*, 70 (1984), 193-205.

Darroch, G.A. "Another Look at Ethnicity, Stratification and Social Mobility in Canada," *Canadian Journal of Sociology*, 4 (1979), 1-25.

DeVries, J. *Statistical Indicators of Ethno-cultural Community Integration in Canada*. Ottawa: Multiculturalism and Citizenship Canada, 1988.

Driedger, L. "Class and Economic Status." In *The Ethnic Factor*. Toronto: McGraw-Hill, Ryerson, 1989, 259-292.

Jollife, I.T. *Principal Component Analysis*. New York: Springer-Verlag, 1986.

Lautard, H. and N. Guppy. "The Vertical Mosaic Revisited: Occupational Differentials among Canadian Ethnic Groups." In *Race and Ethnic Relations in Canada*, edited by Peter S. Li. Toronto: Oxford University Press, 1990, 189-208.

Kalbach, W.E. "A Demographic Overview of Racial and Ethnic Groups in Canada." In *Race and Ethnic Relations in Canada*, edited by Peter S. Li. Toronto: Oxford University Press, 18-47, 1980.

Menard, S. "Longitudinal Research," Sage University Paper No. 76. London: Sage Publications, 1991.

Mezzich, J.E., and H. Solomon. "Cluster Analysis of Ethnic Populations." In *Taxonomy and Behavioural Science*. London: Academic Press, 1980, 108-132.

Porter, J.P. "The Societal Context of Occupational Allocation." In *Ascription and Achievement: Studies in Mobility and Status Attainment*, edited by M. Boyd *et al.* Ottawa: Carleton University Press, 1985.

Pendakur, R. *The Changing Role of Post-War Immigrants in Canada's Labour Force: An Examination Across Four Census Periods*. Ottawa: Corporate and Intergovernmental Affairs Group (DGCIA), Department of Canadian Heritage Monograph, 1995.

Reitz, J.G., *et al.* "Ethnic Inequality and Segregation of Jobs." University of Toronto: Centre for Urban and Community Studies, Research paper No. 123, 1981.

Reitz, J.G. "Ethnic Group Control of Groups." University of Toronto: Centre for Urban and Community Studies, Research Paper No. 133, 1982.

Richmond, A.H. *Immigrants and Ethnic Groups in Metropolitan Toronto*. Toronto: York University, Institute for Behavioural Research, 1972.

Richmond A.H. and D. Rhyne. "Social Indicators for Ethnic and Cultural Minorities." Paper presented to the UNESCO symposium, Ottawa, October 25-28, 1982.

Sullivan, T. "Racial-Ethnic Differences in Labour Force Participation." In *The Demography of Racial and Ethnic Groups*, edited by F.D. Bean and W.P. Frisbie. London: Academic Press, 1978.

Thomas, D. "The Social Integration of Immigrants to Canada." In *The Immigration Dilemma*, edited by S. Globerman. Vancouver: The Fraser Institute, 1992, 211-60.

Tables

Table 1– Microdata Samples by Birthplace: Metro Toronto, 1981 and 1991

	Males 1981		Males 1991	
Birthplace	Frequency	Percent	Frequency	Percent
Canada	8038	52.8	14999	51.7
U.S.	199	1.3	337	1.2
U.K.	1325	8.7	1644	5.7
Germany	285	1.9	381	1.3
Italy	1376	9.0	1717	5.9
Portugal	482	3.2	915	3.2
Poland	225	1.5	465	1.6
U.S.S.R.	188	1.2	156	0.5
Other Europe	1197	7.9	1788	6.2
Asia	956	6.3	3766	13.0
Africa	178	1.2	654	2.3
C.S.Amer/Caribb.	714	4.7	2101	7.2
Other Countries	50	0.3	73	0.3
Total	15213	100.0	28996	100.0

	Females 1981		Females 1991	
Birthplace	Frequency	Percent	Frequency	Percent
Canada	6245	54.3	12859	52.9
U.S.	132	1.1	308	1.3
U.K.	1025	8.9	1478	6.1
Germany	221	1.9	316	1.3
Italy	773	6.7	1084	4.5
Portugal	315	2.7	655	2.7
Poland	155	1.3	406	1.7
U.S.S.R.	111	1.0	137	0.6
Other Europe	758	6.6	1299	5.3
Asia	830	7.2	3104	12.8
Africa	141	1.2	431	1.8
C.S.Amer/Caribb.	747	6.5	2164	8.9
Other Countries	42	0.4	45	0.2
Total	**11495**	**100.0**	**24286**	**100.0**

Table 2 – Immigrant Groups by Length of Residence in Canada

Groups	5 or less	6-10	11-15	16-20	21+	Total	N
Males 1981							
U.S.	13.6	20.1	19.6	8.5	38.2	100.0	199
U.K.	8.3	10.8	19.2	10.3	51.3	100.0	1325
Germany	1.4	1.8	8.4	7.7	80.8	100.0	285
Italy	1.4	4.3	18.6	19.5	56.5	100.0	1376
Portugal	11.4	34.9	26.8	16.2	16.6	100.0	482
Poland	4.4	4.4	8.9	9.3	72.9	100.0	225
U.S.S.R.	7.9	5.9	2.1	3.7	80.3	100.0	188
Other Europe	3.9	10.0	21.9	12.6	56.5	100.0	1197
Asia	26.0	40.5	22.2	4.6	6.6	100.0	956
Africa	24.2	39.9	19.1	10.1	6.7	100.0	178
C.S. America/Carib.	19.4	40.8	27.3	5.7	6.6	100.0	714
Other Countries	8.0	24.0	38.0	8.0	22.0	100.0	50
(Table 2 continued on next page)							
Males 1991							
U.S.	6.5	9.8	11.0	20.2	52.6	100.0	337
U.K.	3.8	5.1	8.3	15.3	67.5	100.0	1644
Germany	1.3	4.5	2.6	4.2	87.4	100.0	381
Italy	1.0	0.9	3.0	5.4	89.7	100.0	1717
Portugal	10.5	8.4	10.5	32.6	38.7	100.0	915
Poland	37.0	30.1	3.7	4.7	24.5	100.0	465
U.S.S.R.	17.3	9.0	17.9	6.4	49.4	100.0	156
Other Europe	6.9	5.4	5.4	13.7	68.5	100.0	1788
Asia	27.1	18.8	15.9	17.7	20.6	100.0	3766
Africa	24.6	16.5	13.6	19.1	26.1	100.0	654
C.S. America/Carib.	16.0	13.9	15.7	29.4	25.0	100.0	2101
Other Countries	17.8	4.1	9.6	20.5	48.9	100.0	73
Females 1981							
U.S.	12.9	19.7	22.0	11.4	34.1	100.0	132
U.K.	6.9	12.0	17.5	11.7	51.9	100.0	1025
Germany	2.8	1.4	7.7	13.1	75.2	100.0	221
Italy	1.7	4.5	21.2	19.9	52.6	100.0	773
Portugal	11.2	38.1	26.7	14.3	9.8	100.0	315
Poland	7.1	8.4	14.8	14.2	55.5	100.0	155
U.S.S.R.	8.1	8.1	1.8	3.6	80.2	100.0	111
Other Europe	4.6	13.5	21.4	13.5	47.1	100.0	758
Asia	29.0	40.0	18.9	5.2	6.9	100.0	830
Africa	27.7	39.0	17.0	9.2	7.1	100.0	141
C.S. America/Carib.	17.7	42.4	27.3	7.1	5.5	100.0	747
Other Countries	7.1	21.4	38.1	14.3	19.0	100.0	42
Females 1991							
U.S.	7.5	11.4	16.9	19.2	45.2	100.0	308
U.K.	3.5	5.0	7.1	13.8	70.5	100.0	1478
Germany	2.8	5.1	3.2	7.0	81.9	100.0	316
Italy	0.9	0.7	2.5	7.0	88.9	100.0	1084
Portugal	11.3	7.0	8.9	31.1	41.6	100.0	655
Poland	33.7	26.8	5.2	5.7	28.7	100.0	406
U.S.S.R.	16.1	11.7	12.4	13.9	45.9	100.0	137
Other Europe	6.0	6.1	6.9	13.2	67.8	100.0	1299
Asia	27.4	18.5	17.9	18.2	17.9	100.0	3104
Africa	22.5	12.1	15.8	26.2	23.4	100.0	431
C.S. America/Carib.	14.8	15.9	14.6	27.4	27.2	100.0	2164
Other Countries	11.1	4.4	4.4	13.3	66.7	100.0	45

Table 3 – Economic Indicators by Birthplace

Males 1981

CA	US	UK	GE	IT	PO	PL	SS	OE	AS	AF	LA	OC
93	96	96	95	96	95	95	93	96	92	95	95	97
28	42	27	20	18	19	20	21	30	30	31	19	36
33	52	39	36	11	5	21	28	23	29	44	17	44
37	22	37	45	68	71	49	53	48	41	26	55	38
63	60	70	77	91	76	85	81	75	57	51	43	50
9	13	11	18	15	6	14	12	20	11	17	4	8
21.9	26.6	24.8	24.2	18.5	15.9	22.3	20.7	20.3	15.6	20.7	15.8	21.9
3	3	2	1	3	3	3	2	2	4	1	4	4
46	48	49	48	45	44	47	46	46	45	47	45	46

Males 1991

CA	US	UK	GE	IT	PO	PL	SS	OE	AS	AF	LA	OC
94	93	96	94	95	94	89	88	92	90	92	92	93
33	54	34	28	22	16	24	36	31	32	34	25	41
40	61	49	42	19	11	26	42	31	34	42	22	37
32	17	30	37	58	70	55	35	45	38	29	49	33
66	63	74	78	93	76	44	66	74	61	49	51	56
7	11	7	9	10	3	7	10	11	7	7	4	1
43.2	53.0	50.7	50.1	38.4	31.7	31.4	39.9	39.3	31.0	35.7	29.3	42.3
6	5	4	7	6	8	14	7	7	10	10	11	11
47	47	48	48	46	44	42	42	46	44	45	45	47

Females 1981

CA	US	UK	GE	IT	PO	PL	SS	OE	AS	AF	LA	OC
77	74	74	76	84	82	77	75	75	82	79	84	79
42	51	40	44	23	36	32	32	38	42	40	41	55
26	40	23	25	6	4	24	18	20	22	26	18	45
10	8	9	15	46	38	21	20	26	22	13	22	12
57	58	65	67	92	74	79	78	74	61	48	45	50
3	7	3	8	4	1	7	4	7	6	5	2	5
11.9	12.1	12.0	12.3	9.5	7.8	14.2	12.1	11.0	10.5	9.8	10.0	12.6
4	5	2	3	5	3	1	2	4	3	1	5	7
43	42	45	44	43	42	45	44	44	41	42	43	42

Females 1991

CA	US	UK	GE	IT	PO	PL	SS	OE	AS	AF	LA	OC
80	75	79	78	81	80	79	82	80	83	79	83	87
50	65	50	43	38	42	41	45	45	42	46	47	60
40	55	37	35	18	14	25	41	32	28	34	28	49
6	4	7	8	29	28	25	7	17	21	9	17	9
63	58	70	77	95	78	51	67	76	67	55	48	62
4	7	4	6	3	2	4	4	5	5	5	2	7
27.9	31.6	27.9	29.2	21.6	18.4	20.8	26.6	25.5	21.4	24.4	21.2	25.9
6	5	5	4	6	8	13	4	7	10	11	9	7
45	44	47	45	45	43	41	45	44	43	43	43	43

Row Information:
1. Birthplace Symbol
2. % Worked full-time in previous year
3. % Worked in social service industries
4. % Worked in managerial and professional occupations
5. % Worked in manual occupations
6. % Lived in an owned home
7. % Self-employed
8. Mean income from all sources (in thousands $Canadian)
9. % Unemployed in the reference week
10. Mean number of weeks worked in previous year

Symbols: CA-Canada, US-United States, UK-United Kingdom, GE-Germany, IT-Italy, PO-Portugal, PL-Poland, SS-Soviet Union, OE-Other Europe, AS-Asia, AF-Africa, LA-Central & South America/Caribbean, OC-Other Countries.

99

Table 4 – Correlation Matrices of Economic Indicators

Males

	FUL	SER	PRO	MAN	OWN	SEL	INC	UNP	WKS
FUL	1	-.01	+.10	+.02	+.07	-.04	+.22	-.20	+.48
SER	-.03	1	+.27	-.34	-.01	+.11	+.07	-.06	+.01
PRO	+.07	+.26	1	-.57	+.11	+.06	+.36	-.11	+.14
MAN	+.01	-.33	-.55	1	-.06	-.01	-.21	+.06	-.12
OWN	+.04	-.02	+.08	-.03	1	+.03	+.24	-.12	+.13
SEL	-.01	+.10	+.13	-.07	+.07	1	+.07	-.04	+.01
INC	+.21	+.04	+.40	-.21	+.22	+.12	1	-.17	+.30
UNP	-.12	-.02	-.06	+.03	-.05	-.04	-.14	1	-.25
WKS	+.45	+.01	+.14	-.11	+.08	+.04	+.35	-.21	1

Females

	FUL	SER	PRO	MAN	OWN	SEL	INC	UNP	WKS
FUL	1	-.04	+.07	+.06	-.06	-.07	+.33	-.13	+.37
SER	-.06	1	+.28	-.27	-.00	+.09	+.07	-.07	-.03
PRO	+.04	+.34	1	-.27	+.05	+.06	+.35	-.11	+.08
MAN	+.09	-.29	-.23	1	-.01	-.03	-.13	+.04	-.04
OWN	-.11	-.01	-.01	-.02	1	+.03	+.11	-.08	+.05
SEL	-.03	+.05	+.08	-.02	+.05	1	+.02	-.04	-.01
INC	+.33	+.04	+.32	-.12	+.05	+.04	1	-.18	+.36
UNP	-.08	-.04	-.06	+.05	-.03	-.03	-.14	1	-.22
WKS	+.34	-.06	+.06	-.05	+.04	+.01	+.44	-.16	1

In Lower Diagonal: 1981 Correlation Coefficients
In Upper Diagonal: 1991 Correlation Coefficients

Table 5 – Varimax Rotated Loadings of Three Major Extracted Components

Indicators	Males 1981			Males 1991		
	WP	WC	OS	WP	WC	OS
FUL	+.77	-.06	-.14	+.77	-.07	-.12
SER	-.11	+.66	-.08	-.10	+.63	+.07
PRO	+.18	+.77	+.22	+.21	+.80	+.08
MAN	-.05	-.83	-.05	-.06	.85	+.06
OWN	+.09	-.11	+.78	+.28	+.02	+.53
SEL	-.06	+.13	+.56	-.16	+.03	+.80
INC	+.56	+.30	+.45	+.52	+.32	+.32
UNP	-.42	+.01	-.08	-.48	-.03	-.25
WKS	+.81	+.06	+.01	+.79	+.05	-.02
Eigenvalue	1.6	2.2	1.0	2.4	1.6	1.0
% Var.Expl.	17.3	24.7	11.8	25.4	17.4	11.6

Indicators	Females 1981			Females 1991		
	WP	WC	OS	WP	WC	OS
FUL	+.70	-.13	-.30	+.74	-.09	-.25
SER	-.11	+.76	+.01	-.09	+.72	+.05
PRO	+.22	+.72	+.05	+.25	+.69	+.09
MAN	-.00	-.66	-.02	-.01	-.70	+.01
OWN	-.01	-.11	+.79	+.08	-.10	+.81
SEL	+.01	+.09	+.55	-.10	+.14	+.47
INC	+.76	+.24	+.10	+.70	+.28	+.12
UNP	-.33	-.06	-.30	-.41	-.06	-.36
WKS	+.78	-.04	+.08	+.75	-.02	+.01
Eigenvalue	1.9	1.6	1.1	2.3	1.6	1.1
% Var.Expl.	21.6	17.5	12.1	22.4	16.7	11.8

In circles: component loadings larger or = | .40|
WP – work performance domain
WC – white-collar domain
OS – home ownership & self-employment domain

Table 6 – Male Samples: Means of Component Scores by Birthplace Groups

Males	Work Performance	Economic Domains White Collar Work	Home Ownership& Self-Employment	N
Canada 1981	+.009	+.124	-.058	8012
Canada 1991	+.086	+.107	+.006	14880
U.S. 1981	+.183	+.573	-.030	199
U.S. 1991	+.104	+.642	+.108	335
U.K. 1981	+.184	+.144	+.093	1323
U.K. 1991	+.297	+.211	+.095	1632
Germany 1981	+.178	-.048	+.338	285
Germany 1991	+.218	+.033	+.213	377
Italy 1981	-.040	-.578	+.376	1372
Italy 1991	+.120	-.484	+.387	1710
Portugal 1981	-.126	-.605	-.005	480
Portugal 1991	+.001	-.701	+.017	904
Poland 1981	+.088	-.251	+.342	224
Poland 1991	-.328	-.290	-.231	457
U.S.S.R. 1981	-.013	-.205	+.266	187
U.S.S.R. 1991	-.211	+.140	+.144	154
Other Europe 1981	+.003	-.096	+.207	1195
Other Europe 1991	-.012	-.138	+.210	1779
Asia 1981	-.126	+.075	-.202	949
Asia 1991	-.170	+.011	-.080	3670
Africa 1981	+.054	+.392	-.180	178
Africa 1991	-.098	+.174	-.221	637
C.S.Am./Carib. 1981	-.049	-.238	-.545	712
C.S.Am./Carib. 1991	-.166	-.289	-.276	2078
Other Co. 1981	+.068	+.325	-.291	50
Other Co.1991	+.068	+.162	-.299	71

In circles: scores >|.300|

T-Tests of Paired Samples	Correlation	t Value	Significance	N
Work Performance Score	.492	.88	.394	13
White-Collar Work Score	.570	1.02	.326	13
Home Ownership & Self-employment Score	.575	.69	.501	13

Table 7 – Female Samples: Means of Component Scores by Birthplace Groups

Females	Economic Domains			N
	Work Performance	White Collar Work	Home Ownership & Self-Employment	
Canada 1981	+.026	+.147	-.078	6204
Canada 1991	+.085	+.162	+.003	12745
U.S. 1981	-.012	+.414	+.032	131
U.S. 1991	+.064	+.548	+.050	305
U.K. 1981	+.072	+.079	+.098	1021
U.K. 1991	+.119	+.105	+.119	1469
Germany 1981	+.068	+.093	+.227	220
Germany 1991	+.095	-.003	+.277	315
Italy 1981	-.021	-.776	+.419	769
Italy 1991	-.016	-.596	+.473	1069
Portugal 1981	-.180	-.551	+.073	314
Portugal 1991	-.142	-.545	+.170	638
Poland 1981	+.234	-.116	+.427	155
Poland 1991	-.206	-.287	-.248	390
U.S.S.R. 1981	+.068	-.179	+.280	110
U.S.S.R. 1991	+.126	+.098	+.085	134
Other Europe 1981	-.005	-.176	+.301	748
Other Europe 1991	+.013	-.159	+.206	1287
Asia 1981	-.050	-.063	+.027	824
Asia 1991	-.074	-.254	+.020	3007
Africa 1981	-.059	+.091	-.146	140
Africa 1991	-.081	+.076	-.150	415
C.S.Am./Carib. 1981	+.009	-.103	-.340	735
C.S.Am./Carib. 1991	.075	-.111	-.332	2111
Other Co. 1981	+.084	+.486	-.157	41
Other Co. 1991	+.008	+.292	-.031	45

In circles: scores >|.300|

T-Tests of Paired Samples	Correlation	t-Value	Significance	N
Work Performance Score	.710	.66	.524	13
White-Collar Work Score	.911	.04	.969	13
Home Ownership & Self-employment Score	.665	.62	.401	13

Table 8 – Male Samples: Mahalanobis Distance Matrices

Males 1981

	CA	US	UK	GE	IT
US	.2326	.0000			
UK	.0538	.1995	.0000		
GE	.2153	.5215	.0969	.0000	
IT	.6846	1.5407	.6518	.3303	.0000
PO	.5536	1.4854	.6672	.5210	.1533
PL	.3077	.8272	.2273	.0494	.1246
SS	.2137	.7312	.1900	.0662	.1523
OE	.1189	.5363	.1031	.0500	.2631
AS	.0412	.3728	.1877	.3992	.7687
AF	.0888	.0721	.1536	.4784	1.2608
LA	.3717	.9775	.6078	.8681	.9645
OC	.0977	.1429	.1934	.5464	1.2717

	PO	PL	SS	OE	AS
PL	.2922	.0000			
SS	.2465	.0181	.0000		
OE	.3212	.049	.0156	.0000	
AS	.5023	.4487	.3101	.213	.0000
AF	1.0587	.6887	.5603	.3913	.1332
LA	.4326	.8070	.6597	.5886	.2217
OC	.9845	.7328	.5965	.4289	.1077

	AF	AL
LA	.5408	.0000
OC	.0169	.3951

Males 1991

	CA	US	UK	GE	IT
US	.2969	.0000			
UK	.0633	.2239	.0000		
GE	.0662	.3954	.0517	.0000	
IT	.4950	1.3443	.5975	.3060	.0000
PO	.6612	1.8239	.9256	.6253	.1992
PL	.3858	1.1710	.7486	.6010	.6207
SS	.1083	.3530	.2656	.2002	.5559
OE	.1113	.6324	.2300	.0821	.1679
AS	.0824	.5088	.2893	.2378	.5471
AF	.0900	.3682	.2581	.3091	.8494
LA	.3001	1.0876	.6024	.4912	.5591
OC	.0961	.3970	.2100	.3016	.8895

Birthplace and Economic Similarities in the Labour Force: An Analysis of Toronto's Census Microdata

	PO	PL	SS	OE	AS
PL	.3387	.0000			
SS	.7680	.3395	.0000		
OE	.3547	.3178	.1209	.0000	
AS	.5462	.1385	.0686	.1315	.0000
AF	.8326	.2683	.1472	.2904	.0515
LA	.2833	.0281	.3621	.2824	.1284
OC	.8498	.3665	.2748	.3551	.1276

	AF	AL
LA	.2222	.0000
OC	.0341	.2595

Symbols: CA-Canada, US-United States, UK-United Kingdom, GE-Germany, IT-Italy, PO-Portugal, PL-Poland, SS-Soviet Union, OE-Other Europe, AS-Asia, AF-Africa, LA-Central&South America/Caribbean, OC-Other Countries.
In Squares: Greater Similarity (d <.1000)
In Circles: Greater Dissimilarity (d >1.0000)

Table 9 – Female Samples: Mahalanobis Distance Matrices

Females 1981

	CA	US	UK	GE	IT
US	.0847	.0000			
UK	.0379	.1236	.0000		
GE	.0978	.1474	.0168	.0000	
IT	1.1012	1.5654	.8422	.7994	.0000
PO	.5526	.9610	.4611	.4997	.1956
PL	.3683	.4974	.1725	.1113	.5005
SS	.2506	.4288	.1068	.0788	.3791
OE	.2490	.4201	.1120	.0829	.3744
AS	.0610	.2287	.0400	.0778	.6624
AF	.0149	.1379	.0772	.1556	1.0739
LA	.1315	.4061	.2293	.3634	1.0296
OC	.1245	.0501	.2311	.3024	1.9352

	PO	PL	SS	OE	AS
PL	.4864	.0000			
SS	.2519	.0477	.0000		
OE	.2235	.0767	.0054	.0000	
AS	.2573	.2433	.1013	.0895	.0000
AF	.4761	.4582	.2882	.2748	.0543
LA	.4072	.6401	.4186	.4167	.1405
OC	1.1982	.7266	.6504	.6558	.3534

	AF	AL
LA	.0799	.0000
OC	.1760	.3862

Females 1991

	CA	US	UK	GE	IT
US	.1518	.0000			
UK	.0176	.2039	.0000		
GE	.1024	.3570	.0376	.0000	
IT	.8051	1.4948	.6357	.4018	.0000
PO	.5787	1.2520	.4935	.3612	.1107
PL	.3494	.8593	.3940	.4474	.6524
SS	.0124	.2081	.0012	.0482	.6518
OE	.1490	.5271	.0886	.0360	.2633
AS	.1981	.6629	.1756	.1572	.3257
AF	.0583	.2841	.1126	.2194	.8432
LA	.2126	.5992	.2875	.4121	.8880
OC	.0241	.0754	.0697	.1901	1.0435

(Table continued on facing page)

	PO	PL	SS	OE	AS
PL	.2455	.0000			
SS	.4917	.3688	.0000		
OE	.1744	.2707	.0930	.0000	
AS	.1119	.0908	.1672	.0509	.0000
AF	.4909	.1569	.0980	.1902	.1373
LA	.4450	.0551	.2577	.2996	.1447
OC	.7634	.4280	.0652	.2596	.3071

	AF	AL
LA	.0679	.0000
OC	.0687	.2595

Symbols: CA-Canada, US-United States, UK-United Kingdom, GE-Germany, IT-Italy, PO-Portugal, PL-Poland, SS-Soviet Union, OE-Other Europe, AS-Asia, AF-Africa, LA-Central&South America/ Caribbean, OC-Other Countries.

In Squares: Greater Similarity (d <.1000)

In Circles: Greater Dissimilarity (d >1.0000)

Table 10 – Inter-Matrix Correlations of Mahalanobis Distances: Male and Female Samples 1981 and 1991

Samples		Correlation Coefficients			N of Pairs Compared
	Males 1981	Males 1991	Females 1981	Females 1991	
Males 1981	1.00	+.7669*	+.8225*	+.7563*	87
Males 1991		1.000	+.6531*	+.8776*	87
Females 1981			1.0000	+.8086*	87
Females 1991				1.0000	87
Mean Mah. Distance	.3850	.3571	.3278	.2884	
S.D. Mah. Distance	.3584	.3312	.3597	.2971	

* - p <.001 (two-tailed test)

Table 11 – Cluster Memberships: Average Linkage Method Results (4 Cluster Solution)

Samples	Cluster Number	
	Males 1981	Males 1991
Agglomeration Coefficient	.6103	.6791
Canada	1	1
United States	1	2
United Kingdom	1	1
Germany	2	1
Italy	3	3
Portugal	3	3
Poland	2	4
Soviet Union	2	1
Other Europe	2	1
Asia	1	1
Africa	1	1
Central & South America/Caribbean	4	4
Other Countries	1	1

Samples	Females 1981	Females 1991
Agglomeration Coefficient	.7290	.6097
Canada	1	1
United States	2	2
United Kingdom	1	1
Germany	1	1
Italy	3	3
Portugal	3	3
Poland	4	4
Soviet Union	4	1
Other Europe	4	1
Asia	1	1
Africa	1	1
Central & South America/Caribbean	1	4
Other Countries	2	1

Table 12 – Multiple Regression of Component Scores on Selected Socio-Demographic Predictors

Groups	Age	Socio-Demographic Predictors			Small Children In Family	% Variance Explained by Model	N
		Family Size	Married Status	University Degree			
Canadian-Born: Males							
WP							
1981	+.14	-.06	+.27	+.06	-	14	7910
1991	+.12	+.06	+.23	+.06	-	11	14779
WC							
1981	+.07	-.08	+.05	+.30	-	11	7910
1991	+.08	-.04	+.05	+.30	-	11	14779
OS							
1981	+.26	+.32	n.s.	+.13	-	19	7910
1991	+.14	+.18	+.05	+.14	-	9	14779
Foreign-born: Males							
WP							
1981	+.06	-.04	+.19	+.04	-	5	7109
1991	+.12	+.04	+.11	+.05	-	5	13781
WC							
1981	n.s.	-.10	-.01	+.31	-	11	7109
1991	n.s.	-.03	-.02	+.30	-	10	13781
OS							
1981	+.20	+.20	+.06	+.06	-	10	7109
1991	+.17	+.15	+.02	+.05	-	7	13781
Canadian-born: Females							
WP							
1981	+.08	-.19	n.s.	+.10	-.13	10	6170
1991	+.05	-.17	n.s.	+.12	-.08	6	12710
WC							
1981	+.02	-.09	n.s.	+.24	n.s.	7	6170
1991	n.s.	-.09	n.s.	+.25	+.03	6	12710
OS							
1981	+.22	+.21	+.05	+.06	+.15	18	6170
1991	+.15	+.32	+12	+.09	n.s.	19	12710
Foreign-born: Females							
WP							
1981	+.10	-.09	n.s.	+.12	n.s.	4	5188
1991	+.09	-.04	n.s.	+.08	-.05	7	11173
WC							
1981	n.s.	-.09	-.07	+.21	n.s.	7	5188
1991	-.03	-.09	-.06	+.20	+.02	6	11173
OS							
1981	+.19	+.15	+.09	+.06	+.08	11	5188
1991	+.11	+.18	+.12	+.05	n.s.	11	11173

n.s. – Non significant coefficient (p. >.01)
WP – Work Performance Component Score
WC – White-Collar Work Component Score
OS – Home Ownership&Self-employment Component Score
In circles: Beta Coefficients > | .20|

Robin Ostow and Maryka Omatsu

Disenfranchisement and Rehabilitation: Restitution and Rebuilding an Ethnic Community – Japanese Canadians and East German Jews

Abstract

The histories of Japanese Canadians, and of Jews in the territory that was for twelve years Nazi Germany, and then for forty years the German Democratic Republic (GDR), are narratives of disenfranchisement. Each of these communities suffered near destruction and endured thirty years of silence. Starting in the 1980s, simultaneous attempts were made to rebuild each "community," and these attempts at rebuilding coincided with successful campaigns for restitution. This paper investigates the 1984-1988 campaigns by these two groups – including comparative material from the United States and the Federal Republic of Germany – and suggests several hypotheses concerning the postwar state and its minorities.

Negotiations for restitution are frequently accompanied by an ethnic "renewal." Ethnic restitution campaigns may or may not be related to standard processes of western-style parliamentary democracy and "ethnic politics." The press can play an important role in "educating" the public about the need for paying restitution to a small group, a measure that can spark controversy. The success of these recent ethnic restitution claims reflect, among other things, the growing power of ethnic/national appeals in the late twentieth century. More importantly, these two case studies illustrate the ways by which states use ethnic minorities to mediate foreign policy and international trade, and to legitimate their rule at home.

Résumé

L'histoire des Canadiens japonais et celle des juifs dans le territoire qui a été, pendant douze ans, l'Allemagne nazie, puis pendant quarante ans, la République démocratique allemande, sont des récits de privation de droits. Ces deux communautés ont été presque détruites et ont subi trente années de silence. À partir des années 1980, des efforts simultanés ont été déployés pour reconstruire ces communautés et ces tentatives de reconstruction ont coïncidé avec des campagnes de redressement qui ont

été couronnées de succès. Cet article examine les campagnes menées de 1984 à 1988 par ces groupes au Canada et en RDA, et avance plusieurs hypothèses concernant l'État d'après-guerre et ses minorités. Il se base notamment sur des données comparatives provenant des États-Unis et de la République fédérale d'Allemagne.

Les négociations en vue d'obtenir des dédommagements s'accompagnent fréquemment d'un « renouveau » ethnique. Les campagnes de redressement menées par des groupes ethniques ne sont pas nécessairement reliées aux processus standard de la démocratie parlementaire et des « politiques ethniques » occidentales. La presse peut contribuer pour beaucoup à sensibiliser la population à la nécessité de verser des compensations à un petit groupe, une mesure qui peut susciter la controverse. Le succès de ces récentes campagnes de redressement reflète, entre autres choses, le pouvoir croissant du sentiment d'appartenance ethnique/nationale à la fin du vingtième siècle. Ces deux histoires de cas illustrent plus particulièrement la façon dont les États utilisent leurs minorités au profit de leur politique étrangère et de leur commerce international, et pour légitimer leur pouvoir politique à l'échelle nationale.

Ethnic Minorities and the State

The public version of an ethnic group's history, its ethnic "narrative", is typically a story of immigration, settlement, and the building and maintenance of ethnic infrastructure – i.e., *community*. But the tales of Japanese Canadians, and that of Jews in the territory that was for twelve years Nazi Germany and then for forty years the German Democratic Republic (GDR), are, by contrast, one of disenfranchisement, near destruction, thirty years of silence, and, starting in the 1980s, attempts to rebuild the *community*, which took place simultaneously with successful campaigns for restitution. Japanese Canadians constitute a "visible" minority in a western-style democracy characterized today by an official policy of multiculturalism. Jews in the GDR represented an "invisible" minority in a state that was socialist and German. These obvious differences notwithstanding, striking similarities are observable in the histories of these two groups over the last five decades. Perhaps precisely because their stories unfold in such dissimilar surroundings, the losses, struggles, and ultimate gains of these minorities point to some basic dynamics of the state and its ethnic minorities in the postwar period.[1]

The Chronology of Near Destruction and Ethnic Renewal

The experiences of Japanese Canadians and of East German Jews in the

years 1940 to 1988 did not take the form of an encounter of "established" citizens with newly arrived labourers who looked different and observed strange holidays. They represented, rather, the working out of a new set of national social definitions in the context of a major war. By 1941, the Japanese and the Jews, respectively, had been present in Canada and Germany for decades.[2] Both groups had – by the early 1920s – evolved a middle class. Yet, during World War II, they became defined as "enemies" – despite the outstanding military service they had rendered to their (host) countries in World War I[3] – and were subsequently disenfranchised, expropriated, interned, and, in the case of German Jews, largely annihilated.

In the years immediately following the end of World War II, the Japanese Canadians and some surviving German Jews returned from the internment and death camps. The Canadian government unsuccessfully tried to deport the entire Japanese minority of 21,000 back to starving Japan, and to disperse the rest across the country in a programme of forced assimilation. In 1949, however, Japanese Canadians were allowed to return to the West Coast of British Columbia, and were granted citizenship rights.

In the same year, the German Democratic Republic was founded as a home for opponents and victims of "Fascism," including its small Jewish minority of 1,244.[4] A counterpart to the anti-Japanese measures of 1941-1949 in Canada can be seen in the anti-Jewish measures of the GDR government in 1952-1953. This campaign had clear anti-Semitic elements, but it was also part of a more general purge. It included anti-Semitic incitement in the press, the removal of Jews from prominent positions in the government and the Socialist Unity Party,[5] interrogations of the leaders of the Jewish communities, police raids on the homes of all Jews, and the confiscation of their identity cards. Hundreds of Jews fled to the West, and many of those who remained dissociated themselves from the Jewish communities and submerged their Jewishness.

For both Japanese Canadians and Jews in the GDR, the thirty years from 1954 to 1984 were a time of "silence." Members of both minorities suppressed their anger and pain, and attempted to reestablish themselves within the larger society through hard work and ethnic "invisibility."[6] As a result, their communal organizations atrophied.

But from the late 1970s on, both groups began to acquire a revived ethnic awareness. In both cases, the impetus came in part from their respective governments.[7] In Canada, just prior to the calling of a federal election, the media announced that the Liberal Party, headed by Pierre Trudeau, was planning to apologize to Japanese Canadians and to establish a $5 million educational trust fund. Responding to criticism from the Japanese-Canadian community that they had not been consulted, the

opposition leader, Brian Mulroney, pledged to compensate Japanese Canadians if elected. Shortly thereafter, Mulroney became Canada's new Prime Minister.

In the same year, in a much quieter way, the Erich Honecker government implemented a policy of actively encouraging Jewish life in the GDR. The steps taken included negotiations with the American Jewish Committee and the U.S. State Department regarding restitution payments to Jewish survivors of the Nazi period who had lived or owned property within the territory of the GDR, and the recruitment of an American rabbi to serve the GDR Jewish communities. This led to the initiation of contact between the GDR and Israel, although previously the GDR had been the only East Block country that had no ties at all to the Jewish state.

In 1984, after considerable soul searching and internal debate, the National Association of Japanese Canadians (NAJC) publicly demanded restitution for the loss of the freedom, property, and livelihood of Japanese Canadians during the war, and it started mobilizing segments of the Canadian population to support its campaign. In 1985 in East Berlin, as behind-the-scenes negotiations continued, a growing interest in the Jewish community could be observed among many younger (and also some older) Jews in the Socialist Unity Party – the children of the returned Jewish emigrants – who started to meet regularly. The Jewish community responded to the formation of this new constituency by extending and intensifying its cultural and religious programs.

A major breakthrough in the negotiations for restitution in Canada was the release in 1986 of a report, *Economic Losses of Japanese Canadians after 1941*. Prepared by the internationally respected accounting firm, Price Waterhouse, this study estimated that the loss in property and income suffered by Japanese Canadians amounted to $443 million in 1986 Canadian dollars. A similar breakthrough occurred in 1987 when an American rabbi was sent to help rebuild the Jewish communities in the GDR;[8] in addition, the Honecker government committed itself to restoring – at great expense – the bombed out ruin of what was once Berlin's most elegant synagogue, to be used as a centre for archival material and research on German Jewish history.

Finally, in 1988, the Canadian government publicly acknowledged wartime injustices toward Japanese Canadians. It returned citizenship to the 4,000 Japanese Canadians deported or exiled to Japan in 1946-1947, pardoned those convicted of offences having to do with curfew or travel restriction violations, promised to fund a jointly established $24 million race relations institute (a promise fulfilled only in part by the succeeding Liberal government), created a $12 million community fund, and awarded

an additional $3 million to the Japanese community to help implement the agreement. It also made symbolic individual reparations of $21,000 to the 17,500 Japanese-Canadian "survivors". The total settlement was in excess of $300 million.

In 1988, the Honecker government literally mobilized the entire population of the GDR to observe the fiftieth anniversary of the Pogrom of November 1938. This massive commemoration included a special session of the Volkskammer (Parliament) to honour the Jewish victims. The speeches were translated into five languages (including Hebrew), for the benefit of the many foreign dignitaries present, and the entire session was broadcast on GDR television. Special programmes – such as exhibits, lectures, performances, the unveiling of plaques – were organized to mark this occasion in almost all GDR institutions. In October and November, the media carried articles with Jewish content almost every day. After a meeting between GDR Prime Minister Erich Honecker and Edgar Bronfman, president of the World Jewish Congress, the GDR government announced its decision to make a "humanitarian donation" to Jewish survivors of the Holocaust. A more detailed analysis of the actors, strategies, and developments leading to these promises of reparations follows below.

Japanese Canadians and East German Jews

The histories of wartime and postwar suffering, and ultimate restitution, of Japanese Canadians and East German Jews over fifty years are not merely coincidentally parallel chronologies. The two minorities are structurally quite similar. Both ethnic communities are tiny, to the point of demographic insignificance,[9] but are valued by their respective governments because they serve as links to larger powers and trading partners – in the Canadian case to Japan, and in the GDR to the U.S. and (secondarily) to Israel. Internally, by the 1980s, Japanese Canadians and Jews in the GDR maintained only minimal ethnic infrastructures,[10] and were almost completely exogamous. In both cases, this situation caused fear for the groups' survival.

In his discussion of nationalist movements, Everett Hughes (1954) calls attention to Schelling's observation: "It takes some sort of psychological crisis to combine people into a group conscious of both its internal unity and of its separation from other people. In such a crisis people may become anxious lest they, as a group, die." (181)[11] Interestingly enough, the non-ethnic partners, who incorporated the danger of group death, ultimately proved an asset in providing moral support and social links to other groups and resources in the course of the ethnic renewal that took place among both minorities between 1984 and 1988.

In both cases, the new ethnic consciousness involved an intense emo-

tional and political confrontation between the generation that had experienced World War II as adults, and their children born during and after the war. The children wanted to learn more about their parents' experiences during the war and about their ethnic culture. They wanted to articulate the pain and anger their parents had suppressed. In both minorities, the older generation counselled caution, restraint, and a low ethnic profile, while their children favoured "coming out" and making public social demands.[12]

Most important, perhaps, was that by the 1980s both Japanese Canadians and East German Jews were highly literate and articulate minorities; it was precisely the writers, teachers, and lawyers among them who took on leadership roles in the campaigns for restitution and the accompanying ethnic renewal. Benedict Anderson (1983) notes that in several (although not all) regions of Central Europe, the national movements of the nineteenth century were propelled, to a significant extent, by those who made their living through language, i.e., writers, teachers, clergy, and lawyers: their constituencies were the reading public.

Canada and the German Democratic Republic

Japanese Canadians and East German Jews are not only similar groups; the states into which they were integrated as minorities have more in common than the casual observer might suppose. Canada is a Western-style democracy which today boasts an official policy of multiculturalism; the GDR was, for forty years, a state that was socialist and German. But both countries were small, weak nations bordering on larger, more powerful states which shared their history and culture. And in both states this situation informed the rather weak national identity of the larger population. Bodemann (1984) points to S. D. Clark's emphasis on

> *the precarious nature of Canadian society, due to external forces:* this theme is reflected in Clark's treatment of the interaction between the "settled" portions of the country and the frontier... and in what he sees as the recurring threat of being swallowed up by the U.S. (215)

The GDR felt so threatened by its neighbours – especially its neighbour to the west – that it built a tank-proof "protective socialist wall" of reinforced concrete around itself in August 1961.[13] Bodemann relates the "lack of *genuine* national culture" in Canada precisely to its multicultural vision of itself as a "community of communities" as well as to its colonial heritage. (223-225) Borneman (1989) discusses the weakness of national identity in the GDR as it is reflected in the narrated life histories of three generations of East Germans.

But beyond incomplete identities and shared perceptions of weakness vis-a-vis their larger, more powerful neighbours, in the 1980s, in both Canada and the GDR, trade relations and internal stability became major problems. The small, highly articulate, and ethnically well-connected minorities under consideration played a role in their governments' plans to resolve these difficulties. The 1984 announcement of an apology and educational fund for Japanese Canadians was perhaps intended, in part, to facilitate trade relations with Japan, and, in the face of an imminent election, to demonstrate Trudeau's (and the Liberal Party's) commitment to Canada's ethnic communities. Similarly, the Honecker government saw the GDR Jewish communities and the international Jewish organizations as channels of communication and potential mobilizers of local Jewish support in Western countries (particularly the U.S.) for trade with the East.

After 1986, as the East German population became increasingly frustrated and impatient with the Honecker government's unwillingness to undertake political and economic reforms, the Socialist Unity Party encouraged Jewish life to illustrate, even incorporate, its "anti-Fascism" which played a major role in legitimizing its rule. Thus, restitution to Japanese Canadians and to Jews in the GDR served the external and internal, the commercial and the ideological, goals of the governments of their respective states.

Campaigning for Reparations

Canada

We have seen that the long-term chronologies, the structure of the minorities, and some aspects of postwar Canada and the GDR were surprisingly similar. Nevertheless, the strategies and dynamics of the bargaining processes that took place between 1984 and 1988 were quite different.

The Canadian government's 1984 announcement caught its Japanese population by surprise. A shocked and fearful community suddenly awoke from four decades of self-absorption. What angered the moribund National Association of Japanese Canadians (NAJC) was the fact that it had not been consulted and that the sum was so paltry as to be an insult. The first battleground was within the Japanese-Canadian community itself. Ghettoized old-timers, afraid of white backlash, advocated the politics of least resistance, and cautioned the fearful to accept the government's offer. However, a newer generation of leadership raised on the 1960s North American civil and human rights discourse urged the survivors to demand what was rightfully theirs, and to set a precedent that would protect future Canadians from their history.

The first part of the Japanese-Canadian campaign for redress involved rebuilding the "community" by resurrecting the communications network of a minority that was forced to disperse – no more than one Japanese family to a city block – in the 1940s. Small gatherings were held in private homes to talk about the war years; a new Japanese-Canadian newspaper was established, and the dying NAJC was revived.

The renewal of interest in Japanese-Canadian affairs, however, did not bring consensus on a political agenda. The ensuing conflict between the fearful, older generation, with its self-deprecating minimalism, and the younger generation advocating more substantial demands, was largely settled – as the issue had arisen – through an external force. In 1985, after holding public hearings, the Toronto City Council unanimously encouraged the federal government to negotiate with the NAJC, which represented the more militant faction, and it offered the NAJC a $5,000 grant towards the cost of a study of its economic losses. In this way, the Toronto City Council empowered one ethnic organization to speak for the Japanese "community." It determined that the more militant NAJC better represented the community, united Toronto's Japanese Canadians to speak with one voice, and empowered the NAJC to push forward with its demands for individual financial compensation and civil rights protections.

Once this question was resolved, the NAJC pursued its campaign for reparations payments of $400 million through strategies commonly thought of as "ethnic politics." To mobilize support for its demands outside the Japanese community, the NAJC began to "educate" the media. It hired the reputable accounting firm of Price Waterhouse to make an independent study of the losses suffered by Japanese Canadians in the 1940s, and it collected endorsements from other organizations. The city councils of Toronto and Vancouver, the National Congress of Italian Canadians, the National Jewish Congress, the Mennonite Central Committee of Canada, the Chinese-Canadian National Congress, and the National Association of Canadians with Origins in India were among the approximately thirty – mostly ethnic – organizations which supported the NAJC. The major organized and vocal opponents of the Japanese-Canadian claims were the World War II Veterans who still viewed Japanese Canadians as "enemy aliens."

Ultimately, the NAJC succeeded in both revitalizing its own constituency and in creating a national consensus supporting restitution. However, the final decision of 1988 – that the government would publicly apologize to Japanese Canadians and award them $400 million – was made, not through standard parliamentary procedures, but from above, by a prime minister about to face another federal election. In fact, on the date of the announcement only four members of the government were aware of the exact terms of the agreement.

GDR

The campaign for restitution to Jews in the GDR began even before the founding of the East German state in 1949. Within weeks of the "liberation" of Germany in 1945, attempts were made by individual Jews and by Jewish organizations – including ultimately, the state of Israel – to reclaim confiscated Jewish property and to obtain reparations and help for Jewish survivors. Thompson (1978) details the major efforts in this direction including the establishment of the Union of Persecutees of the Nazi Regime (VVN) in 1947 to coordinate restitution efforts in both Germanys.[14] Deutschkron (1970) describes how in April 1948, Otto Grotewohl (soon to become First Minister of the new East German state), in a meeting with Dr. Yachil, the Israeli Consul in Munich, and Dr. Livneh, the representative of the Jewish Agency in Berlin, offered restitution and help in transporting Jews from Berlin's displaced persons camps to the new state of Israel. This help never materialized. Deutschkron assumes that Grotewohl was never authorized to make these promises.

Thompson (1978) sees the reparations policies of the Soviet Military Administration, and later the GDR, from 1945 to 1952 as basically positive, although in some areas inconsistent:

> The GDR Jewish communities were given some state subsidies... Payments were made by the government to commemorate the Jewish victims of fascism. These payments were used to construct or rebuild synagogues that had been destroyed by the Nazis. A number of Jews and non-Jews who were recognized as victims of fascism received payments for loss of employment, liberty, and health during the Nazi period. (84)

But Thompson also shows the reactions of several segments of the East German population to these successful claims:

> Apartments, small shops and factories, and personal belongings remained private property however, when the Jewish survivors claimed them, they received violent opposition from two groups. One group was composed of people who now thought of Jewish possessions as their own and of the Jewish survivors as intruders... This group was so large that the Communists and other parties, except possibly the Social Democrats, defended it against Jewish claims. Jewish claims were often sabotaged, and restitution laws were either weakened by amendments, not enforced, or repealed. This struggle ...was soon accompanied

by open or covert anti-Semitic agitation, and resulted in an increase in anti-Jewish feelings.

An even more formidable opponent of restitution was the Communist bureaucracy, which looked on all confiscated possessions as property of the nation. To the bureaucracy, the Jews who requested restitutions were looters of national property who were attempting to subvert the socialist economy by restoring capitalism. (102-103)

In other words, Thompson sees the social tensions related to restitution as one of the important factors leading to the purge of 1952-1953, the flight of an estimated 550 Jews, and the near destruction of the GDR's Jewish communities. After Stalin died, and the GDR began to rehabilitate its Jews and Jewish communities in 1953, individual Jews living in the GDR were recognized as "Victims of Fascism." They received generous pensions and privileges, and the Jewish communities of the GDR received large government grants to rebuild synagogues and maintain their infrastructure. But "reparations" to Jews or Jewish organizations outside the GDR was out of the question. As late as January 1989, Kurt Löffler, GDR Minister for Church-State Affairs, denied any responsibility of the GDR for the Holocaust, to the point of claiming that the GDR was itself an indirect victim of the Nazis.[15] From 1954 to 1984, this policy caused considerable tension in the GDR's relations with international Jewish organizations.

Starting in 1972, in behind-the-scenes negotiations with government officials, the GDR Jewish communities recommended restitution. But the state rejected the idea, and the Jewish communities, lacking the personnel to administer their formerly extensive real estate holdings and having other priorities, did not press the issue.[16]

Thus, after 1954, the campaign for restitution to Jews from the GDR government was conducted by *external* Jewish organizations, and any successful claims would benefit *external* Jewish interests at least as much as they would benefit Jews within the GDR. Furthermore, when the first promise of a "humanitarian donation" was made by Erich Honecker in 1988, it was made, not to a representative of the GDR's Jewish communities, but to Edgar Bronfman, the Canadian president of the World Jewish Congress.

Hence, from 1984 to 1988, the campaign for restitution proceeded simultaneously with an internal Jewish renewal which was encouraged by both the GDR government and by the international – especially the American – Jewish community. But, unlike their Japanese-Canadian counterparts, the Jews in the GDR did not actively campaign for reparations from their government.

In the restitution negotiations of the 1980s, then, the Jews of the GDR gave largely sideline support to what was, in effect, a foreign policy issue. There were no "ethnic politics," or mobilizing support, within the country, and there was no effect of social empowerment. The reparations promises were not extracted from the government in such a way as to set a precedent for other groups. As in the Canadian case, the restitution was bestowed from above. It did not result from democratic parliamentary procedures.

The Role of the Larger Neighbours

In the cases of both the Japanese Canadians and the East German Jews, prior reparations payments by the U.S. and the FRG played an important role in the negotiations.

The U.S.

In contrast to Canada, Japanese Americans were considered American citizens by their government, even during the war. The U.S. government did not confiscate the property of Japanese Americans, nor did it ban them from the West Coast after 1944.[17] It was assumed that once the war was over, Japanese Americans would return to their homes and communities; hence, there was no forced diaspora, deportations, or exile.

Three decades later, in 1976, U.S. President Gerald Ford apologized publicly to the Japanese Americans for the loss of their civil rights during the war. A year later Canada's Prime Minister, Pierre Trudeau, mistakenly apologized in *Tokyo* to the *Japanese government* for Canada's treatment of Canadians whose ancestors had come from Japan as early as 1877.

The U.S. started compensating Japanese Americans in 1972 when the Social Security Act was revised so that Japanese Americans over eighteen were recognized as having contributed during their internment. Similar steps were taken at other levels of government at regular intervals. Moreover, the Japanese American campaign for reparations was conducted along the standard procedures of "ethnic politics" and U.S. democracy.

In 1979, Mike Lowry, a Demoratic Representative from the State of Washington, introduced a private member's bill, HR 5977, that proposed an award of $15,000 plus fifteen dollars a day to all detainees. Although Lowry's bill failed, it helped to spearhead the establishment of a Congressional bipartisan Commission to review the facts and circumstances surrounding the evacuations and internments, to ascertain the impact on the evacuees, and to recommend appropriate remedies.

The Commission held public hearings around the country, and three years later it released a 467-page report which criticized the American government of the day for its "race prejudice, war hysteria and failure of political

leadership."[18] It recommended: a Congressional apology; the establishment of a $1.5 billion fund to compensate the 60,000 survivors at $20,000 per internee, the remainder going to a community fund; pardons to all Japanese Americans who had been convicted of curfew and detention violations; and restitution for lost benefits to all Japanese Americans who were civil servants during the years 1941-1945.[19]

In 1987, the House of Representatives supported the Commission's recommendations and passed Bill HR 442, the Civil Liberties Act. In April 1988, the Senate also voted to endorse the Bill, but without a two-thirds majority. Consequently, under the American system, for the Act to become law, it required the signature of the President. Until the very end, advisers to President Reagan cautioned him to exercise his veto, but he ultimately signed – on August 10, 1988 – and thereby increased the pressure on Prime Minister Mulroney to settle the reparations issue in Canada.

The FRG

At 8:00 a.m. on 10 September 1952, the Reparations Agreement between the Federal Republic of Germany (FRG) and the State of Israel was signed in the city hall of Luxemburg City, Luxemburg, by Konrad Adenauer, Chancellor of the Federal Republic of Germany, and Moshe Sharett, Foreign Minister of Israel. Only a few journalists attended the historic signing. There were no movie cameras and only a few photographers were present. When a photographer's flash bulb exploded with a loud bang, people thought that an assassination was occurring. The treaty was signed in secrecy because Israel feared the outraged extreme rightists in her own country. Due to the emotional aspect and opposition in both Israel and the FRG, the agreement was signed on neutral territory. (Thompson 1978, 47)

The reparations settlement extracted from the FRG, only seven years after the end of the war, was by far the most dramatic and the largest settlement of the four under consideration here. The FRG agreed to pay 3,000 million DM to the state of Israel and another 450 million DM to the Conference on Jewish Material Claims against Germany. Provisions for reparations to Jewish survivors and the heirs of Jewish victims had already been enacted.

The West German government negotiated its settlement, not with its own Jewish communities, but with international Jewish organizations and with a foreign state. As in the U.S., the agreement was ratified by the Parliament: 239 of the 400 members (59 per cent) voted in favour, 35 against, 86 abstained, and 40 were absent.

The restitution payments from the FRG in the early 1950s were attacked by many Jews who considered any restitution insufficient compensation for

their suffering and losses, and by many Germans who thought the payments excessive. The major West German proponent of restitution was Chancellor Konrad Adenauer. These payments became a central element in his development of a Western-oriented foreign policy for the FRG. As in the GDR, the small and weak West German Jewish communities incorporated and benefited from the restitution payments, but they were not major participants in the negotiations. And, as in the U.S., the West German agreement contributed to the pressure on the GDR to follow its example.

Conclusion: Restitution, the Nation State, and Ethnic Politics

The dynamics of the 1984-1988 campaigns for reparations to Japanese Canadians and to Jews in the German Democratic Republic – and the comparative material from the U.S. and the FRG – suggest several hypotheses concerning the postwar state and its minorities. In both cases, negotiations for restitution were accompanied by an ethnic renewal. In one case, the ethnic group was a major party to the campaign and the final agreement, and in the other, it became more a symbol or incorporation of them.[20]

Ethnic restitution campaigns may or may not be related to standard processes of western-style parliamentary democracy and "ethnic politics." In the U.S., the negotiation and ratification of the agreement took this form, and the bill was passed without the backing of the President. In Canada, ethnic patterns of mobilization were deployed to create a consensus favouring restitution, but the ultimate decision was made by the Prime Minister, and the contents of the agreement were not widely known at the time the settlement was signed. In the GDR, all the deliberations took place at the top level behind closed doors, with little if any input from the ethnic group involved or from the rest of the population.

It follows that in the U.S. and Canada, one presupposition underlying the ethnic mobilization and the favourable social consensus was the idea that a restitution grant to one ethnic group sets a precedent for other groups pressing their demands. In the FRG, the Sinti and Roma, who were also persecuted by the Nazis, are still campaigning for restitution, but with relatively little success.[21] In the GDR, the idea of empowerment played no role at all.

Particularly interesting in both cases is the important role assigned to the press – in Canada by the Japanese Canadians, and in the GDR by the government – to "educate" the public to support a large grant to a small group, a measure which could spark resistance. The potentially destabilizing consequences of this kind of policy are illustrated by the cases of both Germanys in the early postwar period.[22]

The success of three major ethnic restitution claims – in the U.S., Canada, and the GDR – in 1987-1988 reflects the growing power of

ethnic/national appeals in the late twentieth century. In the GDR, the apology to the Jews for German war crimes came only in late autumn 1989, when the entire political discourse of the GDR shifted from class-based internationalism to German nationalism.

All four cases discussed demonstrate the way ethnic minorities mediate foreign policy and international trade relations. Had the U.S., Japan, and Israel not been perceived as desirable trading partners, the negotiations might not have been so successful. In fact, they might not even have been attempted. Neither the U.S. nor Canada made any serious attempts to compensate their Japanese citizens as long as Japan was war-torn and weak.

Finally, states use their ethnic minorities not only to mediate their relations to other states, but to legitimate their rule at home as well. In Canada, the first announcement in 1984 and the final agreement in 1988 both came in the wake of an impending election, and were intended to demonstrate the major parties' commitment to Canada's ethnic communities. Honecker's promise of restitution was made at a time when his government, under the pressure of popular dissatisfaction, attempted to use its Jewish communities to incorporate its policy of "anti-Fascism" – one of the cornerstones of its claim to legitimacy – rather than undertake social and economic reform. The GDR is the most dramatic example, but in Canada too, the restitution policy survived the government which conceived it.

Notes

Many thanks to Volker Meja for his extensive comments on an earlier draft of this paper. The authors, however, assume all responsibility for its contents.

1. See Maryka Omatsu, *Bittersweet Passage: Redress and the Japanese-Canadian Experience* (1992) for a history of the Japanese-Canadian community and its successful struggle for redress of World War Two injustices.
2. The anti-Semitism of the Crusades and Hitler notwithstanding, since the late Middle Ages Jews have maintained a continuous presence in the territory that is today the Federal Republic of Germany. Japanese immigration to Canada began in 1877 and peaked in 1907.
3. During World War I, 197 Japanese Canadians volunteered for the Canadian armed forces. Asked by the government to raise $50,000 in Victory Bonds, the Japanese-Canadian community responded by raising $235,400. One hundred thousand Jews fought for Germany during the war. In 1916 the Prussian War Minister conducted a census of Jews in Germany's armed forces as part of an effort to prove that the Jews were not contributing their share to the war effort. Because the census demonstrated that, in fact, the Jews contributed more than their share, it was never published.
4. Jews were theoretically accepted as full, integrated citizens of the GDR. In

fact, they had a special status. They were in some ways privileged and in others disadvantaged. See Thompson (1978) and Ostow (1989).

5. While the GDR had more than one political party, this party dominated the political life of the nation.

6. Irwin-Zarecka (1989) explores the meanings and implications of this kind of "silence" and "invisibility".

7. In both cases, the new ethnic consciousness has a history starting in the late 1970s. In 1977, celebrations of the centennial of Japanese immigration to Canada awakened ethnic consciousness among Japanese Canadians. These years saw several smaller attempts to bring Jewish history into the political culture of the GDR. In 1976, Schönberg's *Moses und Aron* was first performed in Dresden. In 1978, a Jewish youth group was established in East Berlin. And in 1979, the fiftieth anniversary of the birth of Anne Frank was observed in an evening of song and readings in East Berlin. That same year, though, an attempt to commemorate the 100th anniversary of the birth of Albert Einstein in the East Berlin Jewish community was suppressed.

8. Rabbi Neuman's stay in East Berlin turned out to be rather brief and stormy. His difficulties with the East Berlin Jewish community's board of directors and his departure in May 1988 did not, however, damage the warming relations between the East German and American Jewish communities.

9. In 1989, there were 400 registered members of the Jewish communities and another 4,000 or so citizens of Jewish ancestry in the GDR. Canada's population included 50,000 Japanese Canadians of whom one-third were of "mixed race."

10. See Ostow (1989) and Omatsu (1992).

11. In the GDR, such a psychological crisis and fear of the death of the collectivity, evident in the central role of cemeteries in Jewish discourse, has been observable for at least several years (Ostow 1989).

12. See Ostow (1989) and Omatsu (1992).

13. For a discussion of the relation between boundary threats and immigration, see Borneman (1986).

14. At its height, this organization had 50,000 members in Berlin.

15. A particularly popular joke in the GDR was the following. Question: Which country did Hitler invade first? Answer: the GDR. (Vincent von Wroblewsky, personal communication.)

16. Dr. Peter Kirchner, personal communication, April 30, 1990.

17. One-third of the Japanese-American population – those considered "loyal" – were allowed to work, study, and serve in the U.S. Army. The other two-thirds were in camps from 1942 to 1944.

18. See Commission on Wartime Relocation and Internment of Civilians, *Personal Justice Denied* (U.S. Government Printing Office, Washington, DC), 5.

19. *Ibid.*, Part 2, Recommendations, 8-10.

20. In the case of the GDR, there was no final agreement. Before its official demise on October 3, 1990, the GDR contributed 30 million East German marks

to a new Jewish archival and conference centre in East Berlin and 6.2 million marks to Amcha, an international organization which provides counselling and rehabilitation for Holocaust survivors and their descendants in Israel. Between the end of April and October 3, GDR also admitted approximately 1,000 Jewish refugees from the Soviet Union and granted them residence rights and work permits. The Jewish communities of the united Germany are currently pressing for the restitution of 700 properties in the territory of the former GDR that were confiscated from individual Jews and from Jewish communities by the Nazis and by the GDR government.

21. The best documentation of this can be found in Pross (1990).
22. Borneman (1986) discusses the lack of ideological integration and, especially, the role of the press reports in the difficulties experienced absorbing the (Cuban) Marielitos in the U.S. in 1980.

References

Anderson, Benedict. *Imagined Communities: Reflections on the Origin and Spread of Nationalism.* London: Verso, 1983.

Bodemann, Y. Michal. "Elitism, Fragility, and Commoditism: Three Themes in the Canadian Sociological Mythology." In *Models and Myths in Canadian Sociology,* edited by S.D. Berkowitz. Toronto: Butterworths, 1984.

Borneman, John. "Emigres as Bullets/Immigration as Penetration. Perceptions of the Marielitos." *Journal of Popular Culture,* 20:3 (1986), 73-97.

_____. *Narratives of Belonging in the Two Berlins: Kinship Formation and Nation Building in the Context of the Cold War, 1945-1989.* (Unpublished PhD dissertation, Harvard University.)

Deutschkron, Inge. *Israel und die Deutschen.* Köln: Verlag Wissenschaft und Politik, 1970.

Hohri, William. *Repairing America: An Account of the Movement for Japanese America Redress.* Pullman: Washington State University press, 1988.

Hughes, Everett C. "New Peoples." In *The Sociological Eye.* Chicago: Aldine Atherton, 1954, 174-190.

Irwin-Zarecka, Iwona. *Neutralizing Memory: The Jew in Contemporary Poland.* New Brunswick: Transaction Publishers, 1989.

Kobayashi, Audrey. *A Demographic Profile of Japanese Canadians.* Ottawa: Department of the Secretary of State, 1989.

Omatsu, Maryka. *Bittersweet Passage: Redress and the Japanese-Canadian Experience.* Toronto: Between the Lines, 1992.

Ostow, Robin. *Jews in Contemporary East Germany: The Children of Moses in the Land of Marx.* London: Macmillan, 1989.

Pross, Chistian. *Wiedergutmachung. Der Kleinkrieg gegen die Opfer.* Frankfut/Main: Athenaeum, 1990.

Sunahara, Ann Gomer. *The Politics of Racism: The Uprooting of Japanese Canadians During the Second World War.* Toronto: James Lorimer, 1978.

Eran Razin and André Langlois

Immigrant and Ethnic Entrepreneurs in Canadian and American Metropolitan Areas – A Comparative Perspective

Abstract

This paper presents evidence on the influence of the metropolitan milieu on self-employment among immigrant and ethnic groups in Canada and the U.S. It is based on data of the 1991 Canadian census and on the 1990 American census, and includes Canada's 25 metropolitan areas and America's 16 largest ones. Results show that groups that are clearly distinguished from the mainstream population in terms of race, religion or appearance, and the more entrepreneurial groups, gravitate more to self-employment in peripheral metropolitan areas than in metropolitan areas which offer more abundant opportunities. This is particularly true in Canada, and to a lesser extent the U.S. However, immigrants and minorities in peripheral metropolitan areas cluster in narrower entrepreneurial niches. Non-mainstream entrepreneurial minorities are much larger in the U.S. than in Canada and form extensive ethnic enclaves in large metropolitan areas, which can deviate less from means for the total population. "Protected" opportunities created for non-mainstream entrepreneurs by large non-entrepreneurial groups who reside in crime-ridden areas are also a characteristics niche in the U.S. that explains some of the differences between Canada and the U.S.

Résumé

Cet article examine l'influence du milieu métropolitain sur le développement du travail autonome chez les groupes immigrants et ethniques au Canada et aux États-Unis. Il est basé sur les données du recensement canadien de 1991 et du recensement américain de 1990 et englobe les 25 régions métropolitaines du Canada et les 16 plus grandes agglomérations urbaines des États-Unis. Les résultats indiquent que les groupes qui se distinguent nettement de la population majoritaire en termes de race, de religion ou d'aspect et les groupes dont l'esprit d'entreprise est le plus développé s'orientent davantage vers le travail autonome dans les régions métropolitaines périphériques que dans les régions métropolitaines qui offrent des possibilités plus abondantes. Cette constatation

s'applique davantage au Canada qu'aux États-Unis. Cependant, dans les régions métropolitaines périphériques, les immigrants et les minorités sont concentrés dans des créneaux d'entreprises plus étroits. Les minorités entreprenariales sont beaucoup plus importantes aux États-Unis qu'au Canada et elles forment, dans les grandes régions métropolitaines, de vastes enclaves ethniques qui peuvent présenter un écart moindre par rapport aux moyennes de la population générale. Les débouchés « protégés » qu'offrent aux entrepreneurs minoritaires les importants groupes non entreprenariaux résidant dans des zones où le taux de criminalité est très élevé constituent également un créneau caractéristique des États-Unis qui explique certaines des différences entre le Canada et les États-Unis.

Introduction

The major role of self-employment in the economic mobility routes of successful immigrant groups in North America has been extensively documented (Light and Bonacich 1988; Waldinger *et al.* 1990). The present paper compares two studies which focus on the influence of the metropolitan milieu on self-employment among immigrants and ethnic minorities in Canada and in the U.S.

The first question addressed in both studies deals with the influence of the metropolitan opportunity structure on self-employment among immigrant and ethnic groups. On the one hand, ample opportunity in the small-business economy, reflected by a high rate of self-employment in the metropolitan area, can be expected to positively influence the propensity of immigrants and minorities to become self-employed. On the other hand, rates of self-employment among immigrants and minorities may be high in small and remote metropolitan areas, as a result of the difficulty in penetrating salaried job opportunities in smaller and more ethnically homogeneous localities (Razin and Langlois, forthcoming).

A second question refers to the influence of the size of the ethnic community in each metropolitan area on ethnic self-employment. A large ethnic community which offers large co-ethnic clientele and well-developed community-based entrepreneurial networks can be expected to enhance prospects for entrepreneurship. However, niche saturation and availability of salaried jobs in businesses of co-ethnics can limit prospects for self-employment in large ethnic concentrations (Razin and Langlois, forthcoming).

Thus, variables representing the metropolitan opportunity structure and the size of the local ethnic community can influence ethnic enterprise ei-

ther positively or negatively. We propose that the exact nature of these influences depends on the type of the immigrant or the ethnic group.

One distinction can be made between more and less entrepreneurial minorities. A second can be made between groups that are relatively similar to the mainstream majority population and groups that are clearly distinguished in terms of race, religion or appearance. The more entrepreneurial and the more distinct minorities may carve small-business niches which greatly deviate from the general opportunity structure in specific metropolitan areas, due to the impact of their well-developed local entrepreneurial networks. The more distinct minorities may also be influenced by limited opportunities for salaried employees in small and ethnically homogenous cities. Mainstream groups and the less entrepreneurial may be more influenced by the general opportunity structure, and have higher rates of self-employment where the local economy offers more opportunity (Razin and Langlois, forthcoming).

A final question refers to possible differences between Canada and the U.S. with respect to the relationships proposed above. Both countries show higher similarities than differences when compared to most immigrant absorbing countries in the world. In fact, preliminary examination of data for recent immigrants indicated that ethnic entrepreneurial enclaves are more influenced by differences in metropolitan economies than by differences between the national economies of Canada and the U.S. (Razin 1993). However, some differences between Canadian and American political, economic, social, and geographical characteristics do exist (Goldberg and Mercer 1986; Lipset 1990), and can influence the entrepreneurial behaviour of immigrant and ethnic groups in metropolitan areas.

First, it was assumed that the climate for entrepreneurship in Canada was inferior to that in the U.S. This may no longer be true, but Canada is still characterized by stronger welfare state mechanisms, greater legitimacy given to government intervention and guidance in various aspects of life, including immigrant absorption. Hence, self-employment could have a less crucial role in the mobility routes of immigrants in Canada.

Second, Canada lacks the large, poor, and crime-ridden ghettos that characterize American metropolitan areas. Some of the more prominent non-mainstream entrepreneurial immigrant groups in the U.S. have based their ventures on serving these ghettos as "middleman minorities" (Razin 1993). Serving these large non-entrepreneurial minorities can be expected to produce self-employment opportunities for entrepreneurial non-mainstream groups particularly in large metropolitan areas.

Third, Canada has a much smaller population and a simpler urban hierarchy than the U.S. On the one hand, entrepreneurial non-mainstream

groups, such as Koreans, are much larger in the U.S. than in Canada. Hence, they can deviate less from the industrial structure of the small-business sector in metropolitan areas. On the other hand, whereas Toronto is the prominent centre for most groups in Canada, inter-metropolitan variations among groups in the U.S. have more diverse patterns. Large entrepreneurial groups in the U.S. form complex ethnic enclaves in large concentrations, characterized by wide-scale employment of co-ethnics, a sectorial specialization that usually includes both productive industries and community-based goods and services, and functional linkages among firms of the same ethnicity (Logan *et al.* 1994). Such phenomena as the Cuban enclave in Miami and the Korean enclave in Los Angeles are unparalleled in their magnitude in Canada. These enclaves may be associated with extensive entrepreneurial activity by these groups in large and diversified metropolitan areas, although not necessarily in metropolitan regions at the top of the urban hierarchy. In sum, the generalization that entrepreneurial non-mainstream groups have higher rates of self-employment in peripheral metropolitan areas, which offer relatively few entrepreneurial opportunities, may be less true in the U.S.

Data and Methodology

The Canadian study was based on data of the 1991 Census of Canada. The public use files of the Canadian census suffer not only from the small sample size (2 per cent), but also from aggregation of variables, such as country of birth, and from limited geographical divisions (Langlois and Razin 1989; Razin and Langlois 1992). Hence, we had no choice but to order a large special tabulation that included the experienced labour force in Canada's 25 CMAs (Census Metropolitan Areas). Four variables were included in the table: country of birth/ethnic origin (65 groups), CMA, class of worker, and industry.

The U.S. study was based on the 1990 Census Public Use Microdata 5 per cent Sample and included the labour force in the 16 largest metropolitan regions in the U.S. (CMSAs and MSAs). The labour force in each metropolitan region was divided into 78 groups, mainly defined by country of birth. The race and Hispanic origin variables were used to identify several visible minorities within the American-born population.

The comparisons described in this paper are based on: (1) calculations of rates of self-employment for each group in each metropolitan area (small Canadian CMAs were classified into regional groups), (2) calculation of similar tables for major industry groupings, and (3) calculation of correlation coefficients in order to identify factors explaining inter-metropolitan variations in rates of self-employment for each group.

The Most Entrepreneurial Groups in Canadian and American Metropolitan Areas

The rate of self-employment among the foreign-born population in Canadian metropolitan areas was substantially higher than for those born in Canada (Table 1). Jewish people were the most entrepreneurial group among Canadian-born, and Jews born abroad also displayed a very high propensity to become self-employed (Tables 1 and 2). The Jewish people were prominent as self-employed workers in white-collar industries (Table 4), and to a lesser extent in distribution (Table 5). The success of the Jewish ethno-religious group was apparently linked to a remarkable preservation of ethnic ties across generations. Jews are an example of an entrepreneurial group characterized by high levels of human capital and increasing concentration in white-collar professional occupations, accompanied by retention of ethnic ties and ethnic labour market concentrations (Isajiw 1990; Reitz 1990).

The relatively small Korean-born community in Canada was also extremely entrepreneurial (Table 1), and was highly concentrated in retail. High rates of self-employment also characterized Greek and Israeli immigrants, as well as immigrants of German origin. Greeks had the highest propensity to become self-employed in peripheral CMAs, whereas in the large urban centres, Jewish groups and Koreans had the highest propensity to become self-employed (Table 2).

The most prominent entrepreneurial groups in American metropolitan regions were Greeks and Koreans (Table 3). Greeks were the most entrepreneurial group in six of the 16 metropolitan regions, including four of the five largest ones (New York, Los Angeles, San Francisco and Philadelphia). Koreans were the most entrepreneurial group in Chicago and Washington, but were among the three most entrepreneurial groups in seven metropolitan regions. They were actually more prominent than Greeks, particularly in Los Angeles, where Koreans compose a much larger immigrant group. Koreans, and to a slightly lesser extent Greeks, frequently had the highest rate of self-employment in distribution industries (Table 5), but were remarkably absent from the list of most entrepreneurial groups in white-collar industries (Table 4). Other entrepreneurial groups in various metropolitan regions were Middle Eastern and North African immigrants, including Iranians and Israelis, and several European groups, such as Dutch, Hungarians, Czechoslovakians and Polish.

These data for the most entrepreneurial groups in American metropolitan regions closely resemble the data for Canada, except for the technical fact that the U.S. census does not distinguish the Jewish group.

Inter-Metropolitan Variations in Rates of Self-Employment

Rates of self-employment in both countries were highest in western metropolitan areas, as well as in Sunbelt metropolitan areas in the U.S., and in Toronto in Canada (Table 6). A diversified economy, in which large manufacturing corporations and public organizations did not predominate, explained the high rates in most western and Sunbelt metropolitan areas, whereas Toronto's small businesses benefited from its size and economic and ethnic diversity. The particularly high rate of self-employment in Miami could be attributed to the lack of a traditional base of large manufacturing plants in this metropolitan area, as well as to the prominence of tourism and the recent emergence of the Cuban entrepreneurial enclave and international trade orientation (Portes and Stepick 1993). Small and remote metropolitan areas in the Maritime provinces, Northern Ontario and Queébec were characterized by the lowest rates of self-employment in Canada. In the U.S., rates of self-employment were lowest in metropolitan areas in the manufacturing belt – Detroit, Cleveland, Chicago and Philadelphia – and in Washington, with its unique capital city economy.

On average, rates of self-employment were slightly higher in American metropolitan regions than in Canadian metropolitan areas (Table 6). However, Canadian metropolitan areas, except for Toronto and Montréal, are much smaller than the American metropolitan areas included in the analysis. Hence, low rates of self-employment in Maritime CMAs, Québec CMAs and Northern Ontario CMAs can not be directly compared with those of the 16 largest metropolitan regions in Canada.

Immigrants in all 25 Canadian CMAs had a greater propensity to become self-employed than the Canadian-born population. The gap between immigrants and the Canadian-born population was particularly wide in peripheral CMAs, where the Canadian-born population displayed a low propensity to become self-employed (Table 6).

The data support the assumption that the lack of alternative job opportunities and the lack of co-ethnic competition in the small-business sector lead immigrants and minorities to self-employment in small and non-central Canadian CMAs. Greek immigrant entrepreneurs form a clear example. Highly concentrated in food services, the highest rates of self-employment among Greeks were found in their peripheral communities in Maritime, Québec, western and Prairie CMAs, and the lowest rates in their largest communities – Montréal and Toronto (Table 6). However, Greek entrepreneurs in small CMAs were much more limited to restaurants than in Montréal and Toronto. Hence, whereas the propensity of immigrants to become self-employed is high in peripheral CMAs, they tended to concentrate there in narrower entrepre-

neurial niches. Similar spatial variations characterized Chinese immigrants in Canada (Table 6). Patterns were less clear among Koreans. Still, an extraordinary rate of self-employment (60 per cent) characterized the relatively small Korean communities in Hamilton and St. Catharines-Niagara. Non-entrepreneurial groups such as Vietnamese and Filipinos, as well as immigrants from Latin America and Portugal displayed similar patterns.

However, not all immigrant and ethnic groups in Canada displayed the pattern described above. Among groups such as Hungarian, Czechoslovakian, and Scandinavian immigrants, rates of self-employment were higher in their larger communities in the major metropolitan areas. Canadian-born Francophones and Aboriginal people also had higher rates of self-employment in the large and central CMAs (Razin and Langlois, forthcoming).

Patterns in the U.S. were less clear. The total population of immigrants did not always have higher rates of self-employment than the total American-born population (Table 6). For example, the American-born population had higher rates of self-employment than the total population of immigrants in the large metropolitan regions of California. By contrast, immigrants had a greater propensity to become self-employed than the American-born population in smaller metropolitan regions, such as Washington, Miami, and Atlanta, and in metropolitan regions where the proportion of immigrants was low, such as Detroit, Cleveland, and Philadelphia. Differences between immigrants and the American-born population were influenced in various metropolitan regions by the size of local minority communities characterized by low levels of entrepreneurship.

Most immigrant groups had high rates of self-employment in Miami and Los Angeles. The not so high rate of self-employment of the total population of immigrants in Los Angeles is explained by an ethnic composition which includes large relatively non-entrepreneurial minorities. The highest rate of self-employment among Koreans was in their large ethnic enclave in Los Angeles (Table 6). Among Chinese immigrants in the U.S., rates of self-employment were higher in the smaller metropolitan regions, where they strongly gravitated into eating and drinking places. Canadian immigrants in the U.S. gravitated into self-employment much more than in their home country. In their case, the general opportunity structure, as reflected by the total rate of self-employment in the metro region, did have a clear influence on the propensity to become self-employed, and explained high rates of self-employment in metropolitan areas such as Miami, Los Angeles and San Diego. Among non-mainstream groups, however, similar inter-metropolitan variations could be explained by specific entrepreneurial

opportunities in serving large non-entrepreneurial minority groups in large metropolitan areas.

Correlation Coefficients Analysis

Calculation of correlation coefficients clearly showed that the main factor influencing a group's rate of self-employment in Canadian and American metropolitan areas is the rate of self-employment of all populations of the metropolitan area. However, not all groups were similarly influenced by this factor. The total rates of self-employment in Canadian CMAs had a clear positive influence on self-employment among groups that are relatively similar to Canada's mainstream majority population, such as groups of European origin, and among certain non-entrepreneurial immigrant groups, such as those from Latin America (Table 7). The total rate of self-employment in the CMA did not influence, or even influence negatively, the rates of self-employment among the most entrepreneurial groups and among minorities distinguished from Canada's mainstream majority in terms of race, religion or appearance: immigrants from Korea and Greece, Canadian-born Jews, immigrants from Israel, Lebanon and additional countries in east and south Asia. These groups frequently gravitated to self-employment in metropolitan areas that offered limited small-business opportunities.

These relationships can also be identified in the U.S., but they are less clear (Table 7). The groups most influenced by the total rate of self-employment in American metropolitan regions included mainstream immigrants, such as those born in the UK, Canada, Hungary, Scandinavia, and Germany, as well as some non-entrepreneurial minorities, such as immigrants from Vietnam, Mexico, other Latin American countries and American-born blacks. The groups least influenced by the total rate of self-employment in the metropolitan region were mainly non-mainstream groups, some of them entrepreneurial, such as immigrants from various Muslim and Arab countries, Cuba and Korea, and some of them non-entrepreneurial, such as immigrants from the Philippines.

However, there are quite a few exceptions to this generalization, and some groups such as immigrants from Greece behave differently in Canada and in the U.S. This is due, perhaps, to four major reasons:

(1) The U.S. study included only the largest metropolitan regions and not the smaller ones with only a few hundreds of thousands inhabitants. Thus, small and peripheral metropolitan regions, where immigrants may behave differently than in large metropolitan regions, are missing from the U.S. study.

(2) Among the 16 largest metropolitan regions in the U.S., Miami and

Los Angeles, where the total rate of self-employment is high, are also locations where immigrants and minorities tend to be relatively entrepreneurial.

(3) Large and diversified metropolitan regions in the U.S. offer many self-employment opportunities for non-mainstream immigrants by serving large non-entrepreneurial minorities, such as blacks and Hispanics.

(4) Entrepreneurial non-mainstream groups, such as Koreans, are much larger in the U.S. than in Canada. Hence, they can deviate less from the mean for the total population.

Moreover, a detailed analysis of entrepreneurial niches showed that non-mainstream immigrant groups in American metropolitan regions concentrated in narrower entrepreneurial niches than mainstream groups. The industrial composition of entrepreneurs of non-mainstream groups deviated greatly from the industrial composition of all self-employed workers in the metropolitan regions. This was particularly true for Koreans, Salvadorians, Asian Indians, Iranians, Arabs and Chinese. The tendency of immigrant entrepreneurs of non-mainstream groups to concentrate in narrow niches, such as eating and drinking establishments, grocery stores and automotive repair services was particularly strong in smaller and less diversified metropolitan regions, and not in large ethnic enclaves in large metropolitan regions.

The population size of the ethnic or immigrant group in the metropolitan area as well as the total population of the metropolitan area were not clearly correlated with the group's rate of self-employment, with a few exceptions. Size of the metropolitan area had a greater impact on the industrial composition of the self-employed, such that smaller ones were characterized by stronger ethnic concentrations in narrow niches.

Conclusions

Our study shows that immigrant groups and ethnic minorities that are clearly distinguished from the mainstream majority population in terms of race, religion or appearance, and the more entrepreneurial groups, gravitate to self-employment in peripheral metropolitan areas, where entrepreneurial opportunities are few, than in metropolitan areas which offer more abundant opportunities. This is particularly true in Canada and to a lesser extent in the U.S. However, immigrants and minorities in peripheral metropolitan areas cluster in narrower entrepreneurial niches, such as retail and restaurants, which are characterized by limited growth prospects. Assumptions

concerning the impact of the size of the local ethnic community on self-employment among its members were not verified.

While there is some merit to the argument that entrepreneurship among immigrant and ethnic groups is more greatly influenced by differences in metropolitan economies than by those between Canada and the U.S., marked differences do exist between Canadian and American metropolitan areas. In the U.S., generalizations are more difficult due to the greater complexity of the urban system. Non-mainstream entrepreneurial minorities are much larger in the U.S. and form extensive and diversified ethnic enclaves in large metropolitan regions. While they can deviate less from averages for the total population, due to their size, their prominent enclaves do not fully correspond to the general structure of the metropolitan hierarchy. "Protected" opportunities created for non-mainstream entrepreneurs by large non-entrepreneurial groups who reside in crime-ridden areas are also a niche unique to the U.S. which explains some of the deviation between inter-metropolitan variations in Canada and the U.S.

The comparisons presented in this paper form a first step in a broader analysis of ethnic divisions of labour in Canadian and American metropolitan areas. Further investigation should assess how the position of specific immigrant and ethnic groups in the labour market influences the position of other immigrant and ethnic groups in the labour market. Such influences include competition among several groups in particular niches in certain metropolitan areas, and penetration by groups into niches resulting from the lack of competition by either the mainstream majority population or by large minority groups. The present study suggests that these are parameters where Canadian and American experiences may differ substantially.

References

Goldberg, M.A. and J. Mercer. *The Myth of the North American City*. Vancouver: University of British Columbia Press, 1986.

Isajiw, W.W. "Ethnic-identity Retention." In *Ethnic Identity and Equality: Varieties of Experience in a Canadian City*. Edited by R. Breton, W.W. Isajiw, W.E. Kalbach and J.G. Reitz. Toronto: University of Toronto Press, 1990, 34-91.

Langlois, A., and E. Razin. "Self-Employment Among Ethnic Minorities in Canadian Metropolitan Areas." *Canadian Journal of Regional Science*, 12 (1989), 335-354.

Light, I., and E. Bonacich. *Immigrant Entrepreneurs, Koreans in Los Angeles, 1965-1982*. Berkeley: University of California Press, 1988.

Lipset, S.M. *Continental Divide*. New York: Routledge, 1990.

Logan, J.R., R.D. Alba, and T.L. McNulty. "Ethnic Economies in Metropolitan

Regions: Miami and Beyond." *Social Forces,* 72 (1994), 691-724.

Perlman, J. "Beyond New York: The Occupations of Russian Jewish Immigrants in Providence, RI and in Other Small Jewish Communities." *American Jewish History,* 72 (1983), 369-394.

Portes, A. and A. Stepick. *City on the Edge, The Transformation of Miami.* Berkeley: University of California Press, 1993.

Razin, E. "Immigrant Entrepreneurs in Israel, Canada and California." In *Immigration and Entrepreneurship, Culture, Capital, and Ethnic Networks.* Edited by I. Light and P. Bhachu. New Brunswick, NJ: Transaction, 1993, 97-124.

Razin, E., and A. Langlois. "Location and Entrepreneurship Among New Immigrants in Israel and Canada." *Geography Research Forum.* 12 (1992), 16-36.

Razin, E., and A. Langlois. "Metropolitan Characteristics and Entrepreneurship Among Immigrants and Ethnic Groups in Canada" *International Migration Review,* forthcoming.

Reitz, J.G. "Ethnic Concentrations in Labour Markets and Their Implications for Ethnic Inequality." In *Ethnic Identity and Equality: Varieties of Experience in a Canadian City.* Edited by R. Breton, W.W. Isajiw, W.E. Kalbach and J.G. Reitz. Toronto: University of Toronto Press, 1990, 135-195.

Waldinger, R., *et al. Ethnic Entrepreneurs.* Newbury Park, CA: Sage, 1990.

Acknowledgements

The Canadian study was supported by a grant of the Israel Association for Canadian Studies. The American study was supported by a grant of the United States-Israel Binational Science Foundation.

Table 1: The Experienced Labour Force in Canada's CMAs –
Percent Self-employed by Selected Countries of Birth, 1991.

Country of Birth	% S-E	Country of Birth	% S-E
Canada – Total	8.4		
Born in Canada	7.6		
Born outside of Canada	10.6		
Most entrepreneurial groups		**Least entrepreneurial groups**	
Poland (Jewish eth. or.)	37.5	Portugal	5.4
Korea	36.2	Vietnam	5.3
Canada (Jewish eth. or.)	21.5	Other Caribbean	5.1
USSR (German eth. or.)	21.1	Trinidad and Tobago	4.6
Israel	20.3	Canada (Aboriginals)	4.4
Greece	20.1	Mexico & Central America	4.3
USA (German mother to.)	19.3	Haiti	4.3
Poland (German mother to.)	18.4	Jamaica	4.3
Hungary	17.9	Guyana	3.9
USSR (Jewish eth. or.)	17.6	Other Southern Asia	3.7
USA (Jewish eth. or.)	17.2	Philippines	3.3
Lebanon	16.9	Canada (Portuguese mother to.)	2.5
Netherlands	16.5		
Scandinavia	15.8		
Czechoslovakia	15.7		
Middle East & North Africa	15.3		

Source: Special tabulation from Census of Canada 1991.
% s-e – Percent self-employed.
The self-employed include both those in incorporated and unincorporated businesses.

Table 2: The Experienced Labour Force in Canada's CMAs –

The Most Entrepreneurial Immigrant/Ethnic Groups by CMA, 1991 (percent self-employed).

Maritimes		Québec		Montreal	
1. Greece	39.5	1. Greece	32.5	1. Poland (Jewish)	44.9
2. Lebanon	37.1	2. Italy	22.2	2. Korea	32.8
3. Hong Kong	30.0	3. Portugal	16.2	3. Hungary	22.0
4. Italy	26.0	4. Lebanon	16.0	4. Czechoslovakia	20.7
5. Canada (Jewish)	23.4	5. France	12.4	5. Canada (Jewish)	20.4
6. Ireland	23.1	6. SE Asia/other	12.0	6. USSR (Jewish)	20.4

Ottawa-Hull		Toronto		S. Ontario	
1. Greece	24.2	1. Korea	37.1	1. Korea	51.8
2. Lebanon	23.2	2. Poland (Jewish)	35.1	2. Israel	25.4
3. Yugoslavia	18.2	3. Canada (Jewish)	22.3	3. Canada (Jewish)	23.2
4. Hungary	17.5	4. Israel	22.1	4. Greece	22.5
5. Netherlands	16.8	5. USSR (German)	20.9	5. USSR (Jewish)	21.2
4. Italy	15.5	6. Poland (German)	20.8	6. USA (Jewish)	19.8

N. Ontario		Prairies		Western	
1. China	31.0	1. Korea	33.3	1. Greece	28.8
2. USSR	22.6	2. Greece	31.7	2. USSR (German)	27.1
3. Netherlands	20.9	3. USSR (Jewish)	28.6	3. Poland (German)	24.5
4. India	17.1	4. Poland (Jewish)	23.9	4. Korea	22.7
5. Yugoslavia	13.3	5. USSR (German)	22.6	5. Canada (Jewish)	20.7
6. Germany & Aus.	12.7	6. Canada (Jewish)	21.8	6. Hungary	17.8

Vancouver	
1. Korea	37.5
2. Israel	29.5
3. Canada (Jewish)	24.2
4. Greece	23.9
5. Lebanon	23.2
6. USSR (German)	22.7

Maritime CMAs – St. John's, Saint John, Halifax.
Québec CMAs (n.i. Montreal) – Chicoutimi-Jonquière, Québec, Trois-Rivières, Sherbrooke.
Southern Ontario CMAs (n.i. Toronto) – Oshawa, Hamilton, St. Catharines-Niagara, Kitchener, London, Windsor.
Northern Ontario CMAs – Sudbury, Thunder Bay.
Prairie CMAs – Winnipeg, Regina, Saskatoon.
Western CMAs (n.i. Vancouver) – Calgary, Edmonton, Victoria.
SE Asia/other – East and Southeast Asia, n. i. China, Hong Kong, Vietnam, the Philippines and Korea.

Table 3: The Labour Force in the 15 Largest Metropolitan Regions in the USA –
The Most Entrepreneurial Immigrant Groups, 1990 (percent self-employed)

New York		Los Angeles		Chicago	
1. Greece	23.9	1. Greece	29.7	1. Korea	24.1
2. Iran	23.6	2. Korea	28.3	2. Israel	20.4
3. Korea	22.9	3. Turkey	26.6	3. Greece	19.6
4. Israel	21.3	4. Israel	24.8	4. Netherlands	19.0
5. Hungary	20.0	5. Hungary	24.1	5. S. Africa	(18.3)
6. Netherlands	19.4	6. Iran	23.0	6. Europe-other	17.7
San Francisco		**Philadelphia**		**Detroit**	
1. Greece	32.1	1. Greece	28.0	1. Czechoslov.	(37.0)
2. MidEast-other	27.0	2. S. Amer.-other	26.6	2. MidEast-other	25.6
3. Israel	23.8	3. Korea	24.3	3. Pakistan	25.3
4. Argentina	23.4	4. Cambodia	19.6	4. Greece	24.4
5. Czechoslovakia	22.9	5. MidEast-other	19.1	5. France	19.3
6. Yugoslavia	21.7	6. Pakistan	18.3	6. Italy	19.3
Boston		**Washington**		**Dallas**	
1. Greece	21.6	1. Korea	21.1	1. MidEast-other	21.9
2. Romania	(18.2)	2. Yugoslavia	(20.9)	2. Israel	(21.5)
3. Lebanon	17.6	3. Greece	20.3	3. USSR	19.8
4. Egypt	(16.5)	4. Italy	18.3	4. Poland	19.7
5. South Africa	16.2	5. Brazil	17.9	5. South Africa	(19.5)
6. Turkey	15.3	6. Iran	17.7	6. Pakistan	17.8
Houston		**Miami**		**Atlanta**	
1. Israel	(46.7)	1. Greece	35.2	1. Poland	(30.5)
2. Greece	29.9	2. China	32.5	2. Greece	(26.6)
3. Korea	23.6	3. South Africa	(30.0)	3. Korea	26.3
4. Hungary	(22.5)	4. Hungary	28.4	4. MidEast-other	(20.9)
5. Netherlands	(22.0)	5. Korea	26.2	5. China	20.1
6. China	21.1	6. Poland	25.8	6. USA (Am. Indian)	17.3
Cleveland		**Seattle**		**San Diego**	
1. Iran	(27.2)	1. MidEast-other	(21.1)	1. MidEast-other	29.8
2. Lebanon	22.6	2. Czechoslovakia	(21.1)	2. Italy	27.3
3. Israel	(20.7)	3. Hungary	(20.3)	3. Egypt	(26.6)
4. Greece	19.4	4. Poland	18.3	4. Thailand	(23.2)
5. China	17.6	5. Europe-other	(17.3)	5. Netherlands	23.1
6. Vietnam	(17.5)	6. China	16.8	6. Korea	23.0

Source: 1990 Census Public Use Microdata 5% Sample. (*A figure in parenthesis indicates a small sample.*)
New York – New York/Northern New Jersey/Long Island CMSA; Los Angeles – Los Angeles/Anaheim/ Riverside CMSA; Chicago – Chicago/Gary/Lake County CMSA; San Francisco – San Francisco/ Oakland/San Jose CMSA; Philadelphia – Philadelphia/Wilmington/Trenton CMSA; Detroit – Detroit/ Ann Arbor CMSA; Boston – Boston/Lawrence/Salem CMSA; Washington – Washington MSA; Dallas – Dallas/Fort Worth CMSA; Houston – Houston/Galveston/Brazoria CMSA; Miami – Miami/Fort Lauderdale CMSA; Atlanta – Atlanta MSA; Cleveland – Cleveland/Akron/Lorain CMSA; Seattle – Seattle/Tacoma CMSA; San Diego – San Diego MSA; Minneapolis – Minneapolis/St. Paul MSA.

Immigrant and Ethnic Entrepreneurs in Canadian and American
Metropolitan Areas – A Comparative Perspective

Table 4: The Labour Force in Canadian and American Metropolitan Areas
– The Most Entrepreneurial Immigrant/Ethnic Groups in White-Collar Industries, 1990/1 (percent self-employed in white-collar industries of the total labour-force of the specific group in the specific metropolitan area)

CANADA – 1991

Maritime		Québec		Montreal		Ottawa-Hull	
1. Ireland	21.5	1. Haiti	8.6	1. Poland (Jewish)	17.1	1. Canada (Ukr.)	11.0
2. Canada (Jewish)	15.3	2. Portugal	7.4	2. Canada(Jewish)	11.3	2. S. Africa	10.8
3. Greece	14.0	3. S. America	6.3	3. Czech.	9.9	3. Canada (Jewish)	10.5
4. Hong Kong	12.0	4. France	6.1	4. Hungary	9.0	4. USSR	9.9

Toronto		S. Ontario		N. Ontario		Prairie	
1. Poland (Jewish)	16.2	1. USSR (Jewish)	13.5	1. USSR	17.0	1. Poland (Jewish)	17.4
2. Canada (Jewish)	16.1	2. USA (Jewish)	13.2	2. India	9.8	2. Canada (Jewish)	13.2
3. USA (Jewish)	11.6	3. Canada (Jewish)	12.9	3. Netherlands	7.0	3. USSR (Jewish)	12.7
4. Poland(German)	10.1	4. Scandinavia	8.0	4. China	6.9	4. USA (Jewish)	12.0

Western		Vancouver	
1. Canada (Jewish)	13.3	1. Canada (Jewish)	19.1
2. USA (Jewish)	12.1	2. Israel	16.2
3. USSR (Ukrain.)	9.6	3. USA (Jewish)	13.3
4. South Africa	9.0	4. USSR (Jewish)	9.4

USA – 1990

New York		Los Angeles		Chicago		San Francisco	
1. So.Africa	11.1	1. Haiti	12.2	1. Panama	14.5	1. Czechoslov.	13.1
2. Netherlands	9.7	2. Hungary	9.6	2. Australia	10.2	2. Argentina	11.2
3. Indonesia	9.5	3. Scandinavia	8.5	3. Thailand	8.5	3. USA (Cuban)	10.5
4. USA (Japan.)	8.1	4. Egypt	8.4	4. France	8.0	4. Scandinavia	10.0
5. France	7.1	5. Czechoslovak	7.6	5. Argentina	7.8	5. Brazil	9.9
		6. Argentina	7.6				

Philadelphia		Detroit		Boston		Washington	
1. Israel	11.6	1. USSR	7.8	1. S.America-other	8.4	1. USA (Cuban)	13.2
2. Pakistan	9.5	2. France	7.6	2. Scandinavia	7.9	2. Spain	9.3
3. Iran	8.3	3. India	5.6	3. Ger.&Aust.	6.5	3. Czechoslov.	9.0
4. Philippines	7.6			4. Chile	6.5	4. Hong Kong	8.8
5. France	7.5					5. Ireland	8.7

Dallas		Houston		Miami		Atlanta	
1. USSR	8.3	1. Scandinavia	10.0	1. Hungary	8.6	1. UK	9.4
2. Peru	7.1	2. China	8.8	2. USSR	8.6	2. USA outl.ar.	8.4
3. Columbia	6.8	3. Italy	8.6	3. Africa-other	8.5	3. Panama	8.1
4. Pakistan	6.6	4. Argentina	8.6	4. Portugal	8.1	4. Canada	7.2
5. Poland	6.5	5. USSR	8.4	5. Thailand	8.0		

Cleveland		Seattle		San Diego		Minneapolis	
1. Philippines	12.0	1. Poland	13.3	1. Poland	9.9	1. Japan	10.1
2. India	9.1	2. USSR	8.7	2. Canada	8.7	2. Scandinavia	6.6
3. Czechoslov.	5.8	3. UK	6.7	3. Puerto Rico	8.0	3. USSR	6.3
		4. Australia	6.5	4. India	7.8		

White-collar industries: In Canada – business services, public services, professional services and some personal services. In the USA – business services, professional services, public administration.

141

Table 5: The Labour Force in Canadian and American Metropolitan Areas – the Most Entrepreneurial Immigrant/Ethnic Groups in Distribution Industries,1990/1 (percent self-employed in distribution of the total labour-force of the specific group in the specific metropolitan area).

CANADA – 1991

Maritime		Québec		Montreal		Ottawa-Hull	
1. Lebanon	27.3	1. Greece	32.5	1. Korea	27.8	1. Lebanon	18.0
2. Greece	20.9	2. Lebanon	12.0	2. Poland (Jewish)	17.6	2. Greece	12.8
3. Hong Kong	20.0	3. Italy	11.1	3. Greece	10.9	3. Korea	8.5
4. China	15.6	4. SE Asia-other	9.6	4. USSR (Ukra.)	9.5	4. China	6.6

Toronto		S. Ontario		N. Ontario		Prairie	
1. Korea	28.4	1. Korea	45.3	1. China	27.6	1. Korea	26.3
2. Poland (Jewish)	11.4	2. Greece	17.5	2. Ger. & Aus.	5.8	2. Greece	25.3
3. Greece	10.1	3. Israel	16.9			3. China	12.6
4. Israel	9.2	4. China	8.9			4. India	7.7

Western		Vancouver	
1. Greece	22.6	1. Korea	27.2
2. Korea	18.3	2. Lebanon	14.4
3. Lebanon	10.7	3. Greece	11.8
4. China	9.1	4. Israel	8.6

USA – 1990

New York		Los Angeles		Chicago		San Francisco	
1. Korea	17.6	1. Greece	20.2	1. Korea	19.6	1. Mid.East-other	19.8
2. Greece	13.2	2. Korea	18.9	2. Greece	14.3	2. Greece	18.5
3. Iran	13.0	3. Turkey	16.3	3. Israel	13.0	3. Korea	14.5
4. Israel	12.0	4. Lebanon	12.9	4. Pakistan	9.8	4. Israel	12.8
5. Turkey	11.1	5. MidEast-other	12.4	5. Thailand	8.7	5. Thailand	12.6
6. MidEast-other	10.5	6. Iran	12.0	6. Netherlands	8.6	6. Egypt	9.1
7. Lebanon	10.0						

Philadelphia		Detroit		Boston		Washington	
1. Greece	19.0	1. MidEast-other	21.2	1. Greece	16.3	1. Korea	16.8
2. Korea	18.7	2. Greece	14.6	2. Lebanon	9.4	2. Israel	10.4
3. Cambodia	16.8	3. Pakistan	14.1	3. Turkey	8.0	3. Pakistan	10.3
4.China	14.7	4. Korea	13.4	4. Iran	7.8	4. Greece	10.1
5. MidEast-other	13.2	5. Hungary	11.0			5. Iran	9.6
6. Taiwan	11.5	6. Italy	9.9				

Dallas		Houston		Miami		Atlanta	
1. MidEast-other	13.7	1. Greece	19.2	1. China	23.2	1. Korea	18.6
2. Korea	9.8	2. Korea	18.6	2. Greece	22.7	2. China	16.7
3. Iran	9.0	3. China	11.3	3. Korea	19.4	3. Taiwan	14.3
4. China	8.8	4. Hong Kong	11.2	4. MidEast-other	15.7	4. Iran	10.9
				5. Europe-other	14.7		
				6. Thailand	14.6		
				7. Poland	13.1		

Cleveland		Seattle		San Diego		Minneapolis	
1. Lebanon	15.0	1. Korea	13.6	1. MidEast-other	24.8	1. China	10.7
2. Greece	14.4	2. China	12.4	2. Korea	15.8	2. Cambodia	6.4
3. China	12.2			3. Italy	15.1		
4. Korea	10.9			4. Taiwan	14.5		
5. MidEast-other	10.3						

Distribution industries: In Canada – wholesale, retail, food and beverage services, transportation, communication, etc. In the USA – wholesale, retail, eating and drinking places, repair services, personal services, transportation, etc.

Table 6: The Labour Force in Canadian and American Metropolitan Areas –
Percent Self-employed by Selected Countries of Birth, 1990/1.

	Total labour	Foreign born	Korea	Greece	China	Israel	Lebanon	Canada	USA
Canada – 1991									
Maritimes	5.8	12.8	..	39.5	15.6	..	37.1	5.3	10.3
Québec	6.8	10.9	..	32.5	8.2	..	16.0	6.7	7.5
Montreal	8.4	11.3	32.8	18.4	11.7	16.5	15.0	7.7	11.1
Ottawa-Hull	7.6	10.9	14.9	24.2	8.4	10.7	23.2	6.9	10.0
Toronto	9.1	9.8	37.1	18.9	11.4	22.1	15.5	8.5	12.9
S. Ontario	7.1	9.7	51.8	22.5	14.7	25.4	9.7	6.3	8.7
N. Ontario	6.1	11.2	..	..	31.0	..	..	5.5	6.3
Prairies	7.9	9.3	33.3	31.7	16.6	..	..	7.6	8.3
Western	9.3	11.4	22.7	28.8	13.1	15.4	15.9	8.7	13.1
Vancouver	10.6	12.7	37.5	23.9	13.9	29.5	23.2	9.5	12.2
USA – 1990									
New York	8.6	9.0	22.9	23.9	9.4	21.3	15.0	12.0	8.5
Los Angeles	10.1	9.8	28.3	29.7	16.5	24.8	21.2	15.6	10.2
Chicago	7.0	7.8	24.1	19.6	10.8	20.4	17.3	10.1	6.9
San Francisco	10.1	9.4	20.3	32.1	11.1	23.8	13.6	13.8	10.4
Philadelphia	7.3	10.3	24.3	28.0	17.1	18.1	14.0	10.8	7.1
Detroit	6.5	11.6	18.6	24.4	8.7	5.3	12.8	10.9	6.1
Boston	8.1	7.8	8.5	21.6	5.4	4.9	17.6	9.9	8.2
Washington	7.5	9.0	21.1	20.3	6.8	12.6	16.2	7.2	7.2
Dallas	8.6	7.6	14.9	..	10.6	21.5	5.3	11.9	8.7
Houston	8.6	9.0	23.6	29.9	21.1	46.7	10.4	14.5	8.5
Miami	11.1	12.0	26.2	35.2	32.5	22.6	24.5	18.0	10.5
Atlanta	8.5	11.0	26.3	26.6	20.1	..	..	14.0	8.3
Cleveland	6.7	10.4	15.8	19.4	17.6	20.7	22.6	12.4	6.5
Seattle	9.1	9.9	16.5	14.2	16.8	..	..	13.6	9.0
San Diego	10.1	9.9	23.0	22.3	11.8	17.3	10.0	18.6	10.1
Minneapolis	8.1	8.0	0.6	..	14.2	..	..	11.3	8.1

.. A small sample.

143

Table 7: Immigrant/Ethnic Groups in Canadian and American Metropolitan Areas – Pearson Correlation Coefficients of Rates of Self-employment of the Immigrant/Ethnic Group and the Total Rates of Self-employment in the Metropolitan Area, 1990/1.

CANADA	N	R	USA	N	R
Highest positive correlations					
Mexico & Central America	14	0.79	Greece	12	0.82
Austria & Germany	21	0.76	Dominican Republic	7	0.81
USA	23	0.73	UK	16	0.80
United Kingdom	22	0.69	Canada	16	0.79
Canada (French m. tongue)	25	0.64	Hungary	10	0.79
Haiti	4	0.63	Costa Rica	7	0.75
Hungary	15	0.60	Chile	7	0.73
USSR	12	0.58	Vietnam	15	0.71
Canada (Portuguese m. tongue)	10	0.55	Scandinavia	14	0.70
Portugal	15	0.53	USA (Blacks)	16	0.70
Jamaica	13	0.51	USA (Japanese)	12	0.69
Czechoslovakia	12	0.43	Turkey	8	0.69
Poland	20	0.43	Taiwan	15	0.69
Guyana	11	0.42	Peru	12	0.66
Scandinavia	17	0.41	Argentina	12	0.66
			USA (Puerto Ricans)	15	0.65
			Germany & Austria	16	0.63
			Jamaica	14	0.62
			Mexico	15	0.61
			USSR	16	0.60
			Czechoslovakia	11	0.60
Lowest and negative correlations					
Hong Kong	15	..	USA (Filipino)	10	..
Lebanon	10	..	Lebanon	13	..
Israel	6	-0.10	Trinidad and Tobago	7	..
India	18	-0.14	USA (Mexicans)	16	..
China	19	-0.17	Cuba	13	..
Greece	14	-0.18	Panama	13	-0.10
Canada (Jewish ethnic origin)	11	-0.18	Cambodia	13	-0.10
Vietnam	16	-0.19	USA (Cubans)	11	-0.26
Korea	10	-0.28	Philippines	16	-0.51
			Pakistan	12	-0.61

.. – R < /0.10/

N – number of metropolitan areas included in the calculations.

Marilyn J. Rose

Translating/Transliterating the Ethnic: Florence Livesay's *Songs of Ukraina* and Keibo Oiwa's *Stone Voices*

Abstract

Translative acts are incorrigibly local. They arise from and represent responses to their own political moment and as such are always deeply ideological. In the case of the translation of minority or ethnic writing, careful consideration of the "politics of translation" is particularly important, for the power relations between the less privileged language of origin and the culturally dominant language of translation will inevitably be unequal, and that power differential will have to be carefully negotiated by the translator/interpreter. Indeed, comparing the cases of an early twentieth-century "translation" of ethnic material and a recent translation of ethnic voices suggests that even in our own time the translation of ethnic texts remains a slippery business which inevitably verges on cultural imperialism – in the sense of bowing to hegemonic interests – whatever its good intentions.

Résumé

Les actes traductionnels sont incorrigiblement locaux. Ils constituent des réactions à leur propre moment politique – dont ils émanent – et, à ce titre, sont toujours profondément idéologiques. Dans le cas de la traduction de textes originant de groupes minoritaires ou ethniques, il est particulièrement important de bien considérer la « politique de la traduction », car les rapports de pouvoir entre la langue de départ moins privilégiée et la langue d'arrivée culturellement dominante seront inévitablement inégaux, et cette différence de pouvoir devra être traitée avec le plus grand soin par le traducteur/interprète. En effet, si l'on compare une « traduction » datant du début du siècle et une traduction récente de textes « ethniques », on constate que, même à notre époque et malgré les meilleures intentions, la traduction de textes « ethniques » demeure une entreprise délicate qui frôle inévitablement l'impérialisme culturel – au sens d'une soumission à des intérêts hégémoniques.

Few would argue that translation is approximate at best, given the essentially slippery nature of language itself. If, as contemporary literary theory maintains, there can be no certain or "pure" correspondence between words and things signified within a single language, how can one aspire to unequivocal transferrals of meaning across linguistic frontiers? The natural limitations of language in and of themselves proscribe the ideal – the dream of meaning being carried readily and precisely from text to text through translative acts.

Quite apart from linguistic or *intrinsic* concerns, however, there is another, *extrinsic* impediment to the idea of pure or unfettered translation, and that is the cultural or contextual slippage which also invariably accrues to translative acts: the way in which the construction and reception of translations will tend to reflect the political or ideological cognates of the translative moment. As writing is "translated," in other words, it is also "transliterated," which is to say shifted from one cultural "alphabet" or "register" to another. It is trans*posed* or dis*placed*, as it is literally moved from one value-laden context, that of its original production and reception, to another whose values and concerns will inevitably be different.

Moreover, recognition of the *locality* of translative acts – the way that translations arise from and respond to their own political moment and hence are intensely culturally nuanced – is especially important when it comes to the translation of ethnic voices. Writing which emerges from a culturally discrete immigrant community whose first language is "unofficial" will inevitably be read and reconstructed ideologically when transliterated or shifted into the discourse of a dominant linguistic group. In fact, because of the power differential between the separate cultural contexts represented by the language of origin and the language of translation, a skewing of ethnic translations towards the "politics of the powerful" which surround them (which is to say towards the position of the translator and his or her relationship to the cultural apparatus that is the publishing world) is virtually inevitable – though less visible, perhaps, the closer its audience is to the political moment of the translative act.

I would hasten to add (lest all of this be taken as an attack on translation in light of its "contextual contaminations") that I do see the translation of ethnic writing as a good thing – indeed as an inevitably radical, culturally disruptive political act which serves to insert into the mainstream other voices and other experiences which, once heard, cannot be ignored. When formerly quiescent immigrant or ethnic voices are translated into a "master tongue," into the language of hegemony at a particular point in time, "Other" voices are called into being so far as the mainstream is concerned. Such voices may then compel attention and

invite redress, demanding that the "centre" yield to the marginal, at least to the extent of seeing and acknowledging its own self-"centredness" with respect to this particular hithertofore-silenced ethnic community. And this is good – so long as the political freight which attaches itself to the processes of construction and reception with respect to ethnic translations is perceived and acknowledged.

As cases in point, I will consider two historically distanced translations, Florence Livesay's *Songs of Ukraina* (1916) and Keibo Oiwa's *Stone Voices: Wartime Writings of Japanese Canadian Issei* (1991) in light of the contextual pressures which can be seen to affect both their construal of the ethnic material which they translate into English and their subsequent reception as translated texts. The former, so clearly freighted with ideas dismissable as unsophisticated and out-of-date, is rather easy to situate – and perhaps to reject as outworn and propagandistic at conception and in reception. The latter, however, also raises serious questions about translation as cultural practice, despite its currency and greater sophistication, for it too embodies and evinces cultural desire in its design and its reception, though no one, to date, has noted such properties in this text.

Songs of Ukraina,[1] a collection of Ukrainian folk songs and poems, is clearly problematic as a "translation." The book was published in 1916 under the name of, and solely attributed to, its English-Canadian "translator," Florence Randal Livesay – but quite corruptly so, as Livesay herself could neither speak nor read the Ukrainian language at the time of its publication.[2] Rather, according to Dorothy Livesay, Florence's daughter, her mother, having developed an interest in Ukrainian folk music, had been referred to the Reverend Paul Crath, a Ukrainian émigré and Baptist minister who was also a writer and self-styled linguist. Crath began to come to the house weekly, providing Florence Livesay with crude translations in his "stumbling English" which Florence set herself to reworking.[3] Nor was the resulting translation unflawed in terms of the precision of its language or the transferral of meaning, according to later scholars,[4] but this is not surprising as accuracy was not a primary goal in preparing the text.

Instead, it becomes clear from the reception of *Songs of Ukraina* that Livesay was expected to fine-tune, indeed to substantially alter, her primary material, a rough-hewn peasant poetry presumed to be in need of the touch of an accomplished "poetess," a "pioneer social editress" like "Mrs. Livesay."[5] Hence Florence Livesay's delicacy, as a lady poet of refined sensibility whose poetic touch could negotiate an "alien" vision[6] in appropriate language, was everywhere insisted upon. In responding to *Songs of Ukraina*, John Garvin praised Livesay's practiced artistic touch,[7] the New York *Review of Reviews* her ability to produce "distinct creations in Eng-

lish verse,"[8] and J.D. Logan and D.G. French her skilful "turning of phrase and imagery" as well as "a grace and music which are all her own."[9]

Indeed her latitude in translating (which is to say, her inaccuracy) was actually seen as desirable: Logan and French declared that Livesay's poems were not mere translations, but had "such original elements of form and matter" as to be "no more translations in the ordinary meaning than is Fitzgerald's *Rubaiyat*."[10] The fact that the songs were "free translations," to quote Carole Gerson,[11] meant they could be praised as "really interpretive throughout"[12] – an indication of Livesay's reviewers' sense of the translations' superiority over the presumed roughness and inelegance of the folk-verse originals.

In fact, in passing such ore through the sieve of English-Canadian poetic convention – so as to extract, smooth, polish, buff and set some unexpected gems into the crown of English literature on the Canadian prairies – Livesay was applauded as a kind of translative Lady Bountiful. Her work was configured as inadvertent and altruistic in its genesis, as Livesay, a sweet, motherly woman, was seen to have stumbled upon her project accidentally when her heart was moved by the plaintive songs of her Ukrainian-speaking domestic[s]. Livesay herself encouraged such portraiture, by recounting in interview after interview how

> Sometimes when Natalka [who variously appears as "Russalka"] was ironing I would get her to sing song after song. Many were interesting, but not in all could I find what I was seeking. And then with an inward exclamation of joy, I would suddenly see an old story glow out from the mist of the foreign setting.[13]

Clearly Livesay's womanly "sympathetic genius,"[14] her capacity to enter "into the spirit of" her servants,[15] her ability to identify with "the best of the Cossack spirit,"[16] and to do so purely, without "the self-seeking motives, the ill-defined ambitions" of others[17] who might have attempted the translations, legitimized for her contemporary readers her womanly interest in the texts of these disadvantaged "Others." Some went so far as to see her as a natural *medium* for the project, a kind of untutored (so far as Ukrainian language and culture were concerned) genius whose success in working with Ukrainian texts bordered on the uncanny. Contemporary reporters noted that "Mrs. Livesay" had "in some queer way or other... been able to render [her material] into English,"[18] that she had presented, as if intuitively, "directly to our vision the workings of a [Ukrainian] soul free from western trappings."[19]

In doing so, furthermore, Livesay was assumed to have given, not taken, from those whose culture she "translated." She was said to have made

through "her" collection a generous gift to Ukrainian "new Canadians" of "their folksongs in their adopted tongue,"[20] to have "given to [Ukrainian Canadians] again their claim to poetry,"[21] and to have given the "Canadianized grandchildren" of Ukrainian immigrants "the songs of their fathers."[22] A further sign of her beneficence, ironically, was the sense that in doing so Florence Livesay had given Ukrainian-Canadian immigrants something else, a "better understanding between Canadians of British birth and those born under other flags"[23] which would ultimately assist in "the problem of assimilating the foreign element" while at the same time "do[ing] justice to the strangers within our gates."[24]

At this point, with the mention of a needed assimilation to British ways on the part of non-British immigrants to Canada, the contours of a wider political context for *Songs of Ukraina* begin to emerge – the largely un-acknowledged (but often obliquely signalled) location of her project within the dominant Anglo-Saxon imperialist discourse of Livesay's time. Her reviewers routinely situated Livesay as a generous liberator of the silenced Ukrainian ethnic presence in Western Canada and assumed that she had given appropriate (not appropriating) utterance to an otherwise "speech-less" minority. The Saskatoon *Star*, for example, commended the fact that these "fine high-spirited and unusually intelligent people have found in Florence Randal Livesay... a sympathetic voice" to interpret "for them" their "fine sentiment that shall some day become a part of Canadian temperament."[25] The Chicago *Illustrated Post* congratulated Livesay on the way she had shaped the "artistic expression" of a small, oppressed nationality so as to create "an understanding of the likeness in difference."[26] And the *Guardian* hailed her "fine expression," but more especially her sacrifice in "not trim[ming] down at the expense of the native spirit the roughness inevitable to close translation" of the original verse.[27]

The patronizing tone of English-language reviewers, however, is less disturbing, perhaps, than the other side of the imperialist equation, which makes even clearer the inequity of the power relations between the translator's position and that of those whose language had been translated. Ukrainian-Canadian responses to Livesay's translations expressed their humble gratitude that someone of her delicacy and stature had spoken for them: *The Ukrainian Voice* (1917) commented, "WE can only thank Mrs. Livesay and express our sincere wishes for her success in further endeavors [sic] in this field";[28] *The Canadian Ruthenian* declared that her work would "serve to lead to the mutual acquaintance of Ukrainians and English and so will be productive of much good";[29] and George Andreyko of the Ukrainian National Committee declared to Florence Livesay that "the Ukrainian people certainly appreciate their great fortune in having one of your ability

sufficiently interested in Ukrainian literature to translate some of its choice bits into a language intelligible to the greatest and most powerful race on earth."[30]

The extravagance of the commentary, moreover, on both sides, gestures toward the presence of another cultural context with respect to Livesay's translation, and that is a dawning collective recognition by 1916 of the long-standing political and cultural abuse this particular ethnic population had suffered, especially in the Canadian West, between 1898 and 1914. Canada had by then "welcomed" at least two hundred thousand Ukrainians, generally "the poorest and the least educated peasants from the western Ukrainian regions, Galician and Bukovina," by (virtually always) assigning them "second-rate farms on marginal land" or "the lowest paid jobs in railroad building and forest and bush labour."[31] And Anglo-Canadians had justified that assignment, in effect, by configuring these "Ruthvenian"/ "Roumanian"/"Austro-Hungarian"/"Bohemian"/"Polish"/"Ukrainian" immigrants (for these were fairly interchangeable descriptors in the mouths of Western Canadians) as "thundering herds of half-civilized Galicians."[32] What triggered a kind of paradigm shift in English-Canadian thinking about Ukrainian Canadians by 1916, however, was less a matter of collective guilt or pricked conscience, than the shifting of certain political cognates beyond Canada – notably the development of alliances which would culminate during World War I in a reconstitution of the figure of the "Slav" in the consciousness of the Anglo-Western Allies.

The alliances of World War I would lead Britain, Canada and the United States to a kind of pan-English embrace of their new ally, Russia – one tendril of which would be a romanticization of the idea of the "Cossack" warrior. Ukrainians would be cast in this new diorama as "Little Russians" (much to their chagrin), as "a picturesque and attractive people with a glorious tradition" honed by "centuries of war,"[33] to quote one of Livesay's observers. In this context, Florence Livesay would be praised for her translations' success in revealing Ukrainians as noble and heroic, and as taking a non-servile "delight in fighting for fighting's sake."[34]

At this point, then, Livesay's translations can be seen to have been recruited into the discourse of nationalism that surrounds World War I, and made to testify to the admirably bellicose spirit of the Ukrainian people, now configured as "the most devoted and most efficient fighters beneath the banner of the czar."[35] That such readings of the translations are profoundly misleading – much of the emphasis in the poems themselves being on the tragic inability of the Ukrainian people from the seventeenth through the nineteenth centuries to defend their own nation against the encroaching powers of other Eastern Europeans (the Austrians, the Poles, but most of

all the Russians) – is singularly unproblematic to Livesay's reviewers, even when the Ukrainian-Canadian press registers its objections as firmly as it dares: in 1916, the *Ukrainian Voice* protests "the advertisement on the book's cover" where it is implied that from these Ukrainian songs one can more clearly understand the "Soul" of the Russian nation;[36] by 1917, it remonstrates more openly, reminding English readers that "the present Russian government *persecuted* Ukrainians and their Songs – Russians do not consider these their own" and readers should recall that "at present Ukraine is *under* the Russians."[37]

Clearly, then, the historically remote example of Florence Livesay's *Songs of Ukraina* demonstrates the way in which translation, like all other speech acts, is invariably conditioned by its complex relation to what Barbara Herrnstein Smith calls the "contingencies of value"[38] that surround it as it is produced and received within a particular cultural nexus. The reasons for a translation's being called into being, as well as the social apparatus through which translations are publicized and legitimized – prefaces, routine book reviews, book tour coverage, published interviews, not to mention scholarly responses – will tend to embody, should one wish to interrogate them, the specific principles of social and political utility which have governed the production and reception of a particular translative (which is to say "transliterative") act at a particular time.

But are such factors as evident in translations of one's own time, of one's own political moment? Or can "appropriation of voice" be avoided in translation, if and when present-day proprieties are more clearly observed than they were in the case of Livesay's *Songs of Ukraina*?

At this point I wish to turn to a recently published book, Keibo Oiwa's *Stone Voices* (1991). This text avoids many of Livesay's "sins," of course. Oiwa is, to begin with, a native Japanese who was completing a dissertation (on the old Jewish community in Montreal) at Cornell when this project was suggested to him.[39] He has chosen to translate and publish what he sees as "underground" narratives,[40] a "selection of some of the finest written accounts" of the Issei, or first-generation Japanese immigrants to North America.[41] He signals tolerance with respect to any literary deficiencies in the diaries and memoirs he excerpts, any potential sense that they are not "literary" enough, by insisting that the translated narratives were originally constructed as "private" documents, "written with almost no intention of being read by more than a few individuals."[42] He himself will not tinker a great deal with the "simple and ordinary" expression to be found in these documents, for each is written in a "clear yet passionate language" which he celebrates as honest, and, in its honesty, self-vindicating.[43]

Indeed, when it comes to the haiku which are found in one of the ac-

counts he translates, Oiwa refuses to bow to English conventions and re-
produce these in the 17-syllable format *we* expect of all haiku (he refuses
to push them through the sieve of English poetic convention, in other words),
but instead lets the syllables, and their numbers per line, fall where they
may – as in the case of three "haiku" from Kauru Ikeda's "Slocan Diary":

> Spring mud
> Into the wheel tracks
> Cigarette thrown;
>
> Spring mud
> Legs apart
> Edging side to side;
>
> Tail wagging
> Dog leaps
> Into spring mud.[44]

Here, rather than meeting an "Anglo" expectation of 17 syllables per three
lines, with syllabic divisions of 5, 7, and 5 syllables respectively, the haiku
scan as $2 + 5 + 4$ (=11) syllables), $2 + 3 + 5$ (=10) syllables and $3 + 2 + 4$
(=9) syllables respectively when translated into English. It simply does not
matter to Oiwa whether mainstream readerly expectations regarding literary conventions are met.

Response to Oiwa's text has been slight but untroubling. Contemporary reviews are very favourable in fact, suggesting the acceptability of
Oiwa's critical position and basic editorial decisions in our own time. Indeed, his reviewers tend to respond to the book as though its critical/political
apparatus were invisible – as though, in other words, the translations exist
as a *direct* release into speech of silenced Japanese-Canadian wartime voices.
Elaine Kalman Naves, for example, characterizes *Stone Voices*, a translation of four wartime narratives, as "a riveting work that palpates the core of
pain at the centre of Japanese-Canadian history."[45] Eve Drobot commends
Oiwa's "valuable contribution of source material to the literature of Canada's dark period of banishment and internal exile."[46] Pat Barclay refers to
the book as a "testament to the infinite variety and resilience of human
nature" that should be "required reading" not only for Japanese Canadians,
but for "the rest of us, too."[47] What is intriguing about the language of the
reviews, which is to say of the book's reception (in words like "palpates,"
"source material," "testament"), is the apparent assumption that there has
been little or no *mediation* of the written-in-Japanese experience, the Japa-

nese-Canadian voices themselves, on Oiwa's or the text's part, in the process of their transposition into English.

Yet the book itself is a highly political construct, both in its origins and sponsorship and in its actual structure or construction. The "Acknowledgements" record that the text is "a by-product of a larger research project on Japanese-Canadian history which was started by the History Committee of the Japanese Cultural Centre of Montreal in 1982 and is still continuing."[48] The translation was funded by the Multiculturalism Programs branch of Multiculturalism and Citizenship Canada. Oiwa's "Introduction" begins with an eight-page history of Japanese-Canadian experience which is recounted in uncompromisingly partisan language: he speaks of "racial discrimination, both formal and informal," the "deep resentment" of "white society" against Japanese-Canadian citizens, "the humiliating imprisonment" of Japanese Canadians, the "destruction" of Nikkei society in Canada, and so on.[49]

I do not argue that Oiwa's language is inappropriate or untrue, only that it establishes a climate for the reception of the translations which follow, especially when the introduction is situated so as to follow the book's "Foreword," which was written by novelist Joy Kogawa. Kogawa's *Obasan* is widely known as a very successful fictional polemic which was directly instrumental in the achievement of redress for Japanese Canadians in 1988. In her forward to Oiwa, Kogawa's language is intensely emotional as she speaks of "the enemy country of my youth" and her personal "debilitation" by "Canadian racism" – as the background against which *she* received this text.[50] And Kogawa's and Oiwa's words are complemented by full-page black and white period photographs, one of which, for example, records a sign appended to Kelowna, B.C.'s "Kelowna Welcomes You" sign, the attachment reading "Coast Japs, you are not wanted. Get out."[51]

Outrage or affront is not, however, the central issue for Oiwa in designing this book. Rather, there is a larger agenda which we might argue marks the book as a "willing recruit" into the discourse of postmodern pluralism. We might note, for example, the sentence in his introduction where Oiwa refers to Canada's recent embrace of "new national principles of pluralism and multiculturalism," within which "ethnic and racial minorities" can begin to be "actively engaged in tackling discrimination and asserting their rights."[52] This is followed by a statement that the four narratives he has chosen to excerpt and translate were selected on the basis of their pluralism, their diversity and their embodiment of conflicting ideologies.[53] Indeed that is so, as the narratives represent very different Japanese-Canadian constituencies: Koichiro Miyazaki was a right-wing Japanese teacher and patriot who chose prison camp over loyalty to the Canadian nation;

Kensuke Kitagawa turned to traditional Japanese religion in response to his internment at Angler, Ontario; Kaoru Ikeda kept a diary reflecting her domestic life in a camp at Slocan in the interior of British Columbia; Genshichi Takahashi, a life-long labour unionist and socialist, writes, among other things, of his own entrepreneurial successes. Two of the accounts construe Canadian Natives as the first and continuing victims of white Canadian racism and a key to understanding Canadian attitudes toward Japanese Canadians during World War II,[54] while two do not make this connection. The accounts vary in the degree of their hostility toward white Canada and the degree to which they perceive Canada itself as a racist monolith.

Oiwa's main philosophical concern, then, is with a by-product of the "assimilationism" he sees as having been the "dominant ideology" in Canada vis-a-vis Japanese Canadians since the war.[55] Not only were the thriving Powell Street enclave and other West Coast clusters of Japanese Canadians permanently decimated during the internment years, but afterwards its residents were, he says, encouraged to "scatter" themselves throughout the country and keep a "low profile" through silence and cultivated invisibility.[56] An offshoot of such cultural repression, he believes, has been the development of a conveniently monolithic myth about Japanese Canadians on the part of non-Japanese Canadians – a dismissive denial of the essentially "pluralistic nature of Nikkei culture," of the "colourful mosaic of ideologies" which animated and still animates that community.[57] His book is an attempt to demonstrate the existence of such pluralism within the Japanese-Canadian community prior to and during World War II.

Oiwa ultimately locates his work within an even larger context, using an anthropological model (he cites Barbara Myerhoff in particular) which suggests that humankind in general is a kind of *Homo narrans*, an essentially/irresistibly self-narrating species.[58] In *Stone Voices* Oiwa wishes to let individual Issei tell individualistic stories about themselves, while his own record, a collection of those voices, will be distinguished by its multivocality, its varied representationalism. His argument is for history as comprised of histor*ies*, a common enough theme in our time, and one which is especially relevant to acts of ethnic "recovery," such as this text represents. Yet it might be argued that Oiwa, despite his efforts to the contrary, has himself fallen into meta-narrativity or essentialism in this book (that is, he has produced history in other words, rather than histories) through a particular textual apparatus, the polemical framing of the individual translations that his own introductory words, in combination with Kogawa's, represent.

In closing, I wish to reiterate that I do not deny the justice of Keibo Oiwa's position or the intensity of his vision in *Stone Voices*, nor do I mean to attack Florence Livesay for participating in the larger cultural narratives

of *her* own time through her own "act of recovery," *Songs of Ukraina.* The sabotage of sincere translations, each partaking of the political values of its particular historical moment, has not been my agenda in undertaking this study. Rather, my motive has simply been to interrogate translation as a kind of *performance* (a word that suggests interplay between actor, interpretive act and audience) – which is to portray it as an intensely political act bearing traces always of the conflicted material conditions out of which it is produced and within which it is received. We do not "translate" so much as we "transliterate," even today, and hence it is useful to look at the cultural "key" or "register" into which and through which ethnic material is being dispersed into the larger culture through commendable, but never entirely innocent or transparent, translative acts.

Notes

Research for this paper has been funded in part by a grant from the Social Sciences and Humanities Federation of Canada (SSHRC).

1. Florence Randal Livesay (trans.), *Songs of Ukraina, with Ruthenian Poems* (London: J.M. Dent; New York: E.P. Dutton, 1916).
2. That Florence Livesay's inability to speak or understand Ukrainian was widely known at the time of her "translation" is made clear in a number of scrapbook clippings from contemporary newspapers and magazines, which deal with the reception of *Songs of Ukraina* 1914-1918, and which are located in the Province of Manitoba Archives [PMA] (Florence Randal Livesay Collection), box P60, file 13.
3. Preface to Florence Randal Livesay (trans.), *Down Singing Centuries: Folk Literature of the Ukraine*, edited by Louisa Loeb and Dorothy Livesay (Winnipeg: Hyperion, 1981), 11.
4. Louisa Loeb, untitled typescript of thesis prepared for St. John's College, University of Manitoba (1975), 243, located in the Livesay Collection, PMA, box P60, file 31.
5. PMA, Livesay Collection, box P60, file 13, undated clippings.
6. *Ibid.*, undated clipping.
7. John Garvin (ed.), *Canadian Poets* (Toronto: McClelland & Stewart, 1916), 371.
8. Quoted in "Florence Randal Livesay, Poet and Novelist," *Ontario Library Review*, 12 (1927), 41.
9. J. D. Logan and Donald G. French, *Highways of Canadian Literature: A Synoptic Introduction to the Literature History of Canada (English) from 1760-1924* (Toronto: McClelland & Stewart, 1924), 296.
10. *Ibid.*
11. Carole Gerson, "Florence Randal Livesay," *Dictionary of Literary Biography*, 92 (Detroit, New York, London: Gale Research Inc., 1990), 206.

12. PMA, Livesay Collection, box P60, file 13.
13. *Ibid.,* undated clipping, Sheila Rand.
14. *Ibid.,* undated clipping.
15. *Ibid.,* undated clipping.
16. *Ibid.,* undated clipping from the *Guardian.*
17. Loeb, 245.
18. PMA, Livesay Collection, box P60, file 13, undated clipping.
19. *Ibid.,* undated clipping.
20. *Ibid.,* undated clipping.
21. *Ibid.,* undated clipping.
22. *Ibid.,* telegram from Saskatoon, December 3, 1918.
23. *Ibid.,* clipping dated March 15, 1915.
24. *Ibid.,* undated clipping from the *Journal* (Edmonton).
25. *Ibid.,* undated clipping.
26. *Ibid.,* clipping dated October 12, 1917.
27. *Ibid.,* undated clipping.
28. Quoted in Loeb, 222.
29. *Ibid.,* 228.
30. *Ibid.,* 239.
31. Louisa Loeb, "Dorothy Randal Livesay," in Livesay, *Down Singing Centuries,* 180-181.
32. O.W. Garus and J.E. Rea, *The Ukrainians in Canada,* Canadian Ethnic Group Series 10 (Ottawa: Canadian Historical Association, 1985), 9.
33. PMA, Livesay Collection, box P60, file 13, undated clipping from the *Herald* (Calgary), 1916.
34. *Ibid.,* clipping from *The Nation,* November 25, 1916.
35. *Ibid.,* undated clipping.
36. Quoted in Loeb, 222.
37. *Ibid.* Italics mine.
38. Barbara Herrnstein Smith, "Contingencies of Value," in *Canons,* edited by Robert Von Hallberg (Chicago and London: University of Chicago Press, 1984).
39. Keibo Oiwa (ed.), *Stone Voices: Wartime Writings of Japanese Issei* (Montreal: Vehicule Press, 1991), 7.
40. *Ibid.,* 18
41. *Ibid.,* 15.
42. *Ibid.,* 19.
43. *Ibid.*
44. *Ibid.,* 135-37.
45. Elaine Kalman Naves, "Japanese Canadians 'break silence that cannot speak,'" *Montreal Gazette,* February 8, 1992, K3.
46. Eve Drobot, "*Stone Voices* reminds us not to forget," *Globe and Mail* (Toronto), February 22, 1992, C15.
47. Pat Barclay, Review of *Stone Voices, Books in Canada,* 21:5 (1992), 59.

48. Oiwa, 7.
49. *Ibid.*, 9-15.
50. *Ibid.*, 6.
51. *Ibid.*, 13.
52. *Ibid.*, 14.
53. *Ibid.*, 20-1.
54. *Ibid.*, 132, 194-197.
55. *Ibid.*, 21.
56. *Ibid.*, 14.
57. *Ibid.*, 21.
58. *Ibid.*, 22. The reference is to Barbara Meyerhoff, *Number Our Days* (New York, Simon and Schuster, 1980).

Angelika E. Sauer

Christian Charity, Government Policy and German Immigration to Canada and Australia, 1947 to 1952

Abstract

Not unlike displaced persons, the surplus population of postwar Germany constituted a convenient supply of migrants for countries such as Canada and Australia. By focusing on international and national policies, and on Lutheran church involvement in migrant work, this paper takes a closer look at the myth of a charitable, humanitarian gesture towards the masses of Europe. As the intense competition for refugee migrants not only between Canada and Australia, but also between different denominations and even synods within the Lutheran church suggests, they were an asset which added to the strength of the economy and the church alike. This calculation, as much as any spirit of humanitarianism or Christian brotherhood, motivated refugee work. However, the problems arising from the influx of newcomers had to be dealt with at the local level, where both the established community and the individual migrant had to come to terms with mutual expectations and disappointments.

Résumé

À l'instar des personnes déplacées, la population excédentaire de l'Allemagne d'après-guerre constituait un réservoir commode d'immigrants pour des pays comme le Canada et l'Australie. En se concentrant sur les politiques nationales et internationales et sur l'intervention de l'Église luthérienne auprès des immigrants, cet article examine de plus près le mythe des gestes charitables et humanitaires envers les masses européennes. Comme l'indique l'intense concurrence que se livraient non seulement le Canada et l'Australie, mais aussi les différentes confessions religieuses et même les différents synodes de l'Église luthérienne, ces immigrants étaient des atouts qui venaient renforcer l'économie et l'Église. Le travail auprès des réfugiés était motivé par ce calcul, tout autant que par l'esprit humanitaire ou la charité chrétienne. Cependant, les problèmes provoqués par l'influx de nouveaux arrivants devaient être réglés au niveau local, où la communauté établie et les immigrants devaient faire face à leurs attentes et à leurs déceptions réciproques.

In the immediate postwar years, the large pool of uprooted people in Europe constituted a convenient supply of migrants for receiving countries such as Canada and Australia.[1] Australia, for the first time in its history, encouraged the mass migration of people of non-British origin, starting in 1947. In Canada, the diversification of the population had begun about fifty years earlier but was significantly strengthened and rejuvenated in the 1940s and 1950s. In both Commonwealth countries, the ethnically diverse postwar immigration laid the foundation for today's multicultural societies. The political importance of ethnic pluralism in recent years, however, makes us forget that ethnicity was not the only category that described and classified the newcomers in the eyes of the host societies. To the public, they were "DPs", "reffos", or "Balts," regardless of their ethnic origin.[2] To governments and employers, they were labourers and statistics in demographic policies. And in many cases, the migrants' encounters with the host community, including their first contact with the receiving country, were determined not by their nationality but by their denominational affiliation.

Religion-based agencies were deeply involved not only in international refugee work but also in the immigration strategies of many receiving countries.[3] Like other non-governmental organizations, they were actively encouraged by both inter-governmental bodies and by national governments to participate in providing assistance to migrants.[4] Catholic and Protestant churches, with their extensive global infrastructure, were particularly well-suited to working with the inherently international process of migration.[5] Naturally, the interests of church and state did not always coincide. The receiving governments' emphasis on supplying the labour market at the expense of family ties, in particular, was irksome to cooperating churches.[6] In their effort to put a human face on migration, however, religious agencies continued to attempt to iron out injustices. They regularly underwrote passage loans to families and provided the kind of personalized counselling and advice that had no room in mass governmental schemes.[7]

This paper presents a case study of the Lutheran church's involvement in the migration of DPs and German refugees to Canada and Australia. It briefly outlines the international position as well as Canada's and Australia's national policies towards postwar refugees, emphasizing the lesser known case of the *Volksdeutsche* (ethnic Germans who were citizens of other European countries). Lutheran involvement in refugee work on the international, national, and local level is placed in this context. The paper will analyze the international interests of the Lutheran World Federation as well as the national agendas of the Australian and Canadian Lutheran churches. It will then be demonstrated that national differences disappeared in the challenges presented to local congregations by the large influx of migrants.

Overall, the essentially parallel nature of state and church interests will emerge, and the extent of expectations placed upon the individual migrant will become obvious.

*

The presence of not only one million non-German displaced persons (DPs) but up to 10 million ethnic German refugees on German soil was hardly a secret to the occupying powers. However, in a rare display of Western conciliation of Soviet and East European interests, every international refugee body, from United Nations (UNRRA) to the International Refugee Organization (IRO), followed the Soviet suggestion of excluding ethnic German refugees from its mandate and its definition of "displaced person."[8] In what has been aptly called "an international scramble for labour,"[9] the drying up of the steady supply of DPs, combined with an energetic publicity campaign by the new West German state and the hardening of the Cold War fronts, finally lead to an internationalization of the German refugee problem in the 1950s. Questions about their plight were raised by the U.S. Congress and the parliaments of Canada and Australia.[10] In late 1951, 21 non-communist countries met in Brussels and set up a new organization which would primarily look after the transportation of European migrants, including the Volksdeutsche "surplus population" of West Germany.[11]

The initial indifference to the plight of German refugees was partly the result of public ignorance as the issue of German refugees was shrouded in confusion. Many assumed that the DPs – arriving from Germany – were Germans, when in fact, for example, only 15 per cent of the people admitted to Australia between 1947 and 1953 who gave Germany as their last country of residence were German nationals.[12] Adding to public misperceptions was the fact that German was the lingua franca, the "Esperanto" of many DPs. So widespread was the use of the German language among them that governments routinely gave information and instructions in German.[13] The church as well did not hesitate to conduct services and Sunday school in the camps in German.[14] Therefore, the intricacies of official refugee classifications were often lost on the public.

By late 1951, most receiving countries including Canada and Australia were eager to secure a sizable number of German migrants. This had not always been the case. Both nations underwent a similar development in their attitudes towards European refugees in general, and German migrants in particular. Both countries became involved in the discussions about setting up a refugee organization in 1946 with the understanding that membership would carry a moral obligation to accept refugees. In July 1947, despite the resistance of several government departments,[15] the Australian Minister for

Immigration, Arthur Calwell, signed an agreement with the IRO promising the admission of a sizable number of European refugees.[16] It was high time as countries such as Canada had already begun screening immigrants and were, as Calwell explained to the Prime Minister Chifley, "keen competitors for best migrant types."[17]

The competition between the two countries for the "best type" lasted throughout the first postwar decade. The two countries had similar goals and watched each other's policies closely, drawing conclusions from success and failure alike. The publicity given by international organizations to Australia's programme was watched with envy in Ottawa.[18] In the fall of 1951, Canadian immigration officials in Karlsruhe predicted that the majority of German migrants would choose Australia unless the Canadian government reinstated the highly successful Assisted Passage Loan Scheme.[19] Less than two years later, the Australian migration office in Cologne worried about Australia's "prospects of getting a share of the best [East German refugee farmers]" in the face of American and Canadian competition.[20] And in 1957, the Australian government considered canceling its bilateral agreement with Germany because Canada, without such an agreement, was better able to gear annual migration to short-term economic needs.[21]

This agreement points to a major difference in the two countries' approaches to postwar immigration. Australia's policy was based on long-term demographic needs and security-oriented. The Australian government, unlike its Canadian counterpart, published long-term planning figures, which necessitated bilateral agreements with emigration countries. The Canadian government pursued short-term policies tied entirely to labour-market fluctuations. It refused to give an inch on the issue of domestic control of immigration, either by accepting international quotas or spelling out the long-term intake of certain nationalities.[22] Immigration was kept out of the public debate as much as possible; publicity was mostly given to family reunification schemes, which formed a substantial part of the immigrant intake in the postwar years. However, as part of a long tradition, non-governmental agencies were sometimes granted pre-selection privileges and transportation responsibilities. The Australian government, on the other hand, recruited mostly independent migrants and offered assisted passages as an incentive. It kept this process entirely in public hands and surrounded it with public debate and consensus-building to justify the high expenditure of taxpayers' money. Private agencies only entered the picture in the settlement and adjustment stage. In this two-tier model, the government brought the settlers to Australia and placed them in employment, while the community – the churches, Good Neighbour Councils and New Settlers' Leagues – was given the task of assimilating the newcomer.[23]

The Canadian emphasis on family unification allowed a coalition of church-based groups to become first an effective lobby and then an agent in the immigration of ethnic Germans. The Canadian Christian Council for the Resettlement of Refugees (CCCRR), formed at the initiative of the Canadian Lutheran World Relief in June 1947,[24] pointed out to the government that German Canadians were unable to sponsor their relatives because the International Refugee Organization refused to process even those ethnic Germans who were not citizens of Germany and therefore admissible under Canadian regulations. Fearful of losing voters but unwilling to be seen as publicly promoting and assisting *Volksdeutsche* emigration, the Mackenzie King government allowed the CCCRR to step in and care for pre-selection and transportation of German refugee migrants.[25] The organization brought 15,000 ethnic German immigrants by May 1951 and another 15,000 by May 1953.[26]

Canada had thus pioneered a mass immigration scheme for ethnic Germans. In the spring of 1950, the government changed its immigration regulations to admit ethnic Germans without relatives who had not been German citizens before the outbreak of the war. Old ethnic rankings and positive images of the German settler reemerged as the Cold War created new enemies. A poll in early 1950 showed that those Canadians who were in favour of immigration for the most part also approved of German immigrants.[27] Neither the government's lifting of the ban on German citizens in the fall of 1950 nor the subsequent allocation of a high percentage of the newly introduced assisted passages to Germans were much discussed in public.[28] Whether Canadians were largely unaware of what was happening or simply did not care remains open to speculation.[29]

Canadian actions, however, did not go unnoticed in Australia, where the recruitment of Germans was still under consideration.[30] In August 1950, the Minister for External Affairs warned the Immigration Minister that there would be an "early competition from other countries such as Canada which is paying according to my information special attention to Germany."[31] Australian visitors to Germany over the following months confirmed this assessment. One reported that the "Canadians are most active in encouraging German migration, and Canadian officials were enthusiastic in their comments on the German as a migrant."[32] Another visitor observed that Canadian instructions set no limit as to the number of Germans that could be recruited.[33] By mid-1951, even some veterans' organizations implored the government to act quickly, lest Canadian competition diminish Australia's chances to obtain good German settlers.[34]

Unlike the Canadians, the Australian government faced a steep uphill battle over the admission of Germans. There was a public outcry, with mass

protests in Sydney, Melbourne and Perth in early 1951 issuing dire warnings about young, hardened Nazis immigrating by the thousands.[35] The Australian Labor Party, by then in opposition, seized upon this sentiment and made it an election issue.[36] Howard Holt, the new Immigration Minister under the Menzies-Fadden coalition, stood his ground, convinced by his officials that German migrant applicants were "much superior in every way to the displaced persons presented to the selection teams recently." The government also valued Germans over Italians as they assimilated more easily; assisted German migration would counterbalance the number of unskilled Italians that came to Australia as sponsored relatives or friends.[37] After a painstaking consensus-building effort[38] and tough negotiations with the German government,[39] a German-Australian migration agreement was signed on August 29, 1952, at the Palais Schaumburg in Bonn.[40] As a result, over 24,000 Germans had immigrated by the end of 1953.[41]

*

It had been a long way from the defeat of Germany in May 1945, to this massive intake of Germans by Canada and Australia only a few years later. Along the way, church groups, feeling responsible for alleviating the human misery in Europe, tried to influence international organizations and national governments. Most religious organizations concentrated on the general refugee problem. One denomination, however, had special links with Germany, the land of its birth. In the nineteenth century, the Lutheran church had not been known to have been involved in migration. If anything, the strong links between church and state in Europe had led national Lutheran churches to dismiss those who left the fold. In the years leading up to World War II, however, the Lutheran leadership of North America and Europe tried to overcome the isolationist attitude and become a global institution. Although the war briefly arrested this development, the spirit was revived in the postwar period.

As an international body, the Lutheran church stood for reconciliation and humanitarian support for the individual refugee. The churches of the former Allied countries were the first to reach out to the German church, and the Lutheran World Federation (LWF), founded at the Lund Assembly in Sweden in 1947, did its best to mediate tensions between the German and the European exile churches. Protestant world institutions also played an important role in transforming the German refugee problem into an international issue.[42] The Lutheran World Federation and the World Council of Churches, in 1947 and 1948 respectively, condemned the international community's determination to distinguish between refugees on the basis of nationality or ethnic origin. "[T]he refusal to render aid in the case of hu-

man need on an unprecedented scale," the Lund Assembly resolved, was "neither comprehensible nor justifiable."[43]

In the following years, the world bodies encouraged their member churches to lobby national governments and international institutions on behalf of German refugees. Prominent church figures traveled to different countries to publicize the plight of German refugees and to plead for their admission. Pastor Martin Niemöller, for example, who had spent the war in a concentration camp, went to Australia in the southern spring of 1949, and did much to advance the case of German immigration in that country.[44] The Lutheran World Federation, moreover, set an example by establishing in June 1949, within its Refugee Department, a special branch for ethnic Germans, thereby doing "important pioneer work as an international agency in the field of Volksdeutsche settlement and welfare."[45] In order to find new homes for German refugees, the organization was prepared "to mobilize the churches of the world to share the responsibility for absorbing a portion of the Volksdeutsche outside the country."[46]

Undeniably, there was a strong humanitarian component to the Lutheran church's refugee programme, but its leaders wanted it to be understood that refugee work was also spiritual; it involved a proselytizing effort.[47] This agenda was visible in the Lutheran church's insistence on a clearly identifiable separate, confessional role in the refugee work of any ecumenical body.[48] The refugees, according to Stewart Herman, LWF Resettlement Division's executive director, were an important fragment of world Lutheranism; their loss to the church would spell serious injury. "The saving of souls is intimately involved in the process of resettling 'bodies'," he argued.[49] The LWF's task was not only to find new homes for these refugees but "to protect Lutheran interests, and even to channel the stream of emigration into areas where the refugees would not be lost to the church."[50] For this reason, church agencies sought to be present in every stage of the migrant's journey; from life in a camp in Germany to eventual integration into the native church of the receiving country. The image of a "strong chain of hands ... stretched from church to church around the world"[51] symbolized this all-encompassing interest.

To the national member churches of the LWF, the refugee resettlement programme constituted a unique opportunity for growth and was often pursued even at the expense of home mission work and in fierce competition with sister synods.[52] The high numbers of newcomers, however, were also a "real problem"; the "veritable flood" of Lutheran refugees was unparalleled in the history of both the Canadian and the Australian Lutheran churches and posed a challenge of considerable dimension.[53] Both faced "the same problems of vast distances and limited resources." In Australia,

the number of Lutherans increased by 30 per cent between 1947 and 1950 mostly through the influx of DPs; starting in 1951, German migrants became the main source of New Australian Lutherans.[54] Canadian Lutherans claimed an influx of 70,000 Lutheran DPs and German refugees up to 1952, who joined a homegrown population of about 125,000 active Lutheran church members.[55]

Among the newcomers, the Baltic Lutherans (Estonians and Latvians) tended to establish their own congregations. Those groups had formed churches-in-exile and developed camp congregations before their emigration.[56] They brought with them their own pastors from Europe and received financial support from the Lutheran World Federation until their congregations became self-supporting.[57] To the church leadership this was not the ideal solution; in principle it was expected that the traditional identification with a national ecclesiastical body should be transformed into a wider ecumenical appreciation as soon as possible and that refugee congregations should join the indigenous Lutheran church.[58] The difficult task was "to knit together people of various nationalities into one brotherhood with each other and with us."[59] Past experience indicated that it was detrimental to the interests and the image of the church to be divided into national groupings. Segregation along national lines could easily foster "a sterile nationalism"[60] and this, it seems, was particularly repugnant in the case of the Germans. As one Australian pastor wrote: "What might be excusable in the case of the Latvians and Estonians is inexcusable in the case of the Germans, after the unfortunate experiences of two world wars.... [T]hese congregations might become a hotbed of neo-Nazism."[61]

This is not to say that the church did not acknowledge the crucial importance of language. In fact, the Lund Assembly in 1947 had resolved that refugees had a right to spiritual support in their mother tongue[62] as the familiar words and symbols of the liturgy formed a bridge between old and new country. If the church leadership wanted refugees to join existing congregations, it also meant a tacit acknowledgment of the importance of introducing, at least temporarily, foreign-language services. This task, however, thoroughly taxed the resources of the local pastors and made them dependent on outside help.[63] A compromise was reached by offering services, not in several European languages but in German which most refugees seemed to understand. Many congregations in both Australia and Canada were unhappy about this development. There was a deep-seated fear among some Australian pastors of a repetition of the stigma of Germanism being attached to the Australian Lutheran church.[64] Two Lutheran churches in Lethbridge, Alberta, an article reported, had been struggling for years: "They had lived down the stigma of 'German church'! Suddenly they found them-

selves faced with new members and adherents who spoke only the language which most of the former members ... had almost forgotten."[65] A pastor from Calgary reported: "We had considered our congregation over the hump in as far as German work is concerned, but now we are really getting back into the German. Once more many of our congregations will be looked upon as a German Church."[66]

Image problems and the stretching of sparse resources partly offset the joy over a rapid growth in church membership. "The DP influx into the various cities and urban areas has increased our church membership in some cases as high as 20 per cent," rejoiced a pastor in Regina who added rather mournfully: "The DPs have brought German back again into congregations where it would soon have been a thing of the past."[67] Other pastors confirmed that growth was occurring mostly in the area of German-language services. In Calgary, a formerly English-speaking church was now "full for every German service. Once again the German attendance is higher than the English."[68] Reports from Edmonton pointed to a new congregation made up entirely of German-speaking refugees.[69] And a pastor in Winnipeg claimed that "50 per cent of my attendance in the German service is made up of DPs."[70]

Among Australian Lutheran churches the solution to the problem was simple: although there would be temporary concessions such as a German-language newsletter, the migrants were told "that learning to speak the language of their new country is important." Hence, congregations organized English-language classes and encouraged members to invite migrants into their homes for private tutoring.[71] In Canada, there was a more gradual approach to linguistic assimilation, although the continuing use of German had been a thorn in the flesh of the North American church leadership. Blaming ethnic and linguistic exclusivity for declining membership figures, American-born leaders stressed the importance of English for home mission work.[72] Now conciliatory Canadian voices contended that adaptation to a new language in church services was too much to be expected of the immigrants. Newcomers should merely be advised "that an effort to perpetuate the native language in the church beyond one generation will have a most adverse effect on the Lutheran Church in the future."[73] In any case, the assimilationists ought not to have been concerned. As a perceptive pastor noted, the newcomers were making a desperate effort to learn English as quickly as possible. Accordingly, the number of Canadian church services conducted in German dropped from 81 per cent in 1939 to 58 per cent in 1949 and 24.5 per cent in 1959.[74] Obviously, the influx of immigrants did not in the long run arrest the development of the Lutheran church into an English-speaking church.[75]

Despite the obvious challenge the immigrants posed to the Lutheran churches of Canada and Australia, the competition for their souls was intense. On one level, it was played out as an inter-synodical and inter-confessional fight for the allegiance of the newcomers. A pastor in Halifax complained that the Presbyterian and Baptist port workers were "poaching" by taking down names of Lutherans.[76] The Missouri Synod, on the other hand, protested that its congregations and churches were not included in a list given to Lutheran immigrants by the LWF workers in Bremen.[77]

In Australia, there was a similar split between the UELCA, belonging to the LWF, and ELCA, affiliated with the Missouri Synod and "[a]ttempts by the ELCA and other Protestant and secular organizations to share in the care of Lutheran immigrants were at first not welcomed by the UELCA." In Adelaide, a very active UELCA pastor accused other churches of "fishing in our preserves."[78] The two synods realized that unseemly competition complicated an already complex task: "'New Australian' problems are not always easy problems, and the fact that there are two Lutheran synods in Australia does not always make it easier to solve them." Starting in 1949, the migrant boards of both synods met annually to discuss overlapping and duplication of services. By early 1952, an agreement was reached to cooperate as much as possible and to alternate between pastors of the two synods in the reception of German migrant ships.[79]

All churches and other agencies understood the importance of a first impression for lasting attachment of the newcomer.[80] In fact, the new member of the community was often received by an impressive welcoming committee consisting of church officials, officials of the Employment Commission and the Department of Labour, and representatives of employers and transportation companies.[81] The Lutheran church tried to have its representatives on the ships and trains that transported migrants, at ports, train stations, and in reception camps. "The presence of a friendly pastor on a pier or a railway platform in a land full of strange sights and sounds is like the shade of a mighty rock in a dismaying desert," one church leader reported. "More than once this simple service has turned an indifferent DP church-member into a thankful, regular, ardent church-goer in his new hometown."[82] The Lutheran World Relief, in the spirit of the chain of hands, supported such services financially; it helped, for example, the UELCA to hire a chaplain for the reception camp at Bonegilla. Often, however, the most effective way to contact a newcomer was through the local pastor, who relied on the port worker to send him lists of migrants headed for his parish.[83]

The newcomers upon whom such attention was lavished were often overwhelmed by the friendliness and helpfulness. In some cases, the "soul

fishing" was successful and the immigrants were soon considered real assets to their new congregations. In other cases the good feelings disappeared quickly as the newcomer did not live up to the expectations. And there were plenty of problems. On a fundamental level, according to Pastor Zinnbauer in Adelaide, "a strictly denominational church of pietistic background is confronted with the middle class of disintegrating national churches." Many of the newcomers were not committed, active and professing Christians, some not even having been baptized or confirmed.[84] Young German men, who started arriving in greater numbers by late 1951, posed a distinct problem. Not only were they "war-waifs" whose "bitter and hardening experiences of the past" had resulted in "a reluctance to listen." They also came, not fleeing persecution or in search of religious freedom, but looking for work. They pursued worldly pastimes and joined national groups before they tried to find a church.[85] Even nominal Christians brought with them the typical European attitude towards the church as a state-supported body to which one belonged automatically and which was able to carry out impressive welfare programs. In their new environments, migrants had to be "taught the fact that Church and State are separate here."[86] They had to learn that they must actively seek out a congregation and contribute to its existence with offerings. Most importantly they had to be convinced not to join a church simply because it was providing services in the immigrant's mother tongue.[87]

This advice was contained in a handbook for Lutheran immigrants to Canada, but nevertheless many newcomers took the support the Lutheran church had given them in their resettlement for granted and never joined a Lutheran parish.[88] Their new co-religionists did not take this ingratitude well, and in many cases, the parish pastor had to have "the wisdom of Solomon to keep peace between New Canadian Lutherans and Old Canadian Lutherans."[89] Old Australian Lutherans were gently reminded not to expect the newcomer to show the "same interest as those who grew up with the Church here" or "passively to fit themselves in with all that we do."[90] Some pastors became disenchanted with the whole resettlement programme, just as many immigrants were so disappointed with the conditions in Canada or Australia that they wanted to return to Europe right away.[91] Other congregations ended up serving newcomers from both sides of the European conflict and had to reconcile formerly hostile nationalities, for example, Germans and Poles.[92] The crosscurrents of religious and national loyalties occasionally produced conflicting priorities as well; in one instance a pastor complained that the American-directed Lutheran World Action was reluctant to help Germans: "Can we be expected to collect money for the murderers of our brothers, the Czechs and Polacks [sic], but not do any-

thing for our brothers and sisters in blood and in faith?"[93] Thus, while the churches in the receiving countries had much to gain from the influx of refugees and had a distinct self-interest in their support for refugee resettlement programs, the mission came at a price.[94] It was mostly the established congregations at the local level that had to cope with the problems.

On a national level, both the Australian and the Canadian Lutheran churches reaped the rewards. In Canada, refugee work gave parts of the church an opportunity to establish an identity separate from the American parent body. Although the Missouri synod remained largely American-oriented,[95] the establishment of the Canadian Lutheran World Relief was a first step in setting Canadian priorities and spending Canadian money on a Canadian programme. Canadian immigration policies allowed the admission of ethnic Germans since 1947, and through CLWR many could be brought to Canada. The emphasis on refugee resettlement at the expense of an English-language inner mission, displeased many North American oriented church leaders but fitted well into the traditions especially of Western Canadian foreign-language congregations.

The Australian church had identity problems of a different order. Instead of suffering from too little separateness, it was suffering from too much. With its involvement in refugee resettlement programs it managed to strengthen its position in Australian society and to overcome its geographic isolation. The large influx often doubled local churches and provided good publicity. The churches' involvement in assimilating the newcomers earned it credit with the Australian government while the general public learnt more about the world-wide nature of Lutheranism. The Lutheran World Federation supported UELCA efforts with financial contributions to a camp pastor and various refugee pastors. In the case of the ELCA, still suspicious of international or ecumenical developments in 1949, refugee work facilitated a rapprochement with the sister synod and opened a window to the world. By 1952 an ELCA observer attended the Lutheran World Federation Conference in Hanover.[96] For both Australian Lutheran churches, the European refugee was not only "a challenge to compassion, but a stimulus to vigorous home missionary activity and the instrument through which substantial bonds of unity have been forged with the family of world Lutheranism."[97] By the time Germans started arriving in larger numbers, Australian Lutherans were well prepared.

Conclusions

The acceptance of large numbers of refugees after the war has become an integral part of the national myths of both Canada and Australia. In anniversary celebrations, politicians evoke the alleged spirit of humanitarianism

that allowed the governments of the day to offer a new home to the wretched masses of Europe. Although historians continue to provide evidence of opportunism and economic self-interest as governing factors in postwar refugee policies, the self-congratulatory mood – and concomitant expectations of lasting gratitude on the part of the refugee migrants – prevails. By breaking the issue down further and revealing how not only the state but societal groups benefited from, and were transmuted by, the postwar influx of non-German and German refugees, the myth of a charitable act is further unraveled. As this study has shown, refugee work did pose a tremendous challenge, but mostly to the local community. On a national level, the flotsam of Europe was in fact a tremendous asset.

It seems appropriate to point out the parallel interests of church and state. The ideal of international cooperation in solving the refugee problem was matched by the Lutheran World Federation's humanitarian approach in the spirit of Christian brotherhood. However, just as the Lutheran church did not want its contribution to be submerged in a larger ecumenical programme, individual countries rated their domestic priorities generally higher than the spirit of internationalism. The selection of DPs from the camps in Germany and the competition for skilled German labour in the early 1950s followed the dictates of changing labour markets. Immigrants were expected to be economic assets by accepting assigned jobs. To the national church bodies, migrants also represented growth as well and the competition for good Christians took place at an inter-confessional or even inter-synodical level. Finally, just as the expectation of Anglo-conformity was strong in both Canada and Australia,[98] the immigrant was also expected to assimilate into the existing religious mainstream, although the church seemed somewhat more patient and willing to recognize the two-way character of the process. In any case, the assistance given to refugees in the postwar period was well-calculated and came with strings attached.

Notes

1. Research in Australia was made possible by grants of the University of Winnipeg and the German-Canadian Studies Foundation Inc.
2. Barry Humphries, *More Please: An Autobiography* (Ringwood, Victoria: Penguin, 1993),140-1.
3. Clarence M.Cherland, "Canadian Lutheran World Relief and Its Human Involvement," (M.Theology thesis, Wartburg Theological Seminary, 1964), 206.
4. *Ibid.*, 57; John George Stoessinger, *The Refugee and the World Community* (Minneapolis: University of Minnesota Press, 1956), 149-153.
5. Victor Mohr, "Die Geschichte des Raphaels-Werkes – Ein Beispiel für die

Sorge um den Menschen unterwegs," and Helmut Talazko, "Aus der Geschichte der evangelischen Arbeit für Auswanderer und Ausgewanderte," *Zeitschrift für Kulturaustausch,* 39:3 (1989).

6. Mars Dale, "Lutherans in Canada Arise," *Canada Committee Quarterly* 1:4 (December 1950); John Schmidt, "Two Ships Set Sail for Canada," *The Lutheran,* 3 June 1953: "[A]s an agency of the church we are not primarily concerned about supplying a labor market. We are concerned that family ties shall be preserved." The Hanover Assembly of the Lutheran World Federation in July 1952 passed a resolution to safeguard the family unit. National Archives of Canada [NAC], MG28 V120, vol. 30, file LWF-SR, Canadian Lutheran World Relief.

7. *Canada Committee Quarterly,* 3:1, March 1952.

8. Stoessinger, *The Refugee and the World Community,* 50-54.

9. Catherine Panich, *Sanctuary? Remembering Postwar Immigration* (Sydney: Allen & Unwin, 1988),16.

10. Herbert Krimm, *Beistand: Die Tätigkeit des Hilfswerks der Evangelischen Kirchen in Deutschland für Vertriebene und Flüchtlinge nach 1945* (Stuttgart: Evangelisches Verlagswerk, 1974), 75-76; Australian Archives [AA] (ACT) A445/1; 140/4/12, Minutes of the 12th meeting of the Commonwealth Immigration Advisory Council, 5 December 1950; Johannes-Dieter Steinert, *Westdeutsche Wanderungspolitik, internationale Wanderungskooperation und europäische Integration 1945-1961* (Osnabrück, unpublished manuscript, 1991), 182; Canada, House of Commons, *Debates,* 21 March 1950 (Thatcher).

11. Birgit Frieler, and Wiebke Henning, "Auswanderung nach 1945: Hoffnung für Millionen - Schutz und Fürsorge für Auswanderer als staatliche Aufgabe," *Zeitschrift für Kulturaustausch,* 39:3 (1989); Stoessinger, *The Refugee and the World Community,* 174-175.

12. Between 1947 and 1954, according to the census, the German-born population increased by almost 51,000, yet the number of German nationals admitted from 1947-54 was only 37,800. James Jupp and Barry York, *Birthplaces of Australian People: Commonwealth Censuses, 1911-1991* (Canberra: Centre for Immigration and Multicultural Studies, 1993); Barry York, *Admitted 1947-1957: Annual Returns on Persons Admitted into Australia and their Places of Last Permanent Residence* (Canberra: Centre for Immigration and Multicultural Studies, 1993). The relationship between birthplace and nationality in postwar Europe is extremely complicated; a large number of German-born gave Polish as their nationality. See: Jerzy Zubrzycki, *Immigrants in Australia: A Demographic Survey Based Upon the 1954 Census* (Melbourne: Melbourne University Press, 1960).

13. Glenda Sluga, *Bonegilla: 'A Place of no Hope'* (Melbourne: The University of Melbourne History Department, 1988), 44-45, 52; Johannes A. Voigt, *Australia - Germany. Two Hundred Years of Contacts, Relations and Connections* (Bonn: Inter Nationes, 1987), 123. For an example

of a German-language contract, Milda Danys, *DP: Lithuanian Immigration to Canada after the Second World War* (Toronto: Multicultural History Society of Ontario, 1986), 101, 132. For German booklets distributed among DPs, AA (ACT): A445/1, 140/4/11. Minutes of the 11th Meeting of the Commonwealth Immigration Advisory Council, 11 August 1950, Item 21.

14. H.F. Noack, "Preparing the Way at Bathurst," *Australian Lutheran*, 37:5 (16 March 1949), 75; C.D. Nagel, "Missions: Migrant Work," *Australian Lutheran*, 37:6 (30 March 1949), 97.
15. Andrew Markus, "Labour and Immigration 1946-9: The Displaced Persons Program," *Labour History*, 47 (November 1984), 77.
16. AA (ACT): A445/1, 223/2/5, report of the Visit to the Continent of Europe from July 8 to July 22, 1947, of the Minister for Immigration and Information, the Hon. Arthur A.Calwell; Egon F. Kunz, "The Genesis of the Post-War Immigration Programme and the Evolution of the Tied-Labour Displaced Persons Scheme," *Ethnic Studies: An International Journal*, 1 (1977), 36-37.
17. Egon F. Kunz, *Displaced Persons: Calwell's New Australians* (Sydney: Australian National University Press, 1988), 35. Canada had sent its first immigration team into Germany in February 1947. Gerald Dirks, *Canada's Refugee Policy: Indifference or Opportunism?* (Montreal: McGill-Queen's University Press, 1977), 145.
18. NAC, RG25, vol. 8118, file 5475-T-40, pt.18, filepocket, Head of Canadian Delegation to IRO to USSEA, 17 April, 1951.
19. Steinert, *Wanderungspolitik*, 268-269.
20. AA(ACT): A1838, 29/1/3/4, Australian Migration Office Cologne to Department of External Affairs, 25 April, 1953.
21. AA (ACT): A1838, 29/1/3/4, Australian Embassy Bonn to Department of External Affairs, 21 February, 1957.
22. Bilateral agreements were made to regulate the flow of so-called "bulk labour." Franca Iacovetta, "Ordering in Bulk: Canada's Postwar Immigration Policy and the Recruitment of Contract Workers from Italy," *Journal of American Ethnic History*, 11:1 (1991).
23. Ann-Mari Jordens, *Redefining Australians: Immigration, Citizenship and National Identity* (Sydney: Hale & Iremonger, 1995), 77-88; National Library of Australia, Manuscript Collection, no. 932, folder 2B; keynote Address by H.E. Holt to Second Citizenship Convention, January 1951 in Sydney; [AA] (ACT): A445/1; 140/4/11; minutes of the 11th Meeting of the Commonwealth Immigration Advisory Council, 11 August 1950. "Missions: Migrants,' *Australian Lutheran*, 38:12 (14 June 1950), 188.
24. NAC, MG28, V120, vol. 28, files 1-5.
25. Angelika Sauer, "A Matter of Domestic Policy? Canadian Immigration Policy and the Admission of Germans, 1945-50," *Canadian Historical Review*, 74:2 (June 1993).

26. *Canada Committee Quarterly*, 1:3 (September 1950) and 4 (December 1950).
27. *The Lutheran*, 3 May 1950.
28. Steinert, *Wanderungspolitik*, 173, 259-260.
29. Wolfgang G. Friedmann, *German Immigration into Canada* (Toronto: Ryerson Press, 1952), 20-24.
30. For a brief summary of the Australian debate, see Ann-Mari Jordans, *Redefining Australians*, 34-37.
31. AA (ACT): 1838/283, 29/1/3/7, Spender to Holt, 28 August 1950.
32. AA (ACT): A445, 140/4/17, report by H.R. Mitchell of National Mutual to the 17th meeting of Commonwealth Immigration Advisory Council, Summer 1952.
33. AA (ACT): A445, 140/4/15, report by R.D. Huish, President, Queensland Branch of RSSAILA, to the 15th meeting of Commonwealth Immigration Advisory Council, 15 October 1951.
34. "R.S.L. Head Says Bring Germans," *Sydney Morning Herald*, 14 August 1951.
35. "Migration Proposal," *The West Australian*, 22 January 1951; "Germans here Warned that Nazis May Infiltrate," *The Age*, 24 February 1951; "Lively Scene at Meeting: Protest against German Migrants," and "Big Meeting Urges Ban on 'Nazi' German Migrants," *Sydney Morning Herald*, 27 February 1951; "Huge Town Hall meeting demands end to Nazi Migration," *The Tribune* (Sydney), 2 March 1951; Julius Stone, "Mass German Immigration in Australia's Future," *Australian Quarterly*, 23:2 (June, 1951), 20-21; National Library of Australia, Manuscript Collection, no. 932, folder 2B, Keynote Address by H.E. Holt to Second Citizenship Convention, January 1951, in Sydney; "Migrants from Germany: The Nazi Taint," letter to the editor by Julius Stone, *Sydney Morning Herald*, 4 November 1950.
36. The Sydney meeting was addressed by former foreign minister, Dr. Evatt, who led the campaign against German migration. "Evatt Speech Brawl," *The Courier Mail*, 27 February 1951; "Mass Migration of Germans Opposed: Labor Sees Danger of Nazi Elements," *The Age* (Melbourne), 11 April 1951.
37. For example, AA (ACT): A1838, 29/1/3/4, visit to the Federal Republic of Germany by the Prime Minister of Australia, 16-20 July 1956. See also: AA (ACT): A445/1, 140/4/14, minutes of 14th meeting of the Commonwealth Immigration Advisory Council, 2-3 July 1951, item no. 5. Also, A.S. Bohanna letter to the editor, *Sydney Morning Herald*, 20 February 1951.
38. "P.M. Deplores Racial Bias in Migration," *The Age*, 23 February 1951; "German Migrant Policy Defended," *Sydney Morning Herald*, 28 February 1951; editorials "Migrants from Western Germany," *Sydney Morning Herald*, 12 February 1951; and, "German Migration," *The West Australian*, 28 February 1951; AA (ACT): A445/1, 140/4/16, minutes of 16th meeting of Commonwealth Immigration Advisory Council, 29 February 1952.

39. AA (ACT): A1939, 29/1/3/4, memorandum for the Assistant Secretary, Department of External Affairs, 28 April 1952; AA (ACT): A1838, 29/1/3/4, Holt to Menzies, 6 June 1952; and, Australian Embassy Bonn to Department of External Affairs, 30 November 1955; Krimm, *Beistand*, 76.

40. AA (ACT): A1838, 29/1/3/4, visit of Mr. Holt to Berlin and Bonn, 8 September 1952.

41. AA (ACT): A445/1, 140/5/14; York, *Admitted 1947-1957*.

42. Hartmut Rudolph, *Evangelische Kirche und Vertriebene 1945 bis 1972*, 1; *Kirche ohne Land* (Göttingen: Vandenhoeck & Ruprecht, 1984), 44-51.

43. Solberg, *As Between Brothers*, 167; Krimm, *Beistand*, 40-43.

44. *The Christian Century*, 30 March 1949; *Das Hilfswerk*, 34 (January 1950); Voigt, *Australia - Germany*, 121-122. Niemöller was a controversial figure within the church, see *Australian Lutheran*, 37:15 (10 August 1949), 228-229.

45. NAC, MG28 V120, vol. 30, Annual Report of LWF-SR, 1949-1950; Solberg, *As Between Brothers*, 148.

46. Stewart Herman, "Lutheran Service for Refugees," *The Lutheran Quarterly*, 2 (February 1950), 10.

47. As a Canadian involved in Lutheran resettlement work writes, the motive behind Lutheran migration work was "*not primarily* [emphasis added] to transplant Lutherans from Germany to Canada as a mission venture"; T.O.F. Herzer, "DPs Make Impact on Lutheranism in Canada," *The Lutheran Witness*, 8 July 1952.

48. Solberg, *As Between Brothers*, 101.

49. Herman, "Lutheran Service to Refugees," 12.

50. Richard W. Solberg, *Open Doors: The Story of Lutherans Resettling Refugees* (St. Louis, MO: Concordia Publishing House, 1992), 29; H.F. Noack, "Preparing the Way at Bathurst," *Australian Lutheran*, 37:5 (16 March 1949), 75. The German Lutheran church preferred the resettlement of groups to that of individuals, but few countries were willing to accept this type of immigration. Rudolph, *Evangelische Kirche*, 153.

51. NAC, MG28, V120, vol. 30, Annual Report of LWF-SR, 1949-1950.

52. E. Clifford Nelson, *Lutheranism in North America, 1914-1970* (Minneapolis: Augsburg Publishing House, 1972), 147.

53. Paul Eydt, "The Stranger Within Our Gate ... the DP," *The Canada Lutheran*, 37:2 (February 1949): "The mass migrations, both of DPs and ethnic Germans, have provided a special challenge to the relatively small Lutheran churches of Australia, Canada, and South America." See also, Solberg, *As Between Brothers*, 156.

54. *Das Hilfswerk*, 34 (January, 1950); *Australian Lutheran*, 39:24 (28 November 1951), 376; Solberg, *As Between Brothers*, 156.

55. T.O.F. Herzer, "DPs Make Impact on Lutheranism in Canada," *The Lutheran Witness*, 8 July 1952. The overall number of Canadian Lutherans in the 1951 census was more than 400,000.

56. Solberg, *As Between Brothers*, 139-141. On community life in camps, see Norma Eleanor Walmsley, "Canada's Response to the International Problem of 'Displaced Persons' 1947-1951," (M.A. thesis, McGill University, 1954), 38-39.

57. NAC, MG28, V120, vol.30, file 3, Canadian Lutheran World Relief, "Our Ethnic Groups and the Lutheran Church in Canada," unpublished report, n.d.; Stewart Herman, "Lutheran Service to Refugees," *The Lutheran Quarterly*, 2 (February 1950), 13.

58. *Australian Lutheran*, 37:16 (24 August 1949), 245; Margaret Rilett, *And You Took Me In: Alfred and Helga Freund-Zinnbauer, A Biography* (Adelaide: Lutheran Publishing House, 1992), 94.

59. H. Noack, "The New Australian," *Australian Lutheran*, 39:15 (25 July 1951), 233.

60. Herman, "Lutheran Service to Refugees," 14-15.

61. "Lest a false impression should get abroad, may it be stated here that the congregation of our brethren in the capital cities are not national but Lutheran congregations," President's Column, *Australian Lutheran*, 39:9 (2 May 1951), 136. Also, quote from Rilett, *And You Took Me In*, 103-104.

62. Krimm, *Beistand*, 42-43. For the Australian attitude, Rilett, *And You Took Me In*, 103-104.

63. *New Horizons*, 5:1 (January 1954), "To minister to them raises the problem of re-introducing German-language services and other languages also...". See also, "Literature for Migrants," *Australian Lutheran*, 39:3, 37.

64. Rilett, *And You Took Me In*, 103-104; Peter and Elizabeth Koeping, "Religion and Maintenance of Ethnic Identity: (German) Lutherans in a South Australian Town," in *Religion and Ethnic Identity: An Australian Study*, edited by Abe Wade Ata (Richmond, Victoria: Spectrum Publications, 1988), 32.

65. T.O.F. Herzer, "DPs Make Impact on Lutheranism in Canada," *The Lutheran Witness*, 8 July 1952.

66. Pastor Unterschults to Herzer, 2 June 1952, in Cherland, "Canadian Lutheran World Relief," 200-201.

67. Pastor Trait to Herzer, 23 May 1952, in Cherland, "Canadian Lutheran World Relief," 200-201.

68. Pastor Unterschults to Herzer, 2 June 1952, in Cherland, "Canadian Lutheran World Relief," 200-201.

69. T.O.F. Herzer, "DPs Make Impact on Lutheranism in Canada," *The Lutheran Witness*, 8 July 1952.

70. Dr. Kohler to Herzer, 30 May 1952, in Cherland, "Canadian Lutheran World Relief," 200-201.

71. M. Pachur, "Work Among Migrants in Adelaide," *Australian Lutheran*, 40:9 (7 May 1952), 135-136.

72. George O. Evenson, *Adventuring for Christ: The Story of the Evangelical Lutheran Church of Canada* (Calgary: Foothills Lutheran Press 1974), 125-127, 160-161; NAC, Erich Bergbusch papers, MG30 D213, vol. 1, ULCA

Board of Missions to Bergbusch, 6 February 1947.

73. Reuben Baetz, "Resettlement or Assimilation?" *The Canada Committee Quarterly*, 2:1, March 1951.

74. In 1939, only 30 per cent of American Lutheran Church services were conducted in German while the figure in the Canada district was 81 per cent. Almost 40 per cent of Canadian Lutherans in the 1951 census were of German ethnic origin. Evenson, *Adventuring for Christ*, 160.

75. The last regular German service in Australia was held in 1956. Peter and Elizabeth Koeping, "Religion and Maintenance of Ethnic Identity," 47.

76. NAC, MG28 V120, vol. 25, file 55, Monk to Willison, 27 January 1949.

77. Cherland, "Canadian Lutheran World Relief," 200.

78. Rilett, *And You Took Me In*, 98-99.

79. *Australian Lutheran*, 37:16 (24 August 1949), 245; 39:4 (21 February 1951), 53; 40:4 (27 February 1952), 54.

80. Rilett, *And You Took Me In*, 92.

81. *Lethbridge Herald*, 14 May 1953; *Spanner*, May 1951.

82. Stewart Herman, "Lutheran Service to Refugees," *The Lutheran Quarterly*, 2 (February 1950), 6.

83. NAC, MG28 V120, vol. 25, file 55, Monk to Dietrich, 7 November 1952.

84. Rilett, *And You Took Me In*, 111. *Australian Lutheran*, 40:10 (21 May 1952), 149.

85. "Immigration Matters," *Australian Lutheran*, 39:24 (28 November 1951), 376; Mars Dale, "Lutherans in Canada Arise," *Canada Committee Quarterly*, 1:4 (December 1950).

86. Pastor Trait to Herzer, 23 May 1952, in Cherland, "Canadian Lutheran World Relief," 200-201.

87. NAC, MG28 V120, vol. 30, *Handbuch: Helfende Hinweise für Neueinwanderer* (Winnipeg: CLWR, 1960).

88. Krimm, *Beistand*, 77. *Handbuch: Helfende Hinweise für Neueinwanderer*. Not even 50 per cent of migrants who had come to Canada with the help of the Canadian Lutheran World Relief were members of Lutheran churches in 1960. Some Australian figures indicate that only 10 to 20 per cent of newcomers contacted eventually became active members of a congregation. "Report on Migrant Work in Our Congregation," *The Tidings of the Bethlehem Lutheran Church Adelaide*, February 1952.

89. Baetz, "Resettlement or Assimilation?"

90. H. Noack, "The New Australian," *Australian Lutheran*, 39:15 (25 July 1951), 233.

91. NAC, MG30 D213, vol. 1, Bergbusch to Hennig, 19 July 1948; Rilett, *And You Took Me In*, 95-96.

92. Cherland, "Canadian Lutheran World Relief," 208.

93. NAC, MG30 D213, vol.1, Sterzer to Bergbusch, 1 and 9 March 1947.

94. Krimm, *Beistand*, 76-77; *The Canada Committee Quarterly*, 3:1 (March 1952).

95. NAC, MG30 D213, vol. 1, Goos to Monk, 24 March 1948.
96. *Australian Lutheran*, 37:21 (26 October 1949), 325; "Into All the World," 39:2 (24 January 1951), 26; "Overseas Convention," 40:4 (27 February 1952), 54.
97. Solberg, *As Between Brothers*, 157-158.
98. H.B. Murphy, "Assimilating the Displaced Person," *Australian Quarterly*, 24:1 (March 1952).

Bibliography

Monographs and Articles:

Cherland, Clarence M. "Canadian Lutheran World Relief and Its Human Involvement." M.Theology thesis, Wartburg Theological Seminary, 1964.

Danys, Milda. *DP: Lithuanian Immigration to Canada after the Second World War*. Toronto: Multicultural History Society of Ontario, 1986.

Dirks, Gerald. *Canada's Refugee Policy: Indifference or Opportunism?* Montreal: McGill-Queen's University Press, 1977.

Evenson, George O. *Adventuring for Christ: The Story of the Evangelical Lutheran Church of Canada*. Calgary: Foothills Lutheran Press, 1974.

Friedmann, Wolfgang D. *German Immigration into Canada*. Toronto: Ryerson Press, 1952.

Frieler, Birgit, and Wiebke Henning, "Auswanderung nach 1945: Hoffnung für Millionen – Schutz und Fürsorge für Auswanderer als staatliche Aufgabe." *Zeitschrift für Kulturaustausch*, 39:3 (1989).

Humphries, Barry. *More Please: An Autobiography*. Ringwood, Victoria: Penguin, 1993.

Iacovetta, Franca. "Ordering in Bulk: Canada's Postwar Immigration Policy and the Recruitment of Contract Workers from Italy." *Journal of American Ethnic History*, 11:1 (1991).

Jordans, Ann-Mari. *Redefining Australians: Immigration, Citizenship and National Identity*. Sydney: Hale and Iremonger, 1995.

Jupp, James and Barry York. *Birthplaces of Australian People: Commonwealth Censuses, 1911-1991*. Canberra: Centre for Immigration and Multicultural Studies, 1993.

Koeping, Peter and Elizabeth Koeping, "Religion and Maintenance of Ethnic Identity: (German) Lutherans in a South Australian Town." In *Religion and Ethnic Identity: An Australian Study*, edited by Abe Wade Ata. Richmond, Victoria: Spectrum Publications, 1988.

Krimm, Herbert. *Beistand: Die Tätigkeit des Hilfswerks der Evangelischen Kirchen in Deutschland für Vertriebene und Flüchtlinge nach 1945*. Stuttgart: Evangelisches Verlagswerk, 1974.

Kunz, Egon F. *Displaced Persons: Calwell's New Australians*. Sydney: Australian National University Press, 1988.

_____. "The Genesis of the Post-War Immigration Programme and the Evolu-

tion of the Tied-Labour Displaced Persons Scheme." *Ethnic Studies: An International Journal*, 1:1 (1977).

Markus, Andrew. "Labor and Immigration: Policy Formation, 1943-5." *Labour History*, 46 (1984).

_____. "Labour and Immigration 1946-9: The Displaced Persons Program." *Labour History*, 47 (November 1984).

Mohr, Victor. "Die Geschichte des Raphaels-Werkes – Ein Beispiel für die Sorge um den Menschen unterwegs." *Zeitschrift für Kulturaustausch*, 39:3 (1989).

Murphy, H.B. "Assimilating the Displaced Person." *Australian Quarterly*, 24:1 (March 1952).

Nelson, E. Clifford. *Lutheranism in North America, 1914-1970*. Minneapolis: Augsburg Publishing House, 1972.

Panich, Catherine. *Sanctuary? Remembering Postwar Immigration*. Sydney: Allen & Unwin, 1988.

Rilett, Margaret. *And You Took Me In: Alfred and Helga Freund-Zinnbauer, A Biography*. Adelaide: Lutheran Publishing House, 1992.

Rudolph, Hartmut. *Evangelische Kirche und Vertriebene 1945 bis 1972, vol. 1: Kirche ohne Land*. Göttingen: Vandenhoeck & Ruprecht, 1984.

Sauer, Angelika. "A Matter of Domestic Policy? Canadian Immigration Policy and the Admission of Germans, 1945-50." *Canadian Historical Review*, 74:2 (June 1993).

Sluga, Glenda. *Bonegilla: 'A Place of No Hope.'* Melbourne: The University of Melbourne History Department, 1988.

Solberg, Richard W. *As Between Brothers: The Story of Lutheran Response to World Need*. Minneapolis: Augsburg Publishing House, 1957.

_____. *Open Doors: The Story of Lutherans Resettling Refugees*. St.Louis, MO: Concordia Publishing House, 1992.

Steinert, Johannes-Dieter. *Westdeutsche Wanderungspolitik, internationale Wanderungskooperation und europäische Integration 1945-1961*. Osnabrück, unpublished manuscript, 1991.

Stoessinger, John George. *The Refugee and the World Community*. Minneapolis: University of Minnesota Press, 1956.

Stone, Julius. "Mass German Immigration in Australia's Future." *Australian Quarterly*, 23:2 (June 1951).

Talazko, Helmut. "Aus der Geschichte der evangelischen Arbeit für Auswanderer und Ausgewanderte." *Zeitschrift für Kulturaustausch*, 39:3 (1989).

Voigt, Johannes A. *Australia – Germany. Two Hundred Years of Contacts, Relations and Connections*. Bonn: Inter Nationes, 1987.

Walmsley, Norma Eleanor. "Canada's Response to the International Problem of 'Displaced Persons' 1947-1951." M.A. thesis, McGill University, 1954.

York, Barry. *Admitted 1947-1957: Annual Returns on Persons Admitted into Australia and their Places of Last Permanent Residence*. Canberra: Centre for Immigration and Multicultural Studies, 1993.

Zubrzycki, Jerzy. *Immigrants in Australia: A Demographic Survey Based Upon the 1954 Census*. Melbourne: Melbourne University Press, 1960.

Religious newspapers:

The Australian Lutheran
Canada Committee Quarterly
The Canada Lutheran
Das Hilfswerk
The Lutheran
The Lutheran Quarterly
The Lutheran Witness
New Horizons
The Tidings of the Bethlehem Lutheran Church, Adelaide

Newspapers:

Lethbridge Herald
Spanner
The Courier-Mail (Brisbane)
The Age (Melbourne)
Sydney Morning Herald
The Tribune (Sydney)
The West Australian (Perth)

Carlos Teixeira

The Suburbanization of Portuguese Communities in Toronto and Montreal: From Isolation to Residential Integration?

Abstract

The purpose of this paper is to compare the relocation process and the surburbanization of Portuguese communities in Toronto and Montréal. Attention will be focused on the settlement patterns, geographical distribution, residential mobility, and housing choices of Portuguese households who have changed residence. Data was obtained from surveys conducted in Montréal (1984) and in Toronto (1990). Supplementary data was obtained from informal interviews with key members of Portuguese communities in the Toronto and Montréal areas in 1994.

Data collected from the questionnaires, as well as from the informal interviews, indicate that Portuguese communities in Toronto and Montréal are on the move and/or in transition. Portuguese are moving to Mississauga, a western suburb of Toronto, and to Laval, a suburb of Montréal, in search of single family dwellings, located in a better environment in which to raise their children. From this perspective, the move to the suburbs becomes the fulfilment of a long awaited "dream" for Portuguese families – the acquisition of an "ideal" type of house, preferably a newer one, with amenities such as a basement, backyard, garden in front of the house, garage, modern kitchen, and a location in quiet and pleasant surroundings. The data also indicates that resegregation in the suburbs of Toronto (Mississauga) and Montréal (Laval) becomes apparent as some families (particularly Azoreans) chose to live within, or in close proximity to, an existing nucleus of Portuguese concentration and Portuguese religious/cultural institutions. For this particular group, residential integration seems not to have taken place despite their move to the suburbs.

Résumé

Cet article compare le processus de réinstallation et de banlieusardisation des communautés portugaises de Toronto et de Montréal. Il met l'accent sur les tendances d'implantation, la distribution géographique, la mobilité résidentielle et les choix d'habitations des

ménages portugais qui ont changé de résidence. Les données ont été obtenues au moyen de sondages par questionnaire réalisés à Montréal (en 1984) et à Toronto (en 1990). Des données supplémentaires ont été obtenues au moyen d'entrevues informelles réalisées avec les principaux représentants des communautés portugaises de Toronto et de Montréal en 1994.

Les données tirées des sondages et des entrevues informelles indiquent que les communautés portugaises de Toronto et de Montréal sont en mouvement ou en transition. Les Portugais s'installent à Mississauga, une banlieue à l'ouest de Toronto, et à Laval, une banlieue au nord de Montréal, en quête de résidences unifamiliales et d'un environnement plus propice où élever leurs enfants. Dans cette perspective, le déménagement en banlieue devient la réalisation d'un vieux « rêve » pour les familles portugaises, soit l'acquisition de la maison « idéale », de préférence une maison de construction récente, pourvue d'un sous-sol, d'un arrière-cour, d'une pelouse devant la maison, d'un garage et d'une cuisine moderne, et située dans un quartier tranquille et agréable. Les données rassemblées révèlent également une reségrégation apparente dans les banlieues de Toronto (Mississauga) et de Montréal (Laval), du fait que certaines familles portugaises (surtout originaires des Açores) choisissent de vivre au sein ou à proximité des noyaux existants de concentration portugaise et des institutions religieuses et culturelles portugaises. Pour ce groupe particulier de Portugais, l'intégration résidentielle ne semble pas s'être effectuée, malgré leur déménagement en banlieue.

Introduction

Since World War II, Toronto and Montréal have gradually become culturally and racially diverse. According to the 1991 census, 38 per cent of Toronto's population, and 17 per cent of Montréal's, were born abroad. In the last four decades Toronto, and to a lesser degree Montréal, have become important destinations for immigrants arriving in Canada.[1]

One relatively recent ethnic group that has contributed to the country's cultural mosaic are the Portuguese. In the last four decades they have attained a remarkable level of community organization, and their economic, political, social, and cultural impact upon Canadian society has been significant. However, despite the fact that Portuguese Canadians occupy an important place within the ethnic "mosaic" of the country, the number of empirical studies dealing with this group is limited.[2]

The study of ethnicity and ethnic groups in the metropolitan areas of Canada is of particular importance within the context of Canadian

multiculturalism. In contrast to the U.S., with its assimilation model of the "melting pot," Reitz and Breton observe that "the view of Canadian society as a cultural mosaic implies that in Canada ethnic minorities are subject to relatively little pressure to assimilate; they are even encouraged to maintain their identities and cultures."[3] This view has been reflected in the Canadian government's policy of multiculturalism, first announced in 1971, and later embodied in the 1988 Canadian Multiculturalism Act. It declared that the "policy of multiculturalism [is] designed to preserve and enhance the multicultural heritage of Canadians while working to achieve the equality of all Canadians in the economic, cultural and political life of Canada."[4]

Despite these well-intentioned words, multiculturalism has been criticized on both political and ethnic grounds.[5] As Richmond notes, "there is an inevitable tension between the pursuit of multicultural policies and the promotion of a sense of a national unity and commitment particularly in those countries that have experienced substantial immigration."[6] Problems seem to arise from conflicts over recognition and status, not just between ethnic minorities, but also between these minorities and the dominant Anglophone and Francophone cultures. However, the Canadian multiculturalism policy clearly does not aim to segregate ethnic groups into physical and cultural ghettos, but rather acknowledges the unique values/ cohesiveness of ethnic communities and how this can enrich Canadian society as a whole.[7]

The purpose of this study is to compare the relocation process and the suburbanization of Portuguese communities in Toronto and Montréal. Attention will be focused on the settlement patterns, geographical distribution, residential mobility, and housing choices of Portuguese who have changed residence in the Toronto and Montréal area. Data was obtained from questionnaire surveys administered in Montréal (1984) and in Toronto (1990).[8] Supplementary data was obtained from informal interviews with "key" members of Portuguese communities in the Toronto and Montréal areas in 1994.[9]

Portuguese in Canada

While Portuguese contact with Canada dates back to the voyages of early Portuguese navigators in the fifteenth century,[10] immigration to Canada is relatively recent, beginning in the early 1950s (Table 1). At that time the Canadian government promoted Portuguese immigration to supply the demand for agricultural and construction workers. Since the mid-1970s, however, this immigration has gradually diminished due to changes in Canadian legislation.[11]

Today, Portuguese communities are scattered across Canada. It is difficult to estimate the number of Portuguese immigrants (legal and illegal) and their descendants living in Canada, with estimates ranging from 300,000 to almost half a million.[12] Nonetheless, this group is numerically important and the Portuguese language is one of the most important non-official languages in Canada. Figure 1 shows their geographic distribution by province according to the 1991 census. The majority of Portuguese (86.5 per cent) live in the two most populous Canadian provinces – Ontario and Québec. Since the early 1950s, the number of Portuguese immigrants choosing to settle in these two provinces has grown considerably. The 1991 census indicates that approximately 176,000 people in Ontario, and 37,000 in Québec, are of Portuguese ethnic origin (single origin). By far the majority reside in the Toronto and Montréal Census Metropolitan Areas (CMAs).

An important characteristic of the Portuguese in Ontario and Québec is their "urban nature."[13] According to the 1991 census, in Ontario (outside the Toronto CMA, where the majority resides) important Portuguese settlements can be found in the Kitchener (13,755), Hamilton (9,625), and London (6,330) Census Metropolitan Areas. The 1991 census data for Québec show that the population of Portuguese ethnic origin (single origin) for the major Québec Census Metropolitan Areas is distributed as follows: Montréal 32,330; Hull (with Ottawa) 6,580; Québec City 710; Sherbrooke 135; and Chicoutimi-Jonquière 70. Outside of Montréal and Toronto, the cities of Laval (Montréal CMA) and Mississauga (Toronto CMA) became the two most important relocation areas for those Portuguese immigrants who initially settled in the cities of Montréal and Toronto in the last twenty years.

The Establishment of Portuguese Communities: A Case Study – The Portuguese in Toronto and Montréal

The first Portuguese immigrants to Canada arrived alone in the early 1950s, and later sent for their wives, children, and sometimes their extended families. Once in Canada, their main goal has been to reconstitute their families in their new country. In the early years, Canada promoted an immigration policy based on sponsorship and family reunification which was largely responsible for a "chain migration" process. Through this process entire Portuguese families were reunited in Canada. This type of immigration strongly influenced their areas of settlement when, in the late 1950s, the Portuguese began to form communities in several parts of the country.

Toronto and Montréal: "Port of Entry" for Portuguese

Most Portuguese communities in Canada came into being only at the end

of the 1950s. On leaving the farms and railroads, the "pioneers" of Portuguese immigration settled in the cores of major Canadian cities. Toronto and Montréal became the most important destinations for these immigrants, as well as for those who arrived later.[14]

The initial residential experiences of the "pioneers" occurred in physically deteriorated, low income neighbourhoods located in the "hearts" of Toronto and Montréal, on the margins of the emerging central business districts ("Initial Area of Settlement" in Figures 2 and 3).[15] These were poor working-class neighbourhoods with run-down housing, and were already a "port of entry" for other immigrant groups.[16]

Portuguese immigrants who lived in these areas during the 1950s were generally single individuals who resided temporarily in low-rental flats and rooming houses, partly because they were poor, but often also in order to accumulate money with which to buy a house or to finance the immigration of their relatives. These areas, located near the C.B.D. (Central Business District), also possessed the advantage of accessibility to jobs and public transport. The boarding house system was a transitional phase for these boarders and for the Portuguese families who owned the house and wanted to pay their mortgages as soon as possible. Home ownership by Portuguese in Toronto and Montréal increased considerably during the 1960s and 1970s in the "initial areas of settlement" as well as the surrounding neighbourhoods.

The Portuguese "Colonies"

Portuguese "colonies" in Toronto and Montréal evolved mainly during the 1960s ("Core of the Portuguese Community" in Figure 2 and 3). The arrival of entire families due to "chain migration" helped establish Portuguese immigrant communities in areas where ethnic businesses, cultural and religious institutions, and residences were clustered. During the 1960s, however, important changes occurred in the settlement patterns, as well as in the residential location, of the Portuguese. In Toronto, a shift away from the Kensington market area to the south-west of the city took place (Figure 2), while in Montréal the "initial area of settlement" extended north from Sherbrooke Street to Mont-Royal Avenue, between St-Denis and St-Laurent (Figure 3). These neighbourhoods are known as Quartier St-Louis and Quartier Mile-End and have served as a "port of entry" for other ethnic groups such as Jews, Greeks, and Italians.

The questionnaire surveys of Portuguese in Toronto and Montréal indicate that the majority (72.0 per cent and 62 per cent) were "sponsored" by a member of their nuclear or extended family. Information provided by friends and relatives already established in Ontario and Québec played a

crucial role in helping the respondents become established. For example, more than 70 per cent of the Toronto respondents indicated that friends and relatives were "very important" or "important" in helping them find a job (76.9 per cent) and housing (72.7 per cent), as well as in the selection of the city/neighbourhood (90.6 per cent) where they settled after arrival (for the majority of them – the city of Toronto). Similar results were found for the Portuguese in Montréal. Approximately 72 per cent of respondents indicated that they relied on members of their family already established in Montréal when looking for, and selecting, their first residence. In the context of these networks of information, the new immigrants demonstrated preference for the "ethnic" areas (Portuguese colonies – "Little Portugal") of the city.

Among several rural-culture traits transplanted from Portugal was one related to home ownership.[17] The Portuguese take great pride in their houses. The Kensington market area and its surrounding neighbourhoods in Toronto (west of Spadina), and the St-Louis area of Montréal, had affordable housing for sale. In the 1950s and 1960s, houses were bought at low prices and extensive renovations were often made by the new owners. Some of the immigrants were employed in the construction industry and made use of their knowledge of house building when renovating their homes, with the help of members of their families and friends. Mutual help and co-operation among Portuguese immigrants thus became a key factor in the "rejuvenation" of older working-class neighbourhoods in Toronto and Montréal.[18]

The majority of Portuguese immigrants still view home ownership as a secure economic investment today. The questionnaire results from Toronto reveal that, for first-time Portuguese home buyers, housing and home ownership are synonymous with security; they are symbols of security for the immigrant and his family in the new world. More than 90 per cent of the respondents indicated "very important" or "important" to the following reasons why home ownership was so important for them: "to have something of my 'own'"; "as a symbol of security to the family"; "home ownership as an investment"; "it brings greater privacy to the family"; "brings a feeling of having succeeded in this country (Canada)"; and "accomplishment of a 'dream'." Empirical results from the Montréal survey indicate that home ownership is a high priority for that Portuguese community as well. The importance Portuguese families attach to home ownership reflects the immigrants' desire to provide their families with security and privacy in homes of their own.

Portuguese Communities in Toronto and Montréal in the 1990s

In the last two decades, the Portuguese population has undergone impor-

tant changes in urban settlement patterns and distribution. Data from the Toronto and Montréal areas in 1991 (Figure 4 and 5) confirms the gradual dispersion of the group. Nonetheless, the major concentration of the Portuguese continues to be in the traditional areas of reception for immigrants in the two cities. The main concentration of the Portuguese in Toronto is in the west/central part of the city. It is important to note, however, that by 1991, the number of Portuguese living in Toronto had declined to 44,955, as compared to 49,360 in 1981. Within Toronto, the area bounded by Spadina, King, Lansdowne/Canadian National Railways, and St. Clair Avenue formed the major area of concentration for the Portuguese (shown as the "Portuguese Residential Concentration" in Figure 2).

In Montréal, the Portuguese are not evenly distributed throughout the city, but are, instead, concentrated in easily defined locations. Statistics Canada data for 1991 confirmed this non-uniformity of Portuguese distribution (Figure 5). In that year, 15,755 Portuguese were living in the city of Montréal. Even though there are Portuguese in all districts, the majority settled in an area bounded by Sherbrooke Street to the south, St. Denis to the east, Avenue du Parc to the west and the CN/CP railways to the north (see "Core of the Portuguese Community" in Figure 3). These neighbourhoods border the two main French and English communities and, as noted previously, are known as the Quartier St. Louis and the Quartier Mile-End. However, unlike Toronto, the number of Portuguese living in the city of Montréal remained stable (15,755 in 1991, compared to 15,860 in 1981).

The Portuguese communities in Toronto and Montréal have expanded since their original establishment in the immigrant reception areas during the 1960s and 1970s. Two movement patterns have emerged: (a) a northward movement (in both cities) along the traditional "immigrant corridor" in which the Portuguese are replacing Italians; and (b) a movement to the suburbs, especially Mississauga and Laval (Figure 4 and 5). Yet, while the 1991 Canadian census shows a community dispersing, the "heart" (or core) of the Portuguese communities remains.

Different factors seem to have contributed to these major changes in the settlement and residential patterns of the Portuguese communities. First, some of the new immigrants, and particularly those who arrived after 1975, came with better education, skills, and experience, and did not really feel the need to settle in the "core." Also, as a result of the "chain migration" process, many of the new immigrants did not establish residence within the "core," but dispersed on arrival throughout Montréal and Toronto, selecting residences where their sponsors and relatives already lived. Thus, the downtown areas, and particularly the "core" of the Portuguese communities, gradually became less attractive to the new immigrants. This

phenomenon is largely responsible for the new settlements, which are located further from the "core," in different areas of the city and in the suburbs.

Secondly, the Portuguese population has, through residential mobility, also become more dispersed in recent years. Among the major factors contributing to this mobility are the improved economic positions of some Portuguese families of first generation, and their wish to acquire a "dream" house, preferably in the suburbs. For the Portuguese of Montréal and of Toronto, this "dream house" can be had in the suburbs of Laval and Mississauga, their favoured destinations during the last twenty years.

In order to investigate the various reasons behind residential mobility, the surveys in Montréal and Toronto asked for the major reasons why the sampled households left their previous residence. For those in Montréal, the desire to purchase a home (51.9 per cent), and the need for additional housing space (44 per cent), were among the most important reasons given for moving from the previous dwelling. In Toronto, the wish to live in a modern/large house with a backyard ranked first (36.4 per cent), followed by housing prices/investment (21.8 per cent), and the desire to become home-owners (17.3 per cent).

Yet, while the 1991 Canadian census shows the two communities dispersing, the "heart" of these communities remained largely self-contained and self-sufficient. In the last four decades, the Portuguese have constructed a thriving, complex ethnic enclave, with a high degree of "institutional completeness" (using Breton's terminology).[19] This is evident in the appreciable number of social, cultural, and religious institutions that have been established, as well as in the wide range of businesses which provide the group with ethnic products and services in their own language (Table 2).[20] The majority of these are located within the "cores" of the Portuguese communities in Montréal and Toronto, as well as in adjacent neighbourhoods, and they operate mainly for a Portuguese clientele.

In the major metropolitan areas of Canada, and particularly in Toronto and Montréal, the Portuguese show a distinct spatial pattern which is translated into spatial and social isolation from the host society. This voluntary segregation is a major barrier to the integration of first generation Portuguese immigrants into the host society. In 1981, the Portuguese in the Toronto and Montréal CMAs had high indices of dissimilarity in residential patterns (63.2 and 60.0).[21] This high index of dissimilarity for the Portuguese is not a surprise because the majority are relatively recent – that is, first generation – immigrants. Factors such as language barriers, socio-economic status, cultural values, and lifestyle orientation, and a heavy reliance on "ethnic" sources of information in looking for and locating a new dwelling, may explain the concentration of the Portuguese group in

particular neighbourhoods of Toronto and Montréal and their suburbs. All the cultural, social, and religious institutions, and the ethnic businesses presently available to Portuguese, while providing a focus for the community, can also partially explain the high levels of residential concentration of the group in both cities.

The Suburbanization of the Portuguese in Toronto and Montréal

The gradual dispersion of the Portuguese away from Toronto and Montréal is a fairly recent phenomenon. The movement from the "core" to the suburbs, especially to Mississauga and Laval, occurred primarily in the last two decades (see Figures 4 and 5). This movement presents us with the central question facing the future of the Portuguese communities in Toronto and Montréal: "Are they communities in transition from isolation to residential integration?"

For the Portuguese in Toronto and Montréal, the suburbs of Mississauga and Laval have become, in the last twenty years, two of the most important destinations. The Portuguese population of Mississauga has expanded from about 1,465 in 1971, to 14,120 in 1991; the number living in Laval during that same period increased from 635 to 2,780.[22]

In 1991, within both Mississauga and Laval, the Portuguese were not evenly distributed, and pockets, or nuclei, of Portuguese can be identified (Figures 4 and 5). They came to Mississauga and Laval in search of more spacious homes, better neighbourhoods/quality of life, and lower cost housing. The acquisition of the modern "dream" house, usually a single family dwelling with certain amenities such as a basement, backyard, garden in front of the house, garage, modern kitchen, and location in a pleasant neighbourhood with good schools for their children, represents the ultimate goal for Portuguese families. Even if we verify a continuous and gradual movement out of the "core" of the Portuguese communities in Toronto and Montréal, this movement has not yet affected noticeably the vitality of the ethnic institutions, commercial establishments, and community services.

However, while Portuguese may move to different parts of their cities, or to suburbs such Mississauga and Laval, a significant number of them return regularly to the "core" of their old communities to visit relatives and friends, go to church, shop in ethnic businesses, and/or to participate in cultural events. An important question for the future is the degree to which these areas will retain their "Portuguese identity."

With respect to the housing search process, Portuguese home buyers in both Toronto and Montréal relied extensively on "ethnic" sources of information in looking for and locating their residence (Table 3). Ethnic real

estate agents were by far the most important source in locating the present residence. Fifty percent of all Portuguese home buyers in Montréal, and 39.1 per cent of home buyers who relocated to Mississauga, mentioned this source as the most important. The extent of Portuguese home buyers' reliance upon "ethnic" sources is shown in Table 4. Approximately 72 per cent and 56 per cent of all home buyers, in Montréal and Toronto respectively, used an ethnic source as the principal method in locating their present residence.

The majority of Portuguese home buyers spent short periods of time looking for housing, and inspected a limited number of dwellings before the final decision to buy was made. A total of 80.5 per cent of Portuguese home buyers in Montréal, and 85.5 per cent of those who bought houses in Mississauga, spent four months or less searching for a new residence. As well, 66.7 per cent in Montréal, and 41.5 per cent in the Toronto, inspected only 1 to 5 dwellings in their search.

The search strategies undertaken by Portuguese households ultimately led them to different final destinations. Already, there are indications that the Portuguese are more dispersed in the suburbs than they were in the city. Data from the surveys, informal interviews, and data from the 1991 census indicate that resegregation in Mississauga and in Laval becomes apparent for those Portuguese families (particularly Azoreans) who choose to live within or in close proximity to existing pockets or nuclei of Portuguese concentration (e.g., near friends/relatives and/or near the Portuguese church). For other families, geographical dispersion became the most important outcome of their relocation process. Thus, two distinct and separate Portuguese communities seem to be forming in Mississauga and Laval. The heavy reliance by Portuguese home buyers in Toronto and Montréal on "ethnic" sources of information, and particularly on Portuguese agents, show that these sources have played a key role as cultural intermediaries in the home buyer's relocation process. From this perspective, the choice of an "ethnic" source may be a product of a combination of factors, such as language barriers and lack of familiarity with the intricacies of the Toronto and Montréal housing market. Indeed, the use of an ethnic source, especially a Portuguese real estate agent, may be viewed as one aspect of Portuguese immigrants' strategies in adapting to their host society. The most important explanation for Portuguese resegregation in the suburbs of Toronto and Montréal may therefore be found in the "cultural" forces shaping the community from within, rather than on "economic" or "discriminatory" forces in the housing market.

In conclusion, while it is true that the Portuguese group is relatively new to Canada, the majority of its members have come to stay. With vary-

ing degrees of loyalty to their cultural heritage, Portuguese immigrants in Toronto and Montréal seem to be integrating well into the host society. The move to the suburbs cannot be seen as a radical step in an assimilation process, but should be viewed instead as a phase in their gradual integration. These Portuguese, in spite of suburbanization, tend to have frequent contacts with the "core" of their communities in Toronto and Montréal.

It would be impossible to predict the future of the Portuguese in Canada. For the newer generations, the process of defining their cultural identity may the most crucial issue the community will face.[23] Deciding whether they are "Canadian," "Portuguese-Canadian," or "Portuguese" will likely remain an unsolved dilemma for many. The Portuguese, in both Toronto and Montréal, are in control of their own mobility and, whatever changes the community may undergo, these will reflect Portuguese needs and aspirations in their new home of Canada.

Notes

The author would like to express his gratitude to Robert Murdie of the Geography Department, York University, for his support and encouragement in the last few years. Also, I would like to thank all the Portuguese families and "key" persons within the Portuguese communities of Toronto and Montréal whom I interviewed and who shared with me their "immigrant experiences" in Canada.

1. Larry Bourne, *et al., Canada's Ethnic Mosaic: Characteristics and Patterns of Ethnic Origin Groups in Urban Areas* (Toronto: Centre for Urban and Community Studies, University of Toronto, 1986); Conseil des Communautés Culturelles et de l'Immigration, *Statistiques: Démographie, immigration et communautés culturelles au Québec depuis 1871* (Montréal: Conseil des Communautés Culturelles et de l'Immigration, 1993); Wayne Davies and Robert A. Murdie, "The Social Complexity of Canadian Metropolitan Areas in 1986: A Multivariate Analysis of Census Data," in F. Frisken (ed.), *The Changing Canadian Metropolis: A Public Policy Perspective* (Toronto: Canadian Urban Institute, 1994), 203-236.

2. Carlos Teixeira and Gilles Lavigne, *The Portuguese in Canada: A Bibliography/Les Portuguais au Canada : une bibliographie* (North York, Ontario: Institute for Social Research, York University, 1992); David Higgs, "Some Review Notes on a Decade of Portuguese Canadian Studies," *Canadian Ethnic Studies*, 13:2 (1981), 124-130.

3. Jeffrey G. Reitz and Raymond Breton, *The Illusion of Difference: Realities of Ethnicity in Canada and the United States* (Toronto: C.D. Howe Institute, 1994), 41.

4. For further information on Canadian multiculturalism, see Multiculturalism and Citizenship Canada, *Operation of the Canadian Multiculturalism Act – Annual Report 1991-1992* (Ottawa: Multiculturalism and Citizenship

Canada, 1993); K. Victor Ujimoto, "Multiculturalism and the Global In-formation Society," in Vic Satzewich (ed.), *Deconstructing a Nation: Immigration, Multiculturalism & Racism in '90s Canada* (Halifax: Fernwood, 1992), 351-357.

5. See, Augie Fleras and Jean L. Elliott, *The Challenge of Diversity: Multiculturalism in Canada* (Toronto: Nelson Canada, 1992); Neil Bissoondath, *Selling Illusions: The Cult of Multiculturalism in Canada* (Toronto: Penguin Books, 1994).

6. Anthony H. Richmond, *Global Apartheid: Refugees, Racism, and the New World Order* (Toronto: Oxford University Press, 1994), 44.

7. V.M.P. Da Rosa and Carlos Teixeira, "Portugueses do Quebeque e Multiculturalismo Canadense," *Canadart* (Forthcoming).

8. Of the 110 Portuguese who participated in the questionnaire survey in To-ronto, almost all (97.3 per cent) were born in Portugal, and 70 per cent spoke Portuguese at home. Similarly, of the 60 Portuguese respondents in Montréal, all were first generation immigrants born in Portugal. 60.7 per cent of the Portuguese respondents in Toronto were born in the Azores, while 51.7 per cent of the Montréal respondents came from these islands. 67.4 per cent of the Toronto group, and 60 per cent of the Montréal group, ar-rived in Canada during the period 1966-1975. 43 per cent of the Toronto respondents emigrated mainly for economic reasons, while 40.2 per cent came to join members of their families already in Canada. In contrast, in Montréal, 76.7 per cent of the respondents emigrated for economic reasons, while only 13.3 per cent came to join family members already in Canada. Of the 110 Portuguese respondents in Toronto, 79.1 per cent were already homeowners, and 59.1 per cent lived in the city of Toronto before moving to Mississauga. In Montréal, of the 60 respondents, 60 per cent were al-ready homeowners at the time of the interviews. All of these Montréal respondents lived previously in the city of Montréal, and moved to another residence within the boundaries of the city of Montréal. For further details concerning the methodology and the socio-demographic characteristics of the Portuguese samples see, Carlos Teixeira, "The Role of 'Ethnic' Sources of Information in the Relocation Decision-Making Process: A Case Study of the Portuguese in Mississauga" (PhD Thesis, Department of Geography, York University, 1992); Carlos Teixeira, "La mobilité résidentielle intra-urbaine des Portugais de première génération à Montréal" (M.Sc. Thesis, Département de géographie, Université du Québec à Montréal, n.d.)

9. Key informants in the Toronto and Montréal areas (including Mississauga and Laval) were interviewed in the months of June and July (Toronto and Mississauga), and in October (Montréal and Laval) of 1994. Unstructured (guided) indepth interviews were used as the research method to obtain information from key persons (e.g., Portuguese priests, social workers, entrepreneurs, real estate agents/brokers, and pioneers of Portuguese im-migration). The most important topics covered during the interviews were:

housing/home ownership; community structure; ethnic businesses; the Portuguese real estate industry; and the residential mobility of the Portuguese group to the suburbs of Toronto and Montréal (particularly to the cities of Mississauga and Laval).

10. For further information concerning contacts with the East Coast of Canada, and particularly with Newfoundland, see, Eduardo Brazao, *La découverte de Terre-Neuve* (Montréal : Les Presses de l'Université de Montréal, 1964); Grace M. Anderson and David Higgs, *A Future to Inherit: The Portuguese Communities of Canada* (Toronto: McClelland and Stewart, 1976); J.A. Alpalhao and V.M.P. Da Rosa, *A Minority in a Changing Society: The Portuguese Communities of Québec* (Ottawa: University of Ottawa Press, 1980); John Mannion and Selma Barkham, "The 16th-Century Fishery," (Plate 22) in R. Cole Harris (ed.), *Historical Atlas of Canada: From the Beginning to 1800* (Toronto: University of Toronto Press, 1987), 58-59; Priscilla A. Doel, *Port O' Call: Memories of the Portuguese White Fleet in St. John's, Newfoundland* (St. John's, Newfoundland: Institute of Social and Economic Research, 1992).

11. On Portuguese emigration to Canada see, Grace M. Anderson, *Networks of Contact: The Portuguese and Toronto* (Waterloo, Ontario: Wilfrid Laurier University Publications, 1974); Anderson and Higgs, *A Future to Inherit*; Alpalhao and Da Rosa, *A Minority in a Changing Society;* Domingos Marques and Manuela Marujo, *With Hardened Hands: A Pictorial History of Portuguese Immigration to Canada in the 1950s* (Etobicoke, Ontario: New Leaf Publications, 1993); V.M.P. Da Rosa and Salvato Trigo, *Azorean Emigration: A Preliminary Overview* (Porto: Edicoes da Universidade Fernando Pessoa, 1994).

12. Population data from Statistics Canada and Portuguese authorities in Canada (Embassy and Consulates) are not concordant at all. Current estimates vary considerably. The Portuguese population (first, second, and third generation) in Canada in 1993 was estimated to be approximately 500,000, with 385,000 in Ontario alone. In the province of Québec, the number of Portuguese is estimated to be between 55,000 and 60,000. Data from the Canadian Census is more conservative. According to the 1991 Census only approximately 246,890 Portuguese in Canada were of Portuguese ethnic origin (single response). Difficulties in determining the number of Portuguese in Canada as well as in major Canadian cities (e.g., Montréal and Toronto) are due, in part, to different factors including lack of participation in the Canadian Census.

13. Carlos Teixeira, "Ethnicity, Housing Search, and the Role of the Real Estate Agent: A Study of Portuguese and Non-Portuguese Real Estate Agents in Toronto," *Professional Geographer*, 47:2 (1995), 176-183; Gilles Lavigne, *Les ethniques et la ville : l'aventure urbaine des immigrants Portugais à Montréal* (Montréal: Le Préambule, 1987).

14. Gilles Lavigne and Carlos Teixeira, "Mobilité et ethnicité," *Revue*

européene des migrations internationales, 6:2 (1990), 123-132; *Vide Erratum,* 6:3 (1990), 187; Teixeira and Lavigne, *The Portuguese in Canada.*

15. Figures 2 and 3 were constructed using information collected from interviews with key members of the Portuguese communities in Toronto and Montréal, and from the 1991 Canadian Census. The areas identified in Figures 2 and 3 as "Core of the Portuguese Community" and "Portuguese Residential Concentration," reflect relatively homogeneous and compact socio-spatial units, where a large number of Portuguese live and where most of their institutions, businesses and services are located.

16. Robert A. Murdie, *Factorial Ecology of Metropolitan Toronto, 1951-1961: An Essay on the Social Geography of the City* (Chicago, Illinois: Department of Geography, Research Paper No. 116, The University of Chicago, 1969); Lavigne, *Les ethniques et la ville.*

17. Concerning the importance of home ownership for Portuguese families in Montréal and Toronto see, Lavigne, *Les ethniques et la ville*; Teixeira, "Ethnicity, Housing Search, and the Role of the Real Estate Agent."

18. On the "rejuvenation" of neighbourhoods, both in Montréal and Toronto, see Anderson and Higgs, *A Future to Inherit*; R.G. Krohn, B. Fleming, and M. Manzer, *The Other Economy: The Internal Logic of Local Rental Housing* (Toronto: Peter Martin Associates, 1977); Alpalhao and Da Rosa, *A Minority in a Changing Society*; Claude Marois, "Cultural Transformations in Montréal Since 1970," *Journal of Cultural Geography,* 8:2 (1988), 29-38.

19. Raymond Breton, "Institutional Completeness of Ethnic Communities and the Personal Relations of Immigrants," *American Journal of Sociology,* 70:2 (1964), 193-205.

20. Carlos Teixeira, "The Portuguese," in *The Peoples of Canada: An Encyclopedia for the Country,* edited by P.R. Magocsi and C. Fahey, (Toronto: Multicultural History Society of Ontario/University of Toronto Press, Forthcoming).

21. Larry Bourne, *et al., Canada's Ethnic Mosaic.*

22. According to "key" persons in the Portuguese community that I interviewed in Mississauga and Laval, the number of Portuguese of first generation (born in Portugal) and their descendants (second and third), living in Mississauga and Laval are approximately 40,000 (Mississauga) and 8,000/10,000 (Laval).

23. See, Edite Noivo, "Family Life – Worlds and Social Injuries: Three Generations of Portuguese Canadians," (PhD Thesis, Department of Sociology, Université de Montréal, 1992); Manuela Dias, "Deux langues en contact : le français et le portugais dans les communautés de Paris et de Montréal," (PhD Thesis, French Department, University of Toronto, 1990); Onesimo T. Almeida, "Value Conflicts and the Struggle for Cultural Adjustment: The Case of the Portuguese in Canada," *Gavea-Brown,* 5-6:1-2 (1984-1987), 28-34; Calvin Veltman and Odette Paré, *L'insertion sociolinguistique des québecois d'origine portugaise* (« Études et documents ») (Montréal: INRS-Urbanisation, 1985).

Table 1: Portuguese Immigration to Canada, 1900-1989

Years	Number
1900 - 1949	508
1950 - 1954	2,437
1955 - 1959	14,677
1960 - 1964	20,471
1965 - 1969	39,206
1970 - 1974	55,612
1975 - 1979	24,279
1980 - 1984	12,454
1985 - 1989	25,733

Sources: Canada, Department of Mines and Resources, "Report of Immigration Branch for the fiscal year ending March 31, 1947," 1948; Canada, Department of Citizenship and Immigration, "Report of Immigration Branch 1955," 1957; Canada, Employment and Immigration Canada, 1960-1989.

Table 2: Portuguese Organizations/Institutions and Ethnic Businesses, Ontario and Québec – 1993

	Ontario	Québec	Total
Portuguese Businesses	**3,500	*750	4,250
Portuguese Clubs/Assoc.	111	20	131
Portuguese Community Schools	32	4	36
Churches	***26	4	30

* Alianca dos Profissionais e Empresarios do Québec.
** Federacao Luso-Canadiana de Empresarios e Profissionais
*** Guia Comercial Portugues (Portuguese Telephone Directory), 1993

Sources: Portuguese consulates in Montréal and Toronto, and the Portuguese Embassy in Ottawa.

Table 3: Most Important Information Source Used to Find Present Residence

Percentage of Home Buyers Mentioning Source

	Portuguese			
	Toronto* N=110		Montréal** N=36	
Information Sources	N	%	N	%
Ethnic Agents	43	39.1	18	50.0
Friends/Relatives	17	15.5	7	19.4
Non-Ethnic Agents	16	14.5	1	2.8
Signs on Property/Open House/ Driving Around	16	14.5	9	25.0
Newspapers	5	4.5	1	2.8
Other	13	11.8	-	-

Sources: *Questionnaire Survey (1990); **Questionnaire Survey (1984).

Table 4: Most Important Information Sources Used to Find Present Residence

Percentage of Home Buyers Mentioning Source (Aggregate)

	Portuguese			
	Toronto* N=110		Montréal** N=36	
Most Important Source	N	%	N	%
"Ethnic" Sources (1)	61	55.5	26	72.2
"Non-Ethnic" Sources (2)	49	44.5	10	27.8

(1) Ethnic friends, relatives, ethnic agents, and ethnic newspapers
(2) Non-ethnic friends, non-ethnic agents, daily newspaper, driving around, signs on property/open house, and "other" sources

Sources: *Questionnaire Survey (1990); **Questionnaire Survey (1984).

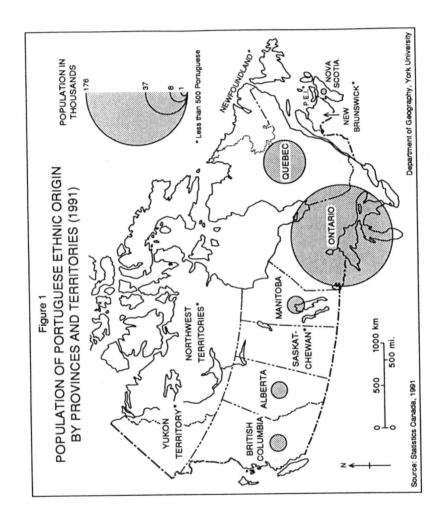

Figure 1

POPULATION OF PORTUGUESE ETHNIC ORIGIN
BY PROVINCES AND TERRITORIES (1991)

Source: Statistics Canada, 1991

Department of Geography, York University

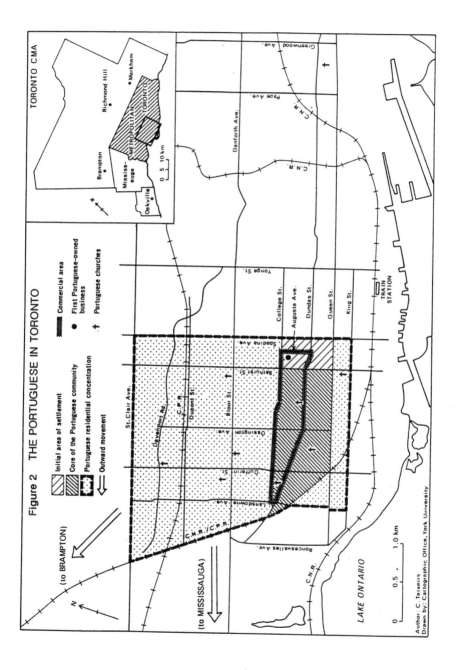

Figure 2 THE PORTUGUESE IN TORONTO

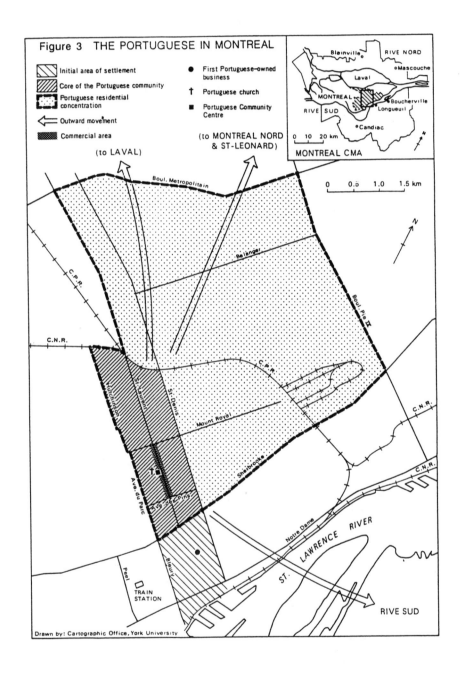

Figure 3   THE PORTUGUESE IN MONTREAL

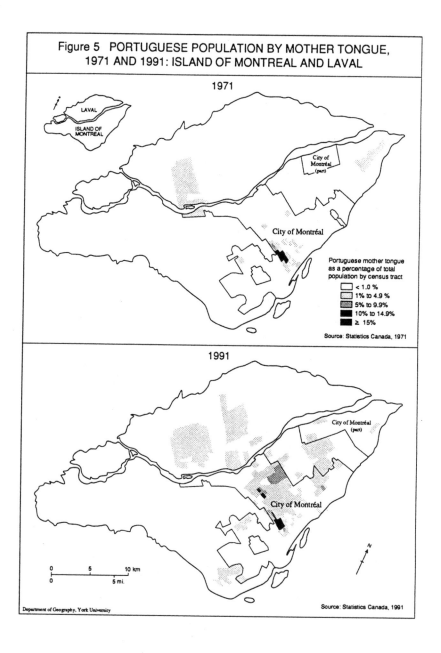

Figure 5   PORTUGUESE POPULATION BY MOTHER TONGUE, 1971 AND 1991: ISLAND OF MONTREAL AND LAVAL

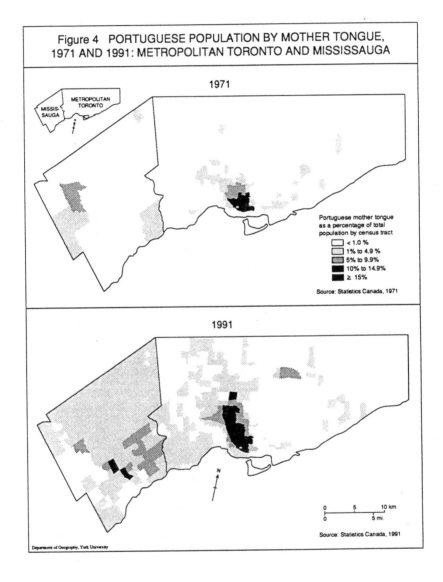

Figure 4   PORTUGUESE POPULATION BY MOTHER TONGUE, 1971 AND 1991: METROPOLITAN TORONTO AND MISSISSAUGA

201

Jiajian Chen (PhD, Social Demography, Western Ontario, 1991) has worked on projections of the Canadian population with working disabilities, on changes in health expectancy, and on the health profile of immigrants in Canada. His current research concerns mortality and health differentials by socio-economic and demographic characteristics.

Oscar E. Firbank is an associate professor at the École de service social and is a member of the Groupe de recherche sur les aspects sociaux de la santé et de la prévention (GRASP) at the Université de Montréal. His current research interests include retirement and the extension of productive working lives for older workers, ethnic communities and their elderly members, and social policy for the aged.

Alexander Freund (MA in History, Simon Fraser University, 1994) is a doctoral student in the Department of History at the University of Bremen, in Germany. The subject of his dissertation is German overseas migration in the 1950s.

Serge Jaumain holds a PhD in History from the Université Libre de Bruxelles (ULB), where he teaches History. He is coeditor of *The Guises of Canadian Diversity: New European Perspectives* (Éditions Rodopi B.V., 1995), a collection of essays culled from a Canadian Studies conferencc for European graduate students, held at the ULB in 1993. He is a specialist in the history of nineteenth-century Canadian-Belgian relations. His current research focuses on the relationships between the Canadian and Belgian federal systems, as well as an analysis of the narratives of nineteenth-century Belgian travellers in North America.

André Langlois is a professor in the Geography Department at the University of Ottawa.

Fernando Mata is a research officer at the Strategic Research and Analysis Directorate of the federal Department of Canadian Heritage. After

obtaining his doctoral degree from York University in 1988, he has undertaken research in different issues related to immigrant integration and multiculturalism.

Edward Ng (PhD, Social Demography, Western Ontario, 1992) has published articles on life table methodology, mortality differentials, intergenerational equity, and distance to hospitals and physicians. His current research concerns life expectancy by educational level, disability of aboriginal Canadians, and immigrant health.

Maryka Omatsu is a Judge with the Ontario Court of Justice, Provincial Division.

Robin Ostow is a professor in the Department of Sociology at the University of Toronto.

Laura Quilici (MA in History, Simon Fraser University, 1995) is working as a counsellor in a transition house for battered women. Her MA thesis was entitled "'I Was a Strong Lady': Italian Housewives with Boarders in Vancouver, 1947-61."

Eran Razin is a senior lecturer of Geography at the Hebrew University of Jerusalem, and a member of the Israel Association for Canadian Studies. He is a coauthor of *The Industrial Geography of Israel* (Routledge, 1993) and of articles on industrial location, local development, and municipal reorganization, as well as on ethnic entrepreneurs in different urban milieux in Canada, the U.S. and Israel. His recent Canadian study was done during a sabbatical year at the University of Ottawa in 1992-1993.

Marilyn J. Rose teaches Canadian Literature and Contemporary Literatures in English in the Department of English at Brock University, where she is also Director of the Canadian Studies Program. Her primary interest is in the working lives of twentieth-century Canadian women writer, particularly matters of locality, cultural inspiration and literary "gatekeeping" with respect to the publication and reception of literary texts in Canada.

Matteo Sanfilippo is an assistant professor in Modern History at the Institute of the Humanities, Faculty of Foreign Languages and Literatures, at the University of Tuscia (Viterbo, Italy). He is co-editor of the journal *Annali Accademici Canadesi*, published by the Canadian Academic Centre in Italy. He has published widely on the subject of Canada and the Vatican, and on historical issues in the *Revue d'histoire de l'Amérique française*, *Social History/Histoire sociale*, *International Journal of Canadian Studies*, and *Cultures du Canada français*.

Angelika E. Sauer received her PhD from the University of Waterloo in 1994 and was awarded the position of Chair in German Canadian Studies at the University of Winnipeg in August 1994. She has published articles on Canadian policy towards postwar Germany and German immigration to Canada. Her current research compares 1950s Germany to Canada and to Australia.

Carlos Teixeira received his PhD in Geography from York University in 1993, and also held a SSHRC postdoctoral research fellowship at York from 1993-1994. His areas of specialization are population, urban and social geography, with an emphasis on migration processes, community and neighbourhood change, housing, ethnic entrepreneurship, and the social structure of Canadian cities.

Russell Wilkins (MUrb, Montréal) has published studies of the demographic, regional, and social dimensions of health expectancy in Canada, and of socioeconomic inequalities in mortality and birth outcomes, based on vital statistics, census, and health and disability survey data for Canada and Québec.

Jiajian Chen (doctorat en démographie sociale, Université Western Ontario, 1991) a travaillé sur les projections d'incapacités de travail au sein de la population canadienne, sur les changements dans l'espérance de vie sans incapacité et sur le profil de santé des immigrants au Canada. Ses recherches actuelles portent sur les différences dans la mortalité et la santé en fonction des caractéristiques socio-économiques et démographiques.

Oscar E. Firbank, Docteur en sociologie, est professeur adjoint à l'École de service social, et chercheur au Groupe de recherche sur les aspects sociaux de la santé et de la prévention (GRASP), à l'Université de Montréal. Ses intérêts de recherche portent sur la retraite et l'extension de la vie productive des travailleurs âgés, les aînés issues des communautés ethniques et les politiques sociales concernant les personnes âgées.

Alexander Freund (maîtrise en histoire, Université Simon Fraser, 1994) est inscrit au doctorat en histoire à l'Université de Brême, en Allemagne. Sa thèse porte sur l'émigration allemande outre-mer dans les années 1950.

Serge Jaumain détient un doctorat en histoire de l'Université Libre de Bruxelles (ULB), où il enseigne l'histoire du Canada. Il a codirigé l'édition de *The Guises of Canadian Diversity: New European Perspectives* (Éditions Rodopi B.V., 1995), un recueil d'essais présentés lors d'un congrès sur les études canadiennes qui s'est tenu en 1993 à l'ULB à l'intention d'étudiants diplômés européens. Il vient de terminer une année sabbatique consacrée à la recherche à l'Université d'Ottawa. Il a également publié des articles sur divers sujets, notamment le genre littéraire des récits de voyage, l'image du Canada en Belgique, l'historiographie canadienne et les colporteurs au Québec.

André Langlois est professeur au Département de géographie de l'Université d'Ottawa.

Fernando Mata est agent de recherche à la Direction de la recherche stra-

tégique et de l'analyse du ministère du Patrimoine canadien. Après avoir obtenu son doctorat de l'Université York en 1988, il a réalisé des recherches sur différentes questions reliées à l'intégration des immigrants et au multiculturalisme.

Edward Ng (doctorat en démographie sociale, Université Western Ontario, 1992) a publié des articles sur la méthodologie des tables de survie, la mortalité différentielle, l'équité intergénérationnelle et l'éloignement par rapport aux hôpitaux et aux médecins. Ses recherches actuelles portent sur l'espérance de vie en fonction du niveau de scolarité, les invalidités chez les autochtones du Canada et la santé des immigrants.

Robin Ostow est professeur au Département de sociologie de l'Université de Toronto.

Maryka Omatsu est juge à la division provinciale de la cour de justice de l'Ontario.

Laura Quilici (maîtrise en histoire, Université Simon Fraser, 1995) travaille comme conseillère dans une maison de transition pour femmes battues. Son mémoire s'intitulait « I Was a Strong Lady : Italian Housewives with Boarders in Vancouver, 1947-61 ».

Eran Razin est professeur au département de géographie à la Hebrew University of Jerusalem et membre de l'Association israélienne d'études canadiennes. Il est coauteur de *The Industrial Geography of Israel* (Routledge 1993) et auteur d'articles sur l'implantation des industries, le développement local et la réorganisation municipale, ainsi que sur les entrepreneurs appartenant à des minorités ethniques dans différents milieux urbains au Canada, aux États-Unis et en Israël. Son étude sur le Canada a été réalisée lors d'une année sabbatique à l'Université d'Ottawa en 1992-1993.

Marilyn J. Rose enseigne la littérature canadienne et les littératures contemporaines de langue anglaise au Département d'anglais de l'Université Brock, où elle dirige également le programme d'études canadiennes. Elle s'intéresse principalement à la vie professionnelle des auteures canadiennes du vingtième siècle, en particulier aux questions de localité, d'inspiration culturelle et de « contrôle » littéraire se rapportant à la publication et à la réception de textes littéraires au Canada.

Matteo Sanfilippo est professeur adjoint d'histoire moderne à l'Institut des humanités, Faculté des langues et des littératures étrangères, de l'Université de Tuscia (Viterbe, Italie). Il est codirecteur de la revue *Annali Accademici Canadesi*, publiée par le Centre académique canadien en Italie. Il a publié

de nombreux articles sur le Canada, le Vatican et l'histoire dans les revues suivantes : *Revue d'histoire de l'Amérique française, Social History/ Histoire sociale, Revue internationale d'études canadiennes* et *Cultures du Canada français.*

Angelika E. Sauer a obtenu son doctorat de l'Université de Waterloo en 1994 et a été nommée directrice de la chaire d'études canadiennes allemandes de l'Université de Winnipeg en août 1994. Elle a publié des articles sur la politique du Canada à l'égard de l'Allemagne d'après-guerre et sur l'immigration allemande au Canada. Ses recherches actuelles comparent l'Allemagne des années 1950 au Canada et à l'Australie.

Carlos Teixeira a obtenu son doctorat en géographie de l'Université York en 1993. Une bourse du Conseil de recherches en sciences humaines du Canada lui a également permis de faire un stage de recherche post-doctoral à cette université en 1993-1994. Ses domaines de spécialisation sont la population, la géographie urbaine et sociale, en particulier les processus de migration, l'évolution des communautés et des quartiers, le logement, l'entrepreneuriat ethnique et la structure sociale des villes canadiennes.

Russell Wilkins (maîtrise en urbanisme, Université de Montréal) a publié des études sur les dimensions démographiques, régionales et sociales de l'espérance de vie sans incapacité au Canada et sur les inégalités socio-économiques dans les taux de mortalité et de natalité, basées sur les statistiques de l'état civil, les recensements et les données d'enquêtes sur la santé et les invalidités au Canada et au Québec.

Due to space limitations, only ten of the papers presented at the Annual Conference of the Association for Canadian Studies are published in this volume of *Canadian Issues*. The following is a list of all the papers presented at the 1995 conference which have not been published in this volume. Some of the papers were not submitted to the editors and thus were not considered for publication; others will no doubt have been published elsewhere. Anyone interested in specific essays should contact the individual authors.

À cause de l'espace limité, seulement dix des communications présentées lors du congrès annuel de l'Association d'études canadiennes ont été publiées cette année. Ce qui suit est une liste des communications présentées au congrès de 1995 qui n'ont pu être imprimées dans ce numéro de *Thèmes canadiens*. Certains articles mentionnés ci-dessous n'ont pas été soumis au comité de rédaction qui n'en a donc pas tenu compte lors de sa sélection; d'autres ont sans doute été publiés ailleurs. Les personnes intéressées par l'un ou l'autre de ces textes doivent s'adresser aux auteurs.

Andrew, Sheila, Claudia Whalen, Nela Rio, and Maria Bartosova (St. Thomas University), "The Canadianisation Process of Immigrant Women."

Badgley, Kerry (Carleton University), "'As Long as He Is an Immigrant from the United Kingdom': Deception, Ethnic Bias and Milestone Commemoration in the Department of Citizenship and Immigration 1953-65."

Bataille, Philippe (Université de Montréal), « La marque du racisme dans la quotidienneté ».

Beaud, Jean-Pierre et Jean-Guy Prévost (Université du Québec à Montréal), « La statistique des origines raciales au Canada pendant l'entre-deux-guerres ».

Bertheleu, Hélène (Université de Montréal et Université de Haute-Bretagne), « Hiérarchies dites ‹ ethniques › en France et au Québec et recomposition

de l'ethnicité : approche comparative ».

Bertheleu, Hélène et Pierre Billion (Université de Montréal et Université de Haute-Bretagne), « Cloisonnement ethnique et solidarités captives : familles Lao dans le quartier Côte-des-Neiges ».

Bischoping, Katherine (York University) and Natalie Fingerhut (Concordia University), "Genocide Scholarship and North American Aboriginal Experiences: Concerns and New Directions."

Butler, Gary R. (York University), "Cultural Adaptation and Retention: The Narrative Tradition of the African-Caribbean Community of Toronto."

Carpenter, Carole H. (York University), "Storying the Immigrant Experience."

Comacchio, Cynthia (Wilfrid Laurier University), "Making Modern Childhood: Mothers, Medicine and the State, 1900-1940."

Cook, Jenny (Dalhousie University), "Migration Into the Upper Saint John Valley Prior to 1850: A Study of the Interaction of Ethnic Groups as Seen in Regional Material Culture."

D'Costa, Ronald (University of Ottawa), "Variations in the Ethnic Diversity of Canada: 1941-1991."

Dean, Kathryn J. (University of Toronto), "Neutral Territory: Deconstructing (and Reconstructing) Niagara."

Dudar, Judy (Saint Mary's University), "Immigration and Imagination: The Autobiographical Presentation of Self."

El Yamani, Myriame (Université de Montréal), « La représentation de ‹ l'autre › dans le cinéma québécois »

El Yamani, Myriame et Jocelyne Dupuis (Université de Montréal), « La construction médiatique du ‹ Bronx › de Montréal ».

Francis, Caroline and Sharon Koehn (Victoria), "Getting Beyond the Threshold: Institutional Barriers to Service for Cambodian Refugees and Elderly Punjabi Sikhs in British Columbia."

Froschauer, Karl (Simon Fraser University), "Immigrant Entrepreneurs: Comparing Tigers?"

Gaffield, Chad (University of Ottawa), "Mass Schooling and the Construction of Masculinities: Hypotheses from 19th-Century Ontario and Québec."

Gravel, Sylvie (Université de Montréal), « Résultats de recherche sur les problèmes sociaux-culturelles des jeunes familles immigrantes de Montréal et leurs recours aux services sociaux publics et communautaires ».

Guilbert, Lucille (Université Laval), « Expression narrative traditionnelle, enculturation selon le genre et stratégies d'adaptation de Vietnamiens et de Vietnamiennes d'origine au Québec ».

Helmy, Guy et Tran Quang Ba (Université de Moncton), « Maintien de l'identité culturelle et intégration nationale : deux groupes ethniques au sud-est du Nouveau-Brunswick ».

Hulslander, Kenneth (Université du Québec à Montréal), « Pris entre ‹ les deux solitudes › : la réponse de deux dramaturges italo-québécois ».

Juteau, Danielle et Sylvie Paré (Université de Montréal), « L'entrepreneurship

‹ ethnique › : cohabitation et enjeux économiques ».

Laaroussi, Michèle, Diane Lessard, Maria Elisa Montejo et Monica Viana (Université de Sherbrooke), « Femmes et immigrantes en région ».

Lanthier, Pierre et Denis Goulet (Université du Québec à Trois-Rivières), « Les relations ethniques dans la profession médicale et dans l'administration municipale au Québec, 1880-1930 : comparaison et hypothèses ».

Le Gall, Josiane, Deirdre Meintel et Christopher McAll (Université de Montréal), « Espaces observés : ethnicité et appropriation territoriale ».

Low, Brian (University of British Columbia), "Graduation Day: Schooling for Mental Health in the Cinematic Society of the National Film Board of Canada, 1940-1980."

Magat, Ilan (University of Alberta), "Home – Places in the Heart."

Mancuso, Rebecca (McGill University), "'Guiding the Girls': The Women's Division of Immigration and Colonization, 1919-1930."

Mann-Feder, Varda and Shahrzad Mojab (Concordia University), "Clash between Generations: An Intervention Model for Ethnic Communities."

Mar, Lisa (University of Toronto), "Madness, Family Violence and Lindsay, Ontario's Anti-Chinese Riot of 1919."

Marshall, Dominique (Carleton University), « Les enfants de l'État providence : pratiques et croyances dans le Québec de l'après-guerre, 1940-1960 ».

Mohan, Chandra (University of Delhi, India), "The Minority Voice of Ethnicity in Narratives: The Native Indians of Canada and the Tribals of India."

Ndoye, Amadou (Université Laval), « Essai d'interprétation des modèles d'identification de la communauté sénégalaise à travers les proverbes et récits traditionnels ».

Neff, Charlotte (Laurentian University), "Pauper Apprenticeship in Pre-Confederation Ontario."

Neijmann, Daisy (University of Manitoba) and David Delafenetre (Université de Paris), "The Netherlandic and Scandinavian Transition in Canada: A Sociological and Literary Perspective."

Newton, Christopher (Multicultural Society of Ontario), "Performing Identity: Comparing Italian Ethnicity in Montréal and Toronto."

Piché, Victor et Jean Renaud (Université de Montréal), « Le quartier Côte-des-Neiges est-il multiethnique? »

Pivato, Joseph (Athabasca University), "Colour in Quebec Writing: Haitian Voices."

Ramirez, Bruno (Université de Montréal), "Leaving Canada Behind: French- and English-Canadian Emigration to the USA, 1900-1930: A Comparative Analysis."

Richardson, Teresa (University of South Florida), "Origins and Implications of Scientific Child Study in North America: American Philanthropy and Canadian Childhood."

Roger, Kerstin (Ontario Institute for the Study of Education), "[Re]-Constructing Whiteness / Defining Other in the Counselling Session."

Saillant, Francine (Université Laval), « Des enfants et des remèdes : la voie marchande de la médicalisation ».

Saldov, Morris (Memorial University), "The Chinese Elderly: Social Integration in Metro Toronto Housing Company Ltd."

Sharma, Nandita (Simon Fraser University), "The True North Strong and Free: Immigration Policy and the Creation of Unfree Wage Labour in Canada."

Simard, Myriam (Université du Québec, INRS-Culture et Société), « La politique québécoise de la régionalisation de l'immigration: réflexions critiques et examen du cas des entrepreneurs agricoles immigrants ».

Simon, Sherry (Université Concordia), « Représentations de l'ethnicité dans le cinéma québécois ».

Symons, Gladys (École nationale d'administration publique), « La communauté, ‹ l'autre › et le travail du contrôle social : la police dans le quartier Côte-des-Neiges »

Taaffe, Ruth (University of Ottawa), Ian Pringle (Carleton University) and Mary Maguire (McGill University), "English Literacy Development of Ethno-linguistic Minority Children: A Comparison of Children Speaking Slavic and Arabic Languages."

Turmel, André (Université Laval), "Science and Normalcy: How Science Contributed at the Turn of the Century to a Redefinition of the Normal Child."

Ulysse, Pierre, Christopher McAll et Deirdre Meintel (Université de Montréal), « Trajectoires quotidiennes de personnes : ethnicité et appropriation territoriale ».

Valtonen, Kathleen (York University), "The Societal Participation of Refugees and Immigrants in Finland, Canada, and Trinidad: A Study of Integration."

Ventresca, Robert (University of Toronto), "'Cowering Women and Combative Men?': Femininity, Masculinity, and Ethnicity on Strike in Two Southern Ontario Towns, 1964-1966."

Verduyn, Christl (Trent University), "Relative(ly) Politic(al)s: Comparing (Examples of) Québec/Canadian 'Ethnic'/'Immigrant' Writings"

Wayland, Sarah (University of Maryland), "Religious Expression in Public Schools: Daggers in Canada, Headscarves in France."

Wilson, Warwick (University of Western Sydney-Macarthur) "Vietnamese Residential Settlement, Adjustment, and Relocation: A Comparison of Sydney (Australia) and Toronto (Canada), 1981-1994."

Zhang, Benzi (Carleton University), "From Trans(re)lation to Trans-Nation: Re-Imagining Nation in Asian Immigrant Literature."

D1507743